Mometrix TEST PREPARATION

MTTC

Mathematics (Secondary) (022) Test Secrets Study Guide

Part 1 of 2

DEAR FUTURE EXAM SUCCESS STORY

First of all, **THANK YOU** for purchasing Mometrix study materials!

Second, congratulations! You are one of the few determined test-takers who are committed to doing whatever it takes to excel on your exam. **You have come to the right place.** We developed these study materials with one goal in mind: to deliver you the information you need in a format that's concise and easy to use.

In addition to optimizing your guide for the content of the test, we've outlined our recommended steps for breaking down the preparation process into small, attainable goals so you can make sure you stay on track.

We've also analyzed the entire test-taking process, identifying the most common pitfalls and showing how you can overcome them and be ready for any curveball the test throws you.

Standardized testing is one of the biggest obstacles on your road to success, which only increases the importance of doing well in the high-pressure, high-stakes environment of test day. Your results on this test could have a significant impact on your future, and this guide provides the information and practical advice to help you achieve your full potential on test day.

Your success is our success

We would love to hear from you! If you would like to share the story of your exam success or if you have any questions or comments in regard to our products, please contact us at **800-673-8175** or **support@mometrix.com**.

Thanks again for your business and we wish you continued success!

Sincerely,
The Mometrix Test Preparation Team

Need more help? Check out our flashcards at:
http://MometrixFlashcards.com/MTTC

Written and edited by the Mometrix Exam Secrets Test Prep Team
Printed in the United States of America

TABLE OF CONTENTS

Introduction

Thank you for purchasing this resource! You have made the choice to prepare yourself for a test that could have a huge impact on your future, and this guide is designed to help you be fully ready for test day. Obviously, it's important to have a solid understanding of the test material, but you also need to be prepared for the unique environment and stressors of the test, so that you can perform to the best of your abilities.

For this purpose, the first section that appears in this guide is the **Secret Keys**. We've devoted countless hours to meticulously researching what works and what doesn't, and we've boiled down our findings to the five most impactful steps you can take to improve your performance on the test. We start at the beginning with study planning and move through the preparation process, all the way to the testing strategies that will help you get the most out of what you know when you're finally sitting in front of the test.

We recommend that you start preparing for your test as far in advance as possible. However, if you've bought this guide as a last-minute study resource and only have a few days before your test, we recommend that you skip over the first two Secret Keys since they address a long-term study plan.

If you struggle with **test anxiety**, we strongly encourage you to check out our recommendations for how you can overcome it. Test anxiety is a formidable foe, but it can be beaten, and we want to make sure you have the tools you need to defeat it.

Secret Key #1 – Plan Big, Study Small

There's a lot riding on your performance. If you want to ace this test, you're going to need to keep your skills sharp and the material fresh in your mind. You need a plan that lets you review everything you need to know while still fitting in your schedule. We'll break this strategy down into three categories.

Information Organization

Start with the information you already have: the official test outline. From this, you can make a complete list of all the concepts you need to cover before the test. Organize these concepts into groups that can be studied together, and create a list of any related vocabulary you need to learn so you can brush up on any difficult terms. You'll want to keep this vocabulary list handy once you actually start studying since you may need to add to it along the way.

Time Management

Once you have your set of study concepts, decide how to spread them out over the time you have left before the test. Break your study plan into small, clear goals so you have a manageable task for each day and know exactly what you're doing. Then just focus on one small step at a time. When you manage your time this way, you don't need to spend hours at a time studying. Studying a small block of content for a short period each day helps you retain information better and avoid stressing over how much you have left to do. You can relax knowing that you have a plan to cover everything in time. In order for this strategy to be effective though, you have to start studying early and stick to your schedule. Avoid the exhaustion and futility that comes from last-minute cramming!

Study Environment

The environment you study in has a big impact on your learning. Studying in a coffee shop, while probably more enjoyable, is not likely to be as fruitful as studying in a quiet room. It's important to keep distractions to a minimum. You're only planning to study for a short block of time, so make the most of it. Don't pause to check your phone or get up to find a snack. It's also important to **avoid multitasking**. Research has consistently shown that multitasking will make your studying dramatically less effective. Your study area should also be comfortable and well-lit so you don't have the distraction of straining your eyes or sitting on an uncomfortable chair.

The time of day you study is also important. You want to be rested and alert. Don't wait until just before bedtime. Study when you'll be most likely to comprehend and remember. Even better, if you know what time of day your test will be, set that time aside for study. That way your brain will be used to working on that subject at that specific time and you'll have a better chance of recalling information.

Finally, it can be helpful to team up with others who are studying for the same test. Your actual studying should be done in as isolated an environment as possible, but the work of organizing the information and setting up the study plan can be divided up. In between study sessions, you can discuss with your teammates the concepts that you're all studying and quiz each other on the details. Just be sure that your teammates are as serious about the test as you are. If you find that your study time is being replaced with social time, you might need to find a new team.

Secret Key #2 – Make Your Studying Count

You're devoting a lot of time and effort to preparing for this test, so you want to be absolutely certain it will pay off. This means doing more than just reading the content and hoping you can remember it on test day. It's important to make every minute of study count. There are two main areas you can focus on to make your studying count.

Retention

It doesn't matter how much time you study if you can't remember the material. You need to make sure you are retaining the concepts. To check your retention of the information you're learning, try recalling it at later times with minimal prompting. Try carrying around flashcards and glance at one or two from time to time or ask a friend who's also studying for the test to quiz you.

To enhance your retention, look for ways to put the information into practice so that you can apply it rather than simply recalling it. If you're using the information in practical ways, it will be much easier to remember. Similarly, it helps to solidify a concept in your mind if you're not only reading it to yourself but also explaining it to someone else. Ask a friend to let you teach them about a concept you're a little shaky on (or speak aloud to an imaginary audience if necessary). As you try to summarize, define, give examples, and answer your friend's questions, you'll understand the concepts better and they will stay with you longer. Finally, step back for a big picture view and ask yourself how each piece of information fits with the whole subject. When you link the different concepts together and see them working together as a whole, it's easier to remember the individual components.

Finally, practice showing your work on any multi-step problems, even if you're just studying. Writing out each step you take to solve a problem will help solidify the process in your mind, and you'll be more likely to remember it during the test.

Modality

Modality simply refers to the means or method by which you study. Choosing a study modality that fits your own individual learning style is crucial. No two people learn best in exactly the same way, so it's important to know your strengths and use them to your advantage.

For example, if you learn best by visualization, focus on visualizing a concept in your mind and draw an image or a diagram. Try color-coding your notes, illustrating them, or creating symbols that will trigger your mind to recall a learned concept. If you learn best by hearing or discussing information, find a study partner who learns the same way or read aloud to yourself. Think about how to put the information in your own words. Imagine that you are giving a lecture on the topic and record yourself so you can listen to it later.

For any learning style, flashcards can be helpful. Organize the information so you can take advantage of spare moments to review. Underline key words or phrases. Use different colors for different categories. Mnemonic devices (such as creating a short list in which every item starts with the same letter) can also help with retention. Find what works best for you and use it to store the information in your mind most effectively and easily.

Secret Key #3 – Practice the Right Way

Your success on test day depends not only on how many hours you put into preparing, but also on whether you prepared the right way. It's good to check along the way to see if your studying is paying off. One of the most effective ways to do this is by taking practice tests to evaluate your progress. Practice tests are useful because they show exactly where you need to improve. Every time you take a practice test, pay special attention to these three groups of questions:

- The questions you got wrong
- The questions you had to guess on, even if you guessed right
- The questions you found difficult or slow to work through

This will show you exactly what your weak areas are, and where you need to devote more study time. Ask yourself why each of these questions gave you trouble. Was it because you didn't understand the material? Was it because you didn't remember the vocabulary? Do you need more repetitions on this type of question to build speed and confidence? Dig into those questions and figure out how you can strengthen your weak areas as you go back to review the material.

Additionally, many practice tests have a section explaining the answer choices. It can be tempting to read the explanation and think that you now have a good understanding of the concept. However, an explanation likely only covers part of the question's broader context. Even if the explanation makes perfect sense, **go back and investigate** every concept related to the question until you're positive you have a thorough understanding.

As you go along, keep in mind that the practice test is just that: practice. Memorizing these questions and answers will not be very helpful on the actual test because it is unlikely to have any of the same exact questions. If you only know the right answers to the sample questions, you won't be prepared for the real thing. **Study the concepts** until you understand them fully, and then you'll be able to answer any question that shows up on the test.

It's important to wait on the practice tests until you're ready. If you take a test on your first day of study, you may be overwhelmed by the amount of material covered and how much you need to learn. Work up to it gradually.

On test day, you'll need to be prepared for answering questions, managing your time, and using the test-taking strategies you've learned. It's a lot to balance, like a mental marathon that will have a big impact on your future. Like training for a marathon, you'll need to start slowly and work your way up. When test day arrives, you'll be ready.

Start with the strategies you've read in the first two Secret Keys—plan your course and study in the way that works best for you. If you have time, consider using multiple study resources to get different approaches to the same concepts. It can be helpful to see difficult concepts from more than one angle. Then find a good source for practice tests. Many times, the test website will suggest potential study resources or provide sample tests.

Practice Test Strategy

If you're able to find at least three practice tests, we recommend this strategy:

Untimed and Open-Book Practice

Take the first test with no time constraints and with your notes and study guide handy. Take your time and focus on applying the strategies you've learned.

Timed and Open-Book Practice

Take the second practice test open-book as well, but set a timer and practice pacing yourself to finish in time.

Timed and Closed-Book Practice

Take any other practice tests as if it were test day. Set a timer and put away your study materials. Sit at a table or desk in a quiet room, imagine yourself at the testing center, and answer questions as quickly and accurately as possible.

Keep repeating timed and closed-book tests on a regular basis until you run out of practice tests or it's time for the actual test. Your mind will be ready for the schedule and stress of test day, and you'll be able to focus on recalling the material you've learned.

Secret Key #4 – Pace Yourself

Once you're fully prepared for the material on the test, your biggest challenge on test day will be managing your time. Just knowing that the clock is ticking can make you panic even if you have plenty of time left. Work on pacing yourself so you can build confidence against the time constraints of the exam. Pacing is a difficult skill to master, especially in a high-pressure environment, so **practice is vital**.

Set time expectations for your pace based on how much time is available. For example, if a section has 60 questions and the time limit is 30 minutes, you know you have to average 30 seconds or less per question in order to answer them all. Although 30 seconds is the hard limit, set 25 seconds per question as your goal, so you reserve extra time to spend on harder questions. When you budget extra time for the harder questions, you no longer have any reason to stress when those questions take longer to answer.

Don't let this time expectation distract you from working through the test at a calm, steady pace, but keep it in mind so you don't spend too much time on any one question. Recognize that taking extra time on one question you don't understand may keep you from answering two that you do understand later in the test. If your time limit for a question is up and you're still not sure of the answer, mark it and move on, and come back to it later if the time and the test format allow. If the testing format doesn't allow you to return to earlier questions, just make an educated guess; then put it out of your mind and move on.

On the easier questions, be careful not to rush. It may seem wise to hurry through them so you have more time for the challenging ones, but it's not worth missing one if you know the concept and just didn't take the time to read the question fully. Work efficiently but make sure you understand the question and have looked at all of the answer choices, since more than one may seem right at first.

Even if you're paying attention to the time, you may find yourself a little behind at some point. You should speed up to get back on track, but do so wisely. Don't panic; just take a few seconds less on each question until you're caught up. Don't guess without thinking, but do look through the answer choices and eliminate any you know are wrong. If you can get down to two choices, it is often worthwhile to guess from those. Once you've chosen an answer, move on and don't dwell on any that you skipped or had to hurry through. If a question was taking too long, chances are it was one of the harder ones, so you weren't as likely to get it right anyway.

On the other hand, if you find yourself getting ahead of schedule, it may be beneficial to slow down a little. The more quickly you work, the more likely you are to make a careless mistake that will affect your score. You've budgeted time for each question, so don't be afraid to spend that time. Practice an efficient but careful pace to get the most out of the time you have.

Secret Key #5 – Have a Plan for Guessing

When you're taking the test, you may find yourself stuck on a question. Some of the answer choices seem better than others, but you don't see the one answer choice that is obviously correct. What do you do?

The scenario described above is very common, yet most test takers have not effectively prepared for it. Developing and practicing a plan for guessing may be one of the single most effective uses of your time as you get ready for the exam.

In developing your plan for guessing, there are three questions to address:

- When should you start the guessing process?
- How should you narrow down the choices?
- Which answer should you choose?

When to Start the Guessing Process

Unless your plan for guessing is to select C every time (which, despite its merits, is not what we recommend), you need to leave yourself enough time to apply your answer elimination strategies. Since you have a limited amount of time for each question, that means that if you're going to give yourself the best shot at guessing correctly, you have to decide quickly whether or not you will guess.

Of course, the best-case scenario is that you don't have to guess at all, so first, see if you can answer the question based on your knowledge of the subject and basic reasoning skills. Focus on the key words in the question and try to jog your memory of related topics. Give yourself a chance to bring the knowledge to mind, but once you realize that you don't have (or you can't access) the knowledge you need to answer the question, it's time to start the guessing process.

It's almost always better to start the guessing process too early than too late. It only takes a few seconds to remember something and answer the question from knowledge. Carefully eliminating wrong answer choices takes longer. Plus, going through the process of eliminating answer choices can actually help jog your memory.

Summary: Start the guessing process as soon as you decide that you can't answer the question based on your knowledge.

How to Narrow Down the Choices

The next chapter in this book (**Test-Taking Strategies**) includes a wide range of strategies for how to approach questions and how to look for answer choices to eliminate. You will definitely want to read those carefully, practice them, and figure out which ones work best for you. Here though, we're going to address a mindset rather than a particular strategy.

Your odds of guessing an answer correctly depend on how many options you are choosing from.

Number of options left	5	4	3	2	1
Odds of guessing correctly	20%	25%	33%	50%	100%

You can see from this chart just how valuable it is to be able to eliminate incorrect answers and make an educated guess, but there are two things that many test takers do that cause them to miss out on the benefits of guessing:

- Accidentally eliminating the correct answer
- Selecting an answer based on an impression

We'll look at the first one here, and the second one in the next section.

To avoid accidentally eliminating the correct answer, we recommend a thought exercise called **the $5 challenge**. In this challenge, you only eliminate an answer choice from contention if you are willing to bet $5 on it being wrong. Why $5? Five dollars is a small but not insignificant amount of money. It's an amount you could afford to lose but wouldn't want to throw away. And while losing $5 once might not hurt too much, doing it twenty times will set you back $100. In the same way, each small decision you make—eliminating a choice here, guessing on a question there—won't by itself impact your score very much, but when you put them all together, they can make a big difference. By holding each answer choice elimination decision to a higher standard, you can reduce the risk of accidentally eliminating the correct answer.

The $5 challenge can also be applied in a positive sense: If you are willing to bet $5 that an answer choice *is* correct, go ahead and mark it as correct.

Summary: Only eliminate an answer choice if you are willing to bet $5 that it is wrong.

Which Answer to Choose

You're taking the test. You've run into a hard question and decided you'll have to guess. You've eliminated all the answer choices you're willing to bet $5 on. Now you have to pick an answer. Why do we even need to talk about this? Why can't you just pick whichever one you feel like when the time comes?

The answer to these questions is that if you don't come into the test with a plan, you'll rely on your impression to select an answer choice, and if you do that, you risk falling into a trap. The test writers know that everyone who takes their test will be guessing on some of the questions, so they intentionally write wrong answer choices to seem plausible. You still have to pick an answer though, and if the wrong answer choices are designed to look right, how can you ever be sure that you're not falling for their trap? The best solution we've found to this dilemma is to take the decision out of your hands entirely. Here is the process we recommend:

Once you've eliminated any choices that you are confident (willing to bet $5) are wrong, select the first remaining choice as your answer.

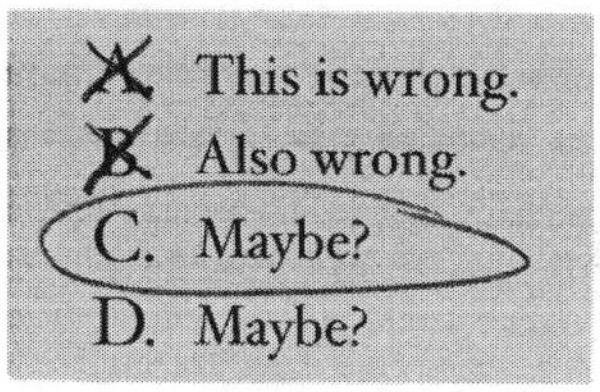

Whether you choose to select the first remaining choice, the second, or the last, the important thing is that you use some preselected standard. Using this approach guarantees that you will not be enticed into selecting an answer choice that looks right, because you are not basing your decision on how the answer choices look.

This is not meant to make you question your knowledge. Instead, it is to help you recognize the difference between your knowledge and your impressions. There's a huge difference between thinking an answer is right because of what you know, and thinking an answer is right because it looks or sounds like it should be right.

Summary: To ensure that your selection is appropriately random, make a predetermined selection from among all answer choices you have not eliminated.

Test-Taking Strategies

This section contains a list of test-taking strategies that you may find helpful as you work through the test. By taking what you know and applying logical thought, you can maximize your chances of answering any question correctly!

It is very important to realize that every question is different and every person is different: no single strategy will work on every question, and no single strategy will work for every person. That's why we've included all of them here, so you can try them out and determine which ones work best for different types of questions and which ones work best for you.

Question Strategies

⊘ Read Carefully

Read the question and the answer choices carefully. Don't miss the question because you misread the terms. You have plenty of time to read each question thoroughly and make sure you understand what is being asked. Yet a happy medium must be attained, so don't waste too much time. You must read carefully and efficiently.

⊘ Contextual Clues

Look for contextual clues. If the question includes a word you are not familiar with, look at the immediate context for some indication of what the word might mean. Contextual clues can often give you all the information you need to decipher the meaning of an unfamiliar word. Even if you can't determine the meaning, you may be able to narrow down the possibilities enough to make a solid guess at the answer to the question.

⊘ Prefixes

If you're having trouble with a word in the question or answer choices, try dissecting it. Take advantage of every clue that the word might include. Prefixes and suffixes can be a huge help. Usually, they allow you to determine a basic meaning. *Pre-* means before, *post-* means after, *pro-* is positive, *de-* is negative. From prefixes and suffixes, you can get an idea of the general meaning of the word and try to put it into context.

⊘ Hedge Words

Watch out for critical hedge words, such as *likely, may, can, sometimes, often, almost, mostly, usually, generally, rarely*, and *sometimes*. Question writers insert these hedge phrases to cover every possibility. Often an answer choice will be wrong simply because it leaves no room for exception. Be on guard for answer choices that have definitive words such as *exactly* and *always*.

⊘ Switchback Words

Stay alert for *switchbacks*. These are the words and phrases frequently used to alert you to shifts in thought. The most common switchback words are *but, although*, and *however*. Others include *nevertheless, on the other hand, even though, while, in spite of, despite*, and *regardless of*. Switchback words are important to catch because they can change the direction of the question or an answer choice.

✓ FACE VALUE

When in doubt, use common sense. Accept the situation in the problem at face value. Don't read too much into it. These problems will not require you to make wild assumptions. If you have to go beyond creativity and warp time or space in order to have an answer choice fit the question, then you should move on and consider the other answer choices. These are normal problems rooted in reality. The applicable relationship or explanation may not be readily apparent, but it is there for you to figure out. Use your common sense to interpret anything that isn't clear.

Answer Choice Strategies

✓ ANSWER SELECTION

The most thorough way to pick an answer choice is to identify and eliminate wrong answers until only one is left, then confirm it is the correct answer. Sometimes an answer choice may immediately seem right, but be careful. The test writers will usually put more than one reasonable answer choice on each question, so take a second to read all of them and make sure that the other choices are not equally obvious. As long as you have time left, it is better to read every answer choice than to pick the first one that looks right without checking the others.

✓ ANSWER CHOICE FAMILIES

An answer choice family consists of two (in rare cases, three) answer choices that are very similar in construction and cannot all be true at the same time. If you see two answer choices that are direct opposites or parallels, one of them is usually the correct answer. For instance, if one answer choice says that quantity x increases and another either says that quantity x decreases (opposite) or says that quantity y increases (parallel), then those answer choices would fall into the same family. An answer choice that doesn't match the construction of the answer choice family is more likely to be incorrect. Most questions will not have answer choice families, but when they do appear, you should be prepared to recognize them.

✓ ELIMINATE ANSWERS

Eliminate answer choices as soon as you realize they are wrong, but make sure you consider all possibilities. If you are eliminating answer choices and realize that the last one you are left with is also wrong, don't panic. Start over and consider each choice again. There may be something you missed the first time that you will realize on the second pass.

✓ AVOID FACT TRAPS

Don't be distracted by an answer choice that is factually true but doesn't answer the question. You are looking for the choice that answers the question. Stay focused on what the question is asking for so you don't accidentally pick an answer that is true but incorrect. Always go back to the question and make sure the answer choice you've selected actually answers the question and is not merely a true statement.

✓ EXTREME STATEMENTS

In general, you should avoid answers that put forth extreme actions as standard practice or proclaim controversial ideas as established fact. An answer choice that states the "process should be used in certain situations, if..." is much more likely to be correct than one that states the "process should be discontinued completely." The first is a calm rational statement and doesn't even make a definitive, uncompromising stance, using a hedge word *if* to provide wiggle room, whereas the second choice is far more extreme.

✓ Benchmark

As you read through the answer choices and you come across one that seems to answer the question well, mentally select that answer choice. This is not your final answer, but it's the one that will help you evaluate the other answer choices. The one that you selected is your benchmark or standard for judging each of the other answer choices. Every other answer choice must be compared to your benchmark. That choice is correct until proven otherwise by another answer choice beating it. If you find a better answer, then that one becomes your new benchmark. Once you've decided that no other choice answers the question as well as your benchmark, you have your final answer.

✓ Predict the Answer

Before you even start looking at the answer choices, it is often best to try to predict the answer. When you come up with the answer on your own, it is easier to avoid distractions and traps because you will know exactly what to look for. The right answer choice is unlikely to be word-for-word what you came up with, but it should be a close match. Even if you are confident that you have the right answer, you should still take the time to read each option before moving on.

General Strategies

✓ Tough Questions

If you are stumped on a problem or it appears too hard or too difficult, don't waste time. Move on! Remember though, if you can quickly check for obviously incorrect answer choices, your chances of guessing correctly are greatly improved. Before you completely give up, at least try to knock out a couple of possible answers. Eliminate what you can and then guess at the remaining answer choices before moving on.

✓ Check Your Work

Since you will probably not know every term listed and the answer to every question, it is important that you get credit for the ones that you do know. Don't miss any questions through careless mistakes. If at all possible, try to take a second to look back over your answer selection and make sure you've selected the correct answer choice and haven't made a costly careless mistake (such as marking an answer choice that you didn't mean to mark). This quick double check should more than pay for itself in caught mistakes for the time it costs.

✓ Pace Yourself

It's easy to be overwhelmed when you're looking at a page full of questions; your mind is confused and full of random thoughts, and the clock is ticking down faster than you would like. Calm down and maintain the pace that you have set for yourself. Especially as you get down to the last few minutes of the test, don't let the small numbers on the clock make you panic. As long as you are on track by monitoring your pace, you are guaranteed to have time for each question.

✓ Don't Rush

It is very easy to make errors when you are in a hurry. Maintaining a fast pace in answering questions is pointless if it makes you miss questions that you would have gotten right otherwise. Test writers like to include distracting information and wrong answers that seem right. Taking a little extra time to avoid careless mistakes can make all the difference in your test score. Find a pace that allows you to be confident in the answers that you select.

⊘ Keep Moving

Panicking will not help you pass the test, so do your best to stay calm and keep moving. Taking deep breaths and going through the answer elimination steps you practiced can help to break through a stress barrier and keep your pace.

Final Notes

The combination of a solid foundation of content knowledge and the confidence that comes from practicing your plan for applying that knowledge is the key to maximizing your performance on test day. As your foundation of content knowledge is built up and strengthened, you'll find that the strategies included in this chapter become more and more effective in helping you quickly sift through the distractions and traps of the test to isolate the correct answer.

Now that you're preparing to move forward into the test content chapters of this book, be sure to keep your goal in mind. As you read, think about how you will be able to apply this information on the test. If you've already seen sample questions for the test and you have an idea of the question format and style, try to come up with questions of your own that you can answer based on what you're reading. This will give you valuable practice applying your knowledge in the same ways you can expect to on test day.

Good luck and good studying!

Mathematical Processes and Number Concepts

Numbers

Classifications of Numbers

Numbers are the basic building blocks of mathematics. Specific features of numbers are identified by the following terms:

Integer – any positive or negative whole number, including zero. Integers do not include fractions $\left(\frac{1}{3}\right)$, decimals (0.56), or mixed numbers $\left(7\frac{3}{4}\right)$.

Prime number – any whole number greater than 1 that has only two factors, itself and 1; that is, a number that can be divided evenly only by 1 and itself.

Composite number – any whole number greater than 1 that has more than two different factors; in other words, any whole number that is not a prime number. For example: The composite number 8 has the factors of 1, 2, 4, and 8.

Even number – any integer that can be divided by 2 without leaving a remainder. For example: 2, 4, 6, 8, and so on.

Odd number – any integer that cannot be divided evenly by 2. For example: 3, 5, 7, 9, and so on.

Decimal number – any number that uses a decimal point to show the part of the number that is less than one. Example: 1.234.

Decimal point – a symbol used to separate the ones place from the tenths place in decimals or dollars from cents in currency.

Decimal place – the position of a number to the right of the decimal point. In the decimal 0.123, the 1 is in the first place to the right of the decimal point, indicating tenths; the 2 is in the second place, indicating hundredths; and the 3 is in the third place, indicating thousandths.

The **decimal**, or base 10, system is a number system that uses ten different digits (0, 1, 2, 3, 4, 5, 6, 7, 8, 9). An example of a number system that uses something other than ten digits is the **binary**, or base 2, number system, used by computers, which uses only the numbers 0 and 1. It is thought that the decimal system originated because people had only their 10 fingers for counting.

Rational numbers include all integers, decimals, and fractions. Any terminating or repeating decimal number is a rational number.

Irrational numbers cannot be written as fractions or decimals because the number of decimal places is infinite and there is no recurring pattern of digits within the number. For example, pi (π) begins with 3.141592 and continues without terminating or repeating, so pi is an irrational number.

Real numbers are the set of all rational and irrational numbers.

> **Review Video: Numbers and Their Classifications**
> Visit mometrix.com/academy and enter code: 461071
>
> **Review Video: Rational and Irrational Numbers**
> Visit mometrix.com/academy and enter code: 280645

THE NUMBER LINE

A number line is a graph to see the distance between numbers. Basically, this graph shows the relationship between numbers. So a number line may have a point for zero and may show negative numbers on the left side of the line. Also, any positive numbers are placed on the right side of the line. For example, consider the points labeled on the following number line:

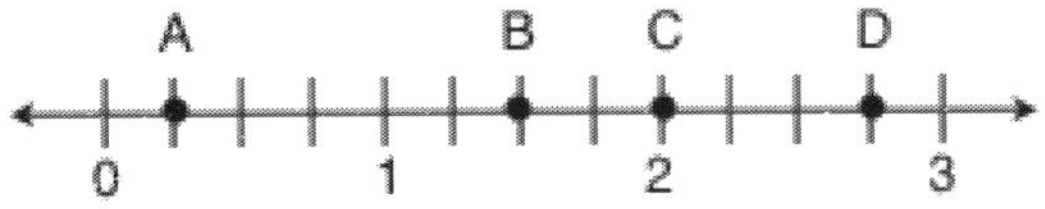

We can use the dashed lines on the number line to identify each point. Each dashed line between two whole numbers is $\frac{1}{4}$. The line halfway between two numbers is $\frac{1}{2}$.

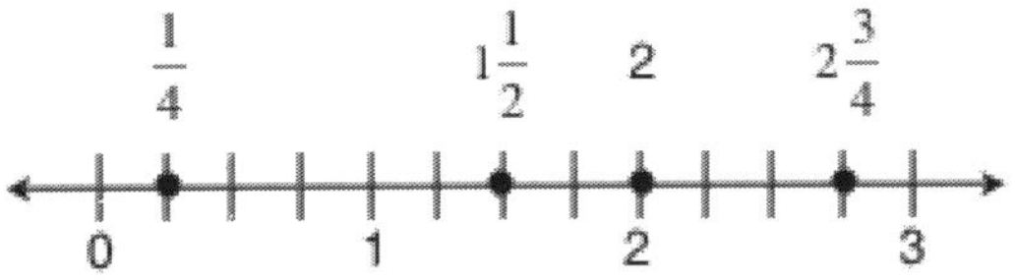

> **Review Video: Negative and Positive Number Line**
> Visit mometrix.com/academy and enter code: 816439

NUMBERS IN WORD FORM AND PLACE VALUE

When writing numbers out in word form or translating word form to numbers, it is essential to understand how a place value system works. In the decimal or base-10 system, each digit of a number represents how many of the corresponding place value – a specific factor of 10 – are contained in the number being represented. To make reading numbers easier, every three digits to the left of the decimal place is preceded by a comma. The following table demonstrates some of the place values:

Power of 10	10^3	10^2	10^1	10^0	10^{-1}	10^{-2}	10^{-3}
Value	1,000	100	10	1	0.1	0.01	0.001
Place	thousands	hundreds	tens	ones	tenths	hundredths	thousandths

For example, consider the number 4,546.09, which can be separated into each place value like this:

4: thousands
5: hundreds
4: tens
6: ones
0: tenths
9: hundredths

This number in word form would be *four thousand five hundred forty-six and nine hundredths.*

Review Video: Number Place Value
Visit mometrix.com/academy and enter code: 205433

Absolute Value

A precursor to working with negative numbers is understanding what **absolute values** are. A number's absolute value is simply the distance away from zero a number is on the number line. The absolute value of a number is always positive and is written $|x|$. For example, the absolute value of 3, written as $|3|$, is 3 because the distance between 0 and 3 on a number line is three units. Likewise, the absolute value of –3, written as $|-3|$, is 3 because the distance between 0 and –3 on a number line is three units. So $|3| = |-3|$.

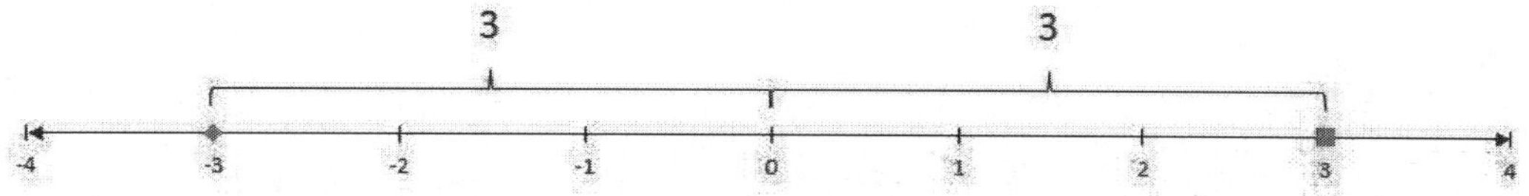

Review Video: Absolute Value
Visit mometrix.com/academy and enter code: 314669

Practice

P1. Write the place value of each digit in 14,059.826

P2. Write out each of the following in words:

(a) 29
(b) 478
(c) 98,542
(d) 0.06
(e) 13.113

P3. Write each of the following in numbers:

(a) nine thousand four hundred thirty-five
(b) three hundred two thousand eight hundred seventy-six
(c) nine hundred one thousandths
(d) nineteen thousandths
(e) seven thousand one hundred forty-two and eighty-five hundredths

Practice Solutions

P1. The place value for each digit would be as follows:

Digit	Place Value
1	ten-thousands
4	thousands
0	hundreds
5	tens
9	ones
8	tenths
2	hundredths
6	thousandths

P2. Each written out in words would be:

(a) twenty-nine
(b) four hundred seventy-eight
(c) ninety-eight thousand five hundred forty-two
(d) six hundredths
(e) thirteen and one hundred thirteen thousandths

P3. Each in numeric form would be:

(a) 9,435
(b) 302, 876
(c) 0.901
(d) 0.019
(e) 7,142.85

Operations

Operations

An **operation** is simply a mathematical process that takes some value(s) as input(s) and produces an output. Elementary operations are often written in the following form: *value operation value*. For instance, in the expression $1 + 2$ the values are 1 and 2 and the operation is addition. Performing the operation gives the output of 3. In this way we can say that $1 + 2$ and 3 are equal, or $1 + 2 = 3$.

Addition

Addition increases the value of one quantity by the value of another quantity (both called **addends**). For example, $2 + 4 = 6$; $8 + 9 = 17$. The result is called the **sum**. With addition, the order does not matter, $4 + 2 = 2 + 4$.

When adding signed numbers, if the signs are the same simply add the absolute values of the addends and apply the original sign to the sum. For example, $(+4) + (+8) = +12$ and $(-4) + (-8) = -12$. When the original signs are different, take the absolute values of the addends and subtract the smaller value from the larger value, then apply the original sign of the larger value to the difference. For instance, $(+4) + (-8) = -4$ and $(-4) + (+8) = +4$.

SUBTRACTION

Subtraction is the opposite operation to addition; it decreases the value of one quantity (the **minuend**) by the value of another quantity (the **subtrahend**). For example, $6 - 4 = 2$; $17 - 8 = 9$. The result is called the **difference**. Note that with subtraction, the order does matter, $6 - 4 \neq 4 - 6$.

For subtracting signed numbers, change the sign of the subtrahend and then follow the same rules used for addition. For example, $(+4) - (+8) = (+4) + (-8) = -4$.

> **Review Video: Addition and Subtraction**
> Visit mometrix.com/academy and enter code: 521157

MULTIPLICATION

Multiplication can be thought of as repeated addition. One number (the **multiplier**) indicates how many times to add the other number (the **multiplicand**) to itself. For example, 3×2 (three times two) $= 2 + 2 + 2 = 6$. With multiplication, the order does not matter: $2 \times 3 = 3 \times 2$ or $3 + 3 = 2 + 2 + 2$, either way the result (the **product**) is the same.

If the signs are the same, the product is positive when multiplying signed numbers. For example, $(+4) \times (+8) = +32$ and $(-4) \times (-8) = +32$. If the signs are opposite, the product is negative. For example, $(+4) \times (-8) = -32$ and $(-4) \times (+8) = -32$. When more than two factors are multiplied together, the sign of the product is determined by how many negative factors are present. If there are an odd number of negative factors then the product is negative, whereas an even number of negative factors indicates a positive product. For instance, $(+4) \times (-8) \times (-2) = +64$ and $(-4) \times (-8) \times (-2) = -64$.

DIVISION

Division is the opposite operation to multiplication; one number (the **divisor**) tells us how many parts to divide the other number (the **dividend**) into. The result of division is called the **quotient**. For example, $20 \div 4 = 5$; if 20 is split into 4 equal parts, each part is 5. With division, the order of the numbers does matter, $20 \div 4 \neq 4 \div 20$.

The rules for dividing signed numbers are similar to multiplying signed numbers. If the dividend and divisor have the same sign, the quotient is positive. If the dividend and divisor have opposite signs, the quotient is negative. For example, $(-4) \div (+8) = -0.5$.

> **Review Video: Multiplication and Division**
> Visit mometrix.com/academy and enter code: 643326

PARENTHESES

Parentheses are used to designate which operations should be done first when there are multiple operations. Example: $4 - (2 + 1) = 1$; the parentheses tell us that we must add 2 and 1, and then subtract the sum from 4, rather than subtracting 2 from 4 and then adding 1 (this would give us an answer of 3).

> **Review Video: Mathematical Parentheses**
> Visit mometrix.com/academy and enter code: 978600

EXPONENTS

An **exponent** is a superscript number placed next to another number at the top right. It indicates how many times the base number is to be multiplied by itself. Exponents provide a shorthand way to write what would be a longer mathematical expression, for example: $2^4 = 2 \times 2 \times 2 \times 2$. A number with an exponent of 2 is said to be "squared," while a number with an exponent of 3 is said to be "cubed." The value of a number raised to an exponent is called its power. So 8^4 is read as "8 to the 4th power," or "8 raised to the power of 4."

The properties of exponents are as follows:

Property	Description
$a^1 = a$	Any number to the power of 1 is equal to itself
$1^n = 1$	The number 1 raised to any power is equal to 1
$a^0 = 1$	Any number raised to the power of 0 is equal to 1
$a^n \times a^m = a^{n+m}$	Add exponents to multiply powers of the same base number
$a^n \div a^m = a^{n-m}$	Subtract exponents to divide powers of the same base number
$(a^n)^m = a^{n \times m}$	When a power is raised to a power, the exponents are multiplied
$(a \times b)^n = a^n \times b^n$ $(a \div b)^n = a^n \div b^n$	Multiplication and division operations inside parentheses can be raised to a power. This is the same as each term being raised to that power.
$a^{-n} = \frac{1}{a^n}$	A negative exponent is the same as the reciprocal of a positive exponent

Note that exponents do not have to be integers. Fractional or decimal exponents follow all the rules above as well. Example: $5^{\frac{1}{4}} \times 5^{\frac{3}{4}} = 5^{\frac{1}{4}+\frac{3}{4}} = 5^1 = 5$.

Review Video: Exponents
Visit mometrix.com/academy and enter code: 600998

Review Video: Laws of Exponents
Visit mometrix.com/academy and enter code: 532558

Roots

A **root**, such as a square root, is another way of writing a fractional exponent. Instead of using a superscript, roots use the radical symbol ($\sqrt{\ }$) to indicate the operation. A radical will have a number underneath the bar, and may sometimes have a number in the upper left: $\sqrt[n]{a}$, read as "the nth root of a." The relationship between radical notation and exponent notation can be described by this equation: $\sqrt[n]{a} = a^{\frac{1}{n}}$. The two special cases of $n = 2$ and $n = 3$ are called square roots and cube roots. If there is no number to the upper left, the radical is understood to be a square root ($n = 2$). Nearly all of the roots you encounter will be square roots. A square root is the same as a number raised to the one-half power. When we say that a is the square root of b ($a = \sqrt{b}$), we mean that a multiplied by itself equals b: ($a \times a = b$).

A **perfect square** is a number that has an integer for its square root. There are 10 perfect squares from 1 to 100: 1, 4, 9, 16, 25, 36, 49, 64, 81, 100 (the squares of integers 1 through 10).

Review Video: Roots
Visit mometrix.com/academy and enter code: 795655

Review Video: Square Root and Perfect Square
Visit mometrix.com/academy and enter code: 648063

ORDER OF OPERATIONS

Order of operations is a set of rules that dictates the order in which we must perform each operation in an expression so that we will evaluate it accurately. If we have an expression that includes multiple different operations, order of operations tells us which operations to do first. The most common mnemonic for order of operations is **PEMDAS**, or "Please Excuse My Dear Aunt Sally." PEMDAS stands for parentheses, exponents, multiplication, division, addition, and subtraction. It is important to understand that multiplication and division have equal precedence, as do addition and subtraction, so those pairs of operations are simply worked from left to right in order.

For example, evaluating the expression $5 + 20 \div 4 \times (2 + 3) - 6$ using the correct order of operations would be done like this:

- **P:** Perform the operations inside the parentheses: $(2 + 3) = 5$
- **E:** Simplify the exponents.
  - The equation now looks like this: $5 + 20 \div 4 \times 5 - 6$
- **MD:** Perform multiplication and division from left to right: $20 \div 4 = 5$; then $5 \times 5 = 25$
  - The equation now looks like this: $5 + 25 - 6$
- **AS:** Perform addition and subtraction from left to right: $5 + 25 = 30$; then $30 - 6 = 24$

Review Video: Order of Operations
Visit mometrix.com/academy and enter code: 259675

SUBTRACTION WITH REGROUPING

A great way to make use of some of the features built into the decimal system would be regrouping when attempting longform subtraction operations. When subtracting within a place value, sometimes the minuend is smaller than the subtrahend, **regrouping** enables you to 'borrow' a unit from a place value to the left in order to get a positive difference. For example, consider subtracting 189 from 525 with regrouping.

Review Video: Subtracting Large Numbers
Visit mometrix.com/academy and enter code: 603350

First, set up the subtraction problem in vertical form:

$$\begin{array}{r} 525 \\ -\ 189 \\ \hline \end{array}$$

Notice that the numbers in the ones and tens columns of 525 are smaller than the numbers in the ones and tens columns of 189. This means you will need to use regrouping to perform subtraction:

$$\begin{array}{cccc} & 5 & 2 & 5 \\ - & 1 & 8 & 9 \\ \hline \end{array}$$

To subtract 9 from 5 in the ones column you will need to borrow from the 2 in the ten's columns:

$$\begin{array}{cccc} & 5 & 1 & 15 \\ - & 1 & 8 & 9 \\ \hline & & & 6 \end{array}$$

Next, to subtract 8 from 1 in the tens column you will need to borrow from the 5 in the hundred's column:

	4	11	15
−	1	8	9
		3	6

Last, subtract the 1 from the 4 in the hundred's column:

	4	11	15
−	1	8	9
	3	3	6

PRACTICE

P1. Demonstrate how to subtract 477 from 620 using regrouping.

P2. Simplify the following expressions with exponents:

(a) 37^0
(b) 1^{30}
(c) $2^3 \times 2^4 \times 2^x$
(d) $(3^x)^3$
(e) $(12 \div 3)^2$

Practice Solutions

P1. First, set up the subtraction problem in vertical form:

	6	2	0
−	4	7	7

To subtract 7 from 0 in the ones column you will need to borrow from the 2 in the tens column:

	6	1	10
−	4	7	7
			3

Next, to subtract 7 from the 1 that's still in the tens column you will need to borrow from the 6 in the hundreds column:

	5	11	10
−	4	7	7
		4	3

Lastly, subtract 4 from the 5 remaining in the hundreds column:

	5	11	10
−	4	7	7
	1	4	3

P2. Using the properties of exponents and the proper order of operations:

(a) Any number raised to the power of 0 is equal to 1: $37^0 = 1$
(b) The number 1 raised to any power is equal to 1: $1^{30} = 1$
(c) Add exponents to multiply powers of the same base: $2^3 \times 2^4 \times 2^x = 2^{(3+4+x)} = 2^{(7+x)}$
(d) When a power is raised to a power, the exponents are multiplied: $(3^x)^3 = 3^{3x}$
(e) Perform the operation inside the parentheses first: $(12 \div 3)^2 = 4^2 = 16$

Factoring

Factors and Greatest Common Factor

Factors are numbers that are multiplied together to obtain a **product**. For example, in the equation $2 \times 3 = 6$, the numbers 2 and 3 are factors. A **prime number** has only two factors (1 and itself), but other numbers can have many factors.

A **common factor** is a number that divides exactly into two or more other numbers. For example, the factors of 12 are 1, 2, 3, 4, 6, and 12, while the factors of 15 are 1, 3, 5, and 15. The common factors of 12 and 15 are 1 and 3.

A **prime factor** is also a prime number. Therefore, the prime factors of 12 are 2 and 3. For 15, the prime factors are 3 and 5.

The **greatest common factor** (GCF) is the largest number that is a factor of two or more numbers. For example, the factors of 15 are 1, 3, 5, and 15; the factors of 35 are 1, 5, 7, and 35. Therefore, the greatest common factor of 15 and 35 is 5.

Review Video: Factors
Visit mometrix.com/academy and enter code: 920086

Review Video: Greatest Common Factor (GCF)
Visit mometrix.com/academy and enter code: 838699

Multiples and Least Common Multiple

Often listed out in multiplication tables, **multiples** are integer increments of a given factor. In other words, dividing a multiple by the factor will result in an integer. For example, the multiples of 7 include: $1 \times 7 = 7$, $2 \times 7 = 14$, $3 \times 7 = 21$, $4 \times 7 = 28$, $5 \times 7 = 35$. Dividing 7, 14, 21, 28, or 35 by 7 will result in the integers 1, 2, 3, 4, and 5, respectively.

The least common multiple (**LCM**) is the smallest number that is a multiple of two or more numbers. For example, the multiples of 3 include 3, 6, 9, 12, 15, etc.; the multiples of 5 include 5, 10, 15, 20, etc. Therefore, the least common multiple of 3 and 5 is 15.

Review Video: Multiples
Visit mometrix.com/academy and enter code: 626738

Rational Numbers

Fractions

A **fraction** is a number that is expressed as one integer written above another integer, with a dividing line between them $\left(\frac{x}{y}\right)$. It represents the **quotient** of the two numbers "x divided by y." It can also be thought of as x out of y equal parts.

The top number of a fraction is called the **numerator**, and it represents the number of parts under consideration. The 1 in $\frac{1}{4}$ means that 1 part out of the whole is being considered in the calculation. The bottom number of a fraction is called the **denominator**, and it represents the total number of equal parts. The 4 in $\frac{1}{4}$ means that the whole consists of 4 equal parts. A fraction cannot have a denominator of zero; this is referred to as "*undefined*."

Fractions can be manipulated, without changing the value of the fraction, by multiplying or dividing (but not adding or subtracting) both the numerator and denominator by the same number. If you divide both numbers by a common factor, you are **reducing** or simplifying the fraction. Two fractions that have the same value but are expressed differently are known as **equivalent fractions**. For example, $\frac{2}{10}, \frac{3}{15}, \frac{4}{20}$, and $\frac{5}{25}$ are all equivalent fractions. They can also all be reduced or simplified to $\frac{1}{5}$.

When two fractions are manipulated so that they have the same denominator, this is known as finding a **common denominator**. The number chosen to be that common denominator should be the least common multiple of the two original denominators. Example: $\frac{3}{4}$ and $\frac{5}{6}$; the least common multiple of 4 and 6 is 12. Manipulating to achieve the common denominator: $\frac{3}{4} = \frac{9}{12}; \frac{5}{6} = \frac{10}{12}$.

Proper Fractions and Mixed Numbers

A fraction whose denominator is greater than its numerator is known as a **proper fraction**, while a fraction whose numerator is greater than its denominator is known as an **improper fraction**. Proper fractions have values *less than one* and improper fractions have values *greater than one*.

A **mixed number** is a number that contains both an integer and a fraction. Any improper fraction can be rewritten as a mixed number. Example: $\frac{8}{3} = \frac{6}{3} + \frac{2}{3} = 2 + \frac{2}{3} = 2\frac{2}{3}$. Similarly, any mixed number can be rewritten as an improper fraction. Example: $1\frac{3}{5} = 1 + \frac{3}{5} = \frac{5}{5} + \frac{3}{5} = \frac{8}{5}$.

Review Video: Proper and Improper Fractions and Mixed Numbers
Visit mometrix.com/academy and enter code: 211077

Review Video: Fractions
Visit mometrix.com/academy and enter code: 262335

Adding and Subtracting Fractions

If two fractions have a common denominator, they can be added or subtracted simply by adding or subtracting the two numerators and retaining the same denominator. If the two fractions do not already have the same denominator, one or both of them must be manipulated to achieve a common denominator before they can be added or subtracted. Example: $\frac{1}{2} + \frac{1}{4} = \frac{2}{4} + \frac{1}{4} = \frac{3}{4}$.

Review Video: Adding and Subtracting Fractions
Visit mometrix.com/academy and enter code: 378080

Multiplying Fractions

Two fractions can be multiplied by multiplying the two numerators to find the new numerator and the two denominators to find the new denominator. Example: $\frac{1}{3} \times \frac{2}{3} = \frac{1\times2}{3\times3} = \frac{2}{9}$.

Review Video: Multiplying Fractions
Visit mometrix.com/academy and enter code: 638849

Dividing Fractions

Two fractions can be divided by flipping the numerator and denominator of the second fraction and then proceeding as though it were a multiplication problem. Example: $\frac{2}{3} \div \frac{3}{4} = \frac{2}{3} \times \frac{4}{3} = \frac{8}{9}$.

Review Video: Dividing Fractions
Visit mometrix.com/academy and enter code: 300874

Multiplying a Mixed Number by a Whole Number or a Decimal

When multiplying a mixed number by something, it is usually best to convert it to an improper fraction first. Additionally, if the multiplicand is a decimal, it is most often simplest to convert it to a fraction. For instance, to multiply $4\frac{3}{8}$ by 3.5, begin by rewriting each quantity as a whole number plus a proper fraction. Remember, a mixed number is a fraction added to a whole number and a decimal is a representation of the sum of fractions, specifically tenths, hundredths, thousandths, and so on:

$$4\frac{3}{8} \times 3.5 = \left(4 + \frac{3}{8}\right) \times \left(3 + \frac{1}{2}\right)$$

Next, the quantities being added need to be expressed with the same denominator. This is achieved by multiplying and dividing the whole number by the denominator of the fraction. Recall that a whole number is equivalent to that number divided by 1:

$$= \left(\frac{4}{1} \times \frac{8}{8} + \frac{3}{8}\right) \times \left(\frac{3}{1} \times \frac{2}{2} + \frac{1}{2}\right)$$

When multiplying fractions, remember to multiply the numerators and denominators separately:

$$= \left(\frac{4 \times 8}{1 \times 8} + \frac{3}{8}\right) \times \left(\frac{3 \times 2}{1 \times 2} + \frac{1}{2}\right)$$
$$= \left(\frac{32}{8} + \frac{3}{8}\right) \times \left(\frac{6}{2} + \frac{1}{2}\right)$$

Now that the fractions have the same denominators, they can be added:

$$= \frac{35}{8} \times \frac{7}{2}$$

Finally, perform the last multiplication and then simplify:

$$= \frac{35 \times 7}{8 \times 2} = \frac{245}{16} = \frac{240}{16} + \frac{5}{16} = 15\frac{5}{16}$$

DECIMALS

Decimals are one way to represent parts of a whole. Using the place value system, each digit to the right of a decimal point denotes the number of units of a corresponding *negative* power of ten. For example, consider the decimal 0.24. We can use a model to represent the decimal. Since a dime is worth one-tenth of a dollar and a penny is worth one-hundredth of a dollar, one possible model to represent this fraction is to have 2 dimes representing the 2 in the tenths place and 4 pennies representing the 4 in the hundredths place:

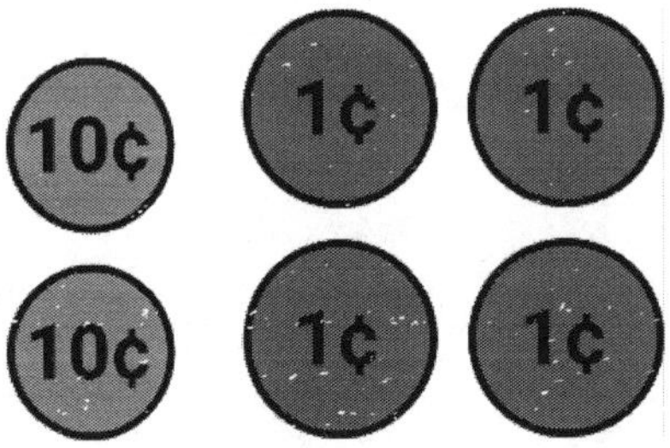

To write the decimal as a fraction, put the decimal in the numerator with 1 in the denominator. Multiply the numerator and denominator by tens until there are no more decimal places. Then simplify the fraction to lowest terms. For example, converting 0.24 to a fraction:

$$0.24 = \frac{0.24}{1} = \frac{0.24 \times 100}{1 \times 100} = \frac{24}{100} = \frac{6}{25}$$

Review Video: Decimals
Visit mometrix.com/academy and enter code: 837268

Operations with Decimals

Adding and Subtracting Decimals

When adding and subtracting decimals, the decimal points must always be aligned. Adding decimals is just like adding regular whole numbers. Example: $4.5 + 2.0 = 6.5$.

If the problem-solver does not properly align the decimal points, an incorrect answer of 4.7 may result. An easy way to add decimals is to align all of the decimal points in a vertical column visually. This will allow one to see exactly where the decimal should be placed in the final answer. Begin adding from right to left. Add each column in turn, making sure to carry the number to the left if a column adds up to more than 9. The same rules apply to the subtraction of decimals.

Review Video: Adding and Subtracting Decimals
Visit mometrix.com/academy and enter code: 381101

Multiplying Decimals

A simple multiplication problem has two components: a **multiplicand** and a **multiplier**. When multiplying decimals, work as though the numbers were whole rather than decimals. Once the final product is calculated, count the number of places to the right of the decimal in both the multiplicand and the multiplier. Then, count that number of places from the right of the product and place the decimal in that position.

For example, 12.3×2.56 has a total of three places to the right of the respective decimals. Multiply 123×256 to get 31,488. Now, beginning on the right, count three places to the left and insert the decimal. The final product will be 31.488.

Review Video: Multiplying Decimals
Visit mometrix.com/academy and enter code: 731574

Dividing Decimals

Every division problem has a **divisor** and a **dividend**. The dividend is the number that is being divided. In the problem $14 \div 7$, 14 is the dividend and 7 is the divisor. In a division problem with decimals, the divisor must be converted into a whole number. Begin by moving the decimal in the divisor to the right until a whole number is created. Next, move the decimal in the dividend the same number of spaces to the right. For example, 4.9 into 24.5 would become 49 into 245. The decimal was moved one space to the right to create a whole number in the divisor, and then the same was done for the dividend. Once the whole numbers are created, the problem is carried out normally: $245 \div 49 = 5$.

Review Video: Dividing Decimals
Visit mometrix.com/academy and enter code: 560690

Percentages

Percentages can be thought of as fractions that are based on a whole of 100; that is, one whole is equal to 100%. The word **percent** means "per hundred." Percentage problems are often presented in three main ways:

- Find what percentage of some number another number is.
  - Example: What percentage of 40 is 8?
- Find what number is some percentage of a given number.

  - Example: What number is 20% of 40?
- Find what number another number is a given percentage of.
  - Example: What number is 8 20% of?

There are three components in each of these cases: a **whole** (W), a **part** (P), and a **percentage** (%). These are related by the equation: $P = W \times \%$. This can easily be rearranged into other forms that may suit different questions better: $\% = \frac{P}{W}$ and $W = \frac{P}{\%}$. Percentage problems are often also word problems. As such, a large part of solving them is figuring out which quantities are what. For example, consider the following word problem:

In a school cafeteria, 7 students choose pizza, 9 choose hamburgers, and 4 choose tacos. What percentage of student choose tacos?

To find the whole, you must first add all of the parts: $7 + 9 + 4 = 20$. The percentage can then be found by dividing the part by the whole ($\% = \frac{P}{W}$): $\frac{4}{20} = \frac{20}{100} = 20\%$.

Review Video: Percentages
Visit mometrix.com/academy and enter code: 141911

Converting Between Percentages, Fractions, and Decimals

Converting decimals to percentages and percentages to decimals is as simple as moving the decimal point. To *convert from a decimal to a percentage*, move the decimal point **two places to the right.** To *convert from a percentage to a decimal*, move it **two places to the left**. It may be helpful to remember that the percentage number will always be larger than the equivalent decimal number. For example:

$$0.23 = 23\% \qquad 5.34 = 534\% \qquad 0.007 = 0.7\%$$
$$700\% = 7.00 \qquad 86\% = 0.86 \qquad 0.15\% = 0.0015$$

To convert a fraction to a decimal, simply divide the numerator by the denominator in the fraction. To convert a decimal to a fraction, put the decimal in the numerator with 1 in the denominator. Multiply the numerator and denominator by tens until there are no more decimal places. Then simplify the fraction to lowest terms. For example, converting 0.24 to a fraction:

$$0.24 = \frac{0.24}{1} = \frac{0.24 \times 100}{1 \times 100} = \frac{24}{100} = \frac{6}{25}$$

Fractions can be converted to a percentage by finding equivalent fractions with a denominator of 100. For example,

$$\frac{7}{10} = \frac{70}{100} = 70\% \quad \frac{1}{4} = \frac{25}{100} = 25\%$$

To convert a percentage to a fraction, divide the percentage number by 100 and reduce the fraction to its simplest possible terms. For example,

$$60\% = \frac{60}{100} = \frac{3}{5} \quad 96\% = \frac{96}{100} = \frac{24}{25}$$

Review Video: Converting Decimals to Fractions and Percentages
Visit mometrix.com/academy and enter code: 986765

Review Video: Converting Fractions to Percentages and Decimals
Visit mometrix.com/academy and enter code: 306233

Review Video: Converting Percentages to Decimals and Fractions
Visit mometrix.com/academy and enter code: 287297

RATIONAL NUMBERS

The term **rational** means that the number can be expressed as a ratio or fraction. That is, a number, r, is rational if and only if it can be represented by a fraction $\frac{a}{b}$ where a and b are integers and b does not equal 0. The set of rational numbers includes integers and decimals. If there is no finite way to represent a value with a fraction of integers, then the number is **irrational**. Common examples of irrational numbers include: $\sqrt{5}$, $(1 + \sqrt{2})$, and π.

Review Video: Rational Numbers
Visit mometrix.com/academy and enter code: 280645

PRACTICE

P1. What is 30% of 120?

P2. What is 150% of 20?

P3. What is 14.5% of 96?

P4. Simplify the following expressions:

(a) $\left(\frac{2}{5}\right)/\left(\frac{4}{7}\right)$
(b) $\frac{7}{8}-\frac{8}{16}$
(c) $\frac{1}{2}+\left(3\left(\frac{3}{4}\right)-2\right)+4$
(d) $0.22+0.5-(5.5+3.3\div 3)$
(e) $\frac{3}{2}+(4(0.5)-0.75)+2$

P5. Convert the following to a fraction and to a decimal: **(a)** 15%; **(b)** 24.36%

P6. Convert the following to a decimal and to a percentage. **(a)** 4/5; **(b)** $3\frac{2}{5}$

P7. A woman's age is thirteen more than half of 60. How old is the woman?

P8. A patient was given pain medicine at a dosage of 0.22 grams. The patient's dosage was then increased to 0.80 grams. By how much was the patient's dosage increased?

P9. At a hotel, $\frac{3}{4}$ of the 100 rooms are occupied today. Yesterday, $\frac{4}{5}$ of the 100 rooms were occupied. On which day were more of the rooms occupied and by how much more?

P10. At a school, 40% of the teachers teach English. If 20 teachers teach English, how many teachers work at the school?

P11. A patient was given blood pressure medicine at a dosage of 2 grams. The patient's dosage was then decreased to 0.45 grams. By how much was the patient's dosage decreased?

P12. Two weeks ago, $\frac{2}{3}$ of the 60 customers at a skate shop were male. Last week, $\frac{3}{6}$ of the 80 customers were male. During which week were there more male customers?

P13. Jane ate lunch at a local restaurant. She ordered a $4.99 appetizer, a $12.50 entrée, and a $1.25 soda. If she wants to tip her server 20%, how much money will she spend in all?

P14. According to a survey, about 82% of engineers were highly satisfied with their job. If 145 engineers were surveyed, how many reported that they were highly satisfied?

P15. A patient was given 40 mg of a certain medicine. Later, the patient's dosage was increased to 45 mg. What was the percent increase in his medication?

P16. Order the following rational numbers from least to greatest: 0.55, 17%, $\sqrt{25}$, $\frac{64}{4}$, $\frac{25}{50}$, 3.

P17. Order the following rational numbers from greatest to least: 0.3, 27%, $\sqrt{100}$, $\frac{72}{9}$, $\frac{1}{9}$, 4.5

P18. Perform the following multiplication. Write each answer as a mixed number.

(a) $\left(1\frac{11}{16}\right) \times 4$
(b) $\left(12\frac{1}{3}\right) \times 1.1$
(c) $3.71 \times \left(6\frac{1}{5}\right)$

P19. Suppose you are making doughnuts and you want to triple the recipe you have. If the following list is the original amounts for the ingredients, what would be the amounts for the tripled recipe?

$1\,^3/_4$	cup	Flour
$1\,^1/_4$	tsp	Baking powder
$^3/_4$	tsp	Salt
$^3/_8$	cup	Sugar
$1\,^1/_2$	Tbsp	Butter
2	large	Eggs
$^3/_4$	tsp	Vanilla extract
$^3/_8$	cup	Sour cream

PRACTICE SOLUTIONS

P1. The word *of* indicates multiplication, so 30% of 120 is found by multiplying 120 by 30%. Change 30% to a decimal, then multiply: $120 \times 0.3 = 36$

P2. The word *of* indicates multiplication, so 150% of 20 is found by multiplying 20 by 150%. Change 150% to a decimal, then multiply: $20 \times 1.5 = 30$

P3. Change 14.5% to a decimal before multiplying. $0.145 \times 96 = 13.92$.

P4. Follow the order of operations and utilize properties of fractions to solve each:

(a) Rewrite the problem as a multiplication problem: $\frac{2}{5} \times \frac{7}{4} = \frac{2 \times 7}{5 \times 4} = \frac{14}{20}$. Make sure the fraction is reduced to lowest terms. Both 14 and 20 can be divided by 2.

$$\frac{14}{20} = \frac{14 \div 2}{20 \div 2} = \frac{7}{10}$$

(b) The denominators of $\frac{7}{8}$ and $\frac{8}{16}$ are 8 and 16, respectively. The lowest common denominator of 8 and 16 is 16 because 16 is the least common multiple of 8 and 16. Convert the first fraction to its equivalent with the newly found common denominator of 16: $\frac{7 \times 2}{8 \times 2} = \frac{14}{16}$. Now that the fractions have the same denominator, you can subtract them.

$$\frac{14}{16} - \frac{8}{16} = \frac{6}{16} = \frac{3}{8}$$

(c) When simplifying expressions, first perform operations within groups. Within the set of parentheses are multiplication and subtraction operations. Perform the multiplication first to get $\frac{1}{2} + \left(\frac{9}{4} - 2\right) + 4$. Then, subtract two to obtain $\frac{1}{2} + \frac{1}{4} + 4$. Finally, perform addition from left to right:

$$\frac{1}{2} + \frac{1}{4} + 4 = \frac{2}{4} + \frac{1}{4} + \frac{16}{4} = \frac{19}{4} = 4\frac{3}{4}$$

(d) First, evaluate the terms in the parentheses $(5.5 + 3.3 \div 3)$ using order of operations. $3.3 \div 3 = 1.1$, and $5.5 + 1.1 = 6.6$. Next, rewrite the problem: $0.22 + 0.5 - 6.6$. Finally, add and subtract from left to right: $0.22 + 0.5 = 0.72$; $0.72 - 6.6 = -5.88$. The answer is -5.88.

(e) First, simplify within the parentheses, then change the fraction to a decimal and perform addition from left to right:

$$\frac{3}{2} + (2 - 0.75) + 2 =$$
$$\frac{3}{2} + 1.25 + 2 =$$
$$1.5 + 1.25 + 2 = 4.75$$

P5. (a) 15% can be written as $\frac{15}{100}$. Both 15 and 100 can be divided by 5: $\frac{15 \div 5}{100 \div 5} = \frac{3}{20}$

When converting from a percentage to a decimal, drop the percent sign and move the decimal point two places to the left: $15\% = 0.15$

(b) 24.36% written as a fraction is $\frac{24.36}{100}$, or $\frac{2436}{10{,}000}$, which reduces to $\frac{609}{2500}$. 24.36% written as a decimal is 0.2436. Recall that dividing by 100 moves the decimal two places to the left.

P6. (a) Recall that in the decimal system the first decimal place is one tenth: $\frac{4 \times 2}{5 \times 2} = \frac{8}{10} = 0.8$

Percent means "per hundred." $\frac{4 \times 20}{5 \times 20} = \frac{80}{100} = 80\%$

(b) The mixed number $3\frac{2}{5}$ has a whole number and a fractional part. The fractional part $\frac{2}{5}$ can be written as a decimal by dividing 5 into 2, which gives 0.4. Adding the whole to the part gives 3.4.

To find the equivalent percentage, multiply the decimal by 100. $3.4(100) = 340\%$. Notice that this percentage is greater than 100%. This makes sense because the original mixed number $3\frac{2}{5}$ is greater than 1.

P7. "More than" indicates addition, and "of" indicates multiplication. The expression can be written as $\frac{1}{2}(60) + 13$. So the woman's age is equal to $\frac{1}{2}(60) + 13 = 30 + 13 = 43$. The woman is 43 years old.

P8. The first step is to determine what operation (addition, subtraction, multiplication, or division) the problem requires. Notice the keywords and phrases "by how much" and "increased." "Increased" means that you go from a smaller amount to a larger amount. This change can be found by subtracting the smaller amount from the larger amount: 0.80 grams $-$ 0.22 grams $=$ 0.58 grams.

Remember to line up the decimal when subtracting:

$$\begin{array}{r} 0.80 \\ -\ 0.22 \\ \hline 0.58 \end{array}$$

P9. First, find the number of rooms occupied each day. To do so, multiply the fraction of rooms occupied by the number of rooms available:

$$\text{Number occupied} = \text{Fraction occupied} \times \text{Total number}$$
$$\text{Number of rooms occupied today} = \frac{3}{4} \times 100 = 75$$
$$\text{Number of rooms occupied} = \frac{4}{5} \times 100 = 80$$

The difference in the number of rooms occupied is: $80 - 75 = 5$ rooms

P10. To answer this problem, first think about the number of teachers that work at the school. Will it be more or less than the number of teachers who work in a specific department such as English? More teachers work at the school, so the number you find to answer this question will be greater than 20.

40% of the teachers are English teachers. "Of" indicates multiplication, and words like "is" and "are" indicate equivalence. Translating the problem into a mathematical sentence gives $40\% \times t = 20$, where t represents the total number of teachers. Solving for t gives $t = \frac{20}{40\%} = \frac{20}{0.40} = 50$. Fifty teachers work at the school.

P11. The decrease is represented by the difference between the two amounts:

$$2 \text{ grams} - 0.45 \text{ grams} = 1.55 \text{ grams.}$$

Remember to line up the decimal point before subtracting.

$$\begin{array}{r} 2.00 \\ -\ 0.45 \\ \hline 1.55 \end{array}$$

P12. First, you need to find the number of male customers that were in the skate shop each week. You are given this amount in terms of fractions. To find the actual number of male customers, multiply the fraction of male customers by the number of customers in the store.

$$\text{Actual number of male customers} = \text{fraction of male customers} \times \text{total customers}$$
$$\text{Number of male customers two weeks ago} = \frac{2}{3} \times 60 = \frac{120}{3} = 40$$
$$\text{Number of male customers last week} = \frac{3}{6} \times 80 = \frac{1}{2} \times 80 = \frac{80}{2} = 40$$

The number of male customers was the same both weeks.

P13. To find total amount, first find the sum of the items she ordered from the menu and then add 20% of this sum to the total.

$$\$4.99 + \$12.50 + \$1.25 = \$18.74$$

$$\$18.74 \times 20\% = (0.20)(\$18.74) = \$3.748 \approx \$3.75$$

$$\text{Total} = \$18.74 + \$3.75 = \$22.49$$

P14. 82% of 145 is $0.82 \times 145 = 118.9$. Because you can't have 0.9 of a person, we must round up to say that 119 engineers reported that they were highly satisfied with their jobs.

P15. To find the percent increase, first compare the original and increased amounts. The original amount was 40 mg, and the increased amount is 45 mg, so the dosage of medication was increased by 5 mg ($45 - 40 = 5$). Note, however, that the question asks not by how much the dosage increased but by what percentage it increased.

$$\begin{aligned}\text{Percent increase} &= \frac{\text{new amount} - \text{original amount}}{\text{original amount}} \times 100\% \\ &= \frac{45\text{ mg} - 40\text{ mg}}{40\text{ mg}} \times 100\% = \frac{5}{40} \times 100\% = 0.125 \times 100\% = 12.5\%\end{aligned}$$

P16. Recall that the term rational simply means that the number can be expressed as a ratio or fraction. Notice that each of the numbers in the problem can be written as a decimal or integer:

$$\begin{aligned}17\% &= 0.1717 \\ \sqrt{25} &= 5 \\ \frac{64}{4} &= 16 \\ \frac{25}{50} &= \frac{1}{2} = 0.5\end{aligned}$$

So, the answer is 17%, $\frac{25}{50}$, 0.55, 3, $\sqrt{25}$, $\frac{64}{4}$.

P17. Converting all the numbers to integers and decimals makes it easier to compare the values:

$$\begin{aligned}27\% &= 0.27 \\ \sqrt{100} &= 10 \\ \frac{72}{9} &= 8 \\ \frac{1}{9} &\approx 0.11\end{aligned}$$

So, the answer is $\sqrt{100}$, $\frac{72}{9}$, 4.5, 0.3, 27%, $\frac{1}{9}$.

Review Video: Ordering Rational Numbers
Visit mometrix.com/academy and enter code: 419578

P18. For each, convert improper fractions, adjust to a common denominator, perform the operations, and then simplify:

(a) Sometimes, you can skip converting the denominator and just distribute the multiplication.

$$\begin{aligned}\left(1\frac{11}{16}\right)\times 4 &= \left(1+\frac{11}{16}\right)\times 4\\ &= 1\times 4+\frac{11}{16}\times 4\\ &= 4+\frac{11}{16}\times\frac{4}{1}\\ &= 4+\frac{44}{16}=4+\frac{11}{4}=4+2\frac{3}{4}=6\frac{3}{4}\end{aligned}$$

(b)

$$\begin{aligned}\left(12\frac{1}{3}\right)\times 1.1 &= \left(12+\frac{1}{3}\right)\times\left(1+\frac{1}{10}\right)\\ &= \left(\frac{12}{1}\times\frac{3}{3}+\frac{1}{3}\right)\times\left(\frac{10}{10}+\frac{1}{10}\right)\\ &= \left(\frac{36}{3}+\frac{1}{3}\right)\times\frac{11}{10}\\ &= \frac{37}{3}\times\frac{11}{10}\\ &= \frac{407}{30}=\frac{390}{30}+\frac{17}{30}=13\frac{17}{30}\end{aligned}$$

(c)

$$\begin{aligned}3.71\times\left(6\frac{1}{5}\right) &= \left(3+\frac{71}{100}\right)\times\left(6+\frac{1}{5}\right)\\ &= \left(\frac{300}{100}+\frac{71}{100}\right)\times\left(\frac{6}{1}\times\frac{5}{5}+\frac{1}{5}\right)\\ &= \frac{371}{100}\times\left(\frac{30}{5}+\frac{1}{5}\right)\\ &= \frac{371}{100}\times\frac{31}{5}\\ &= \frac{11501}{500}=\frac{11500}{500}+\frac{1}{500}=23\frac{1}{500}\end{aligned}$$

P19. Fortunately, some of the amounts are duplicated, so we do not need to figure out every amount.

$$\begin{aligned}1\frac{3}{4}\times 3 &= (1\times 3)+\left(\frac{3}{4}\times 3\right)\\ &= 3+\frac{9}{4}\\ &= 3+2\frac{1}{4}\\ &= 5\frac{1}{4}\end{aligned}$$

$$\begin{aligned}1\frac{1}{4}\times 3 &= (1\times 3)+\left(\frac{1}{4}\times 3\right)\\ &= 3+\frac{3}{4}\\ &= 3\frac{3}{4}\end{aligned}$$

$$\begin{aligned}\frac{3}{4}\times 3 &= \frac{3}{4}\times 3\\ &= \frac{9}{4}\\ &= 2\frac{1}{4}\end{aligned}$$

$$\frac{3}{8} \times 3 = \frac{3}{8} \times 3 = \frac{9}{8} = 1\frac{1}{8}$$

$$1\frac{1}{2} \times 3 = 1 \times 3 + \frac{1}{2} \times 3 = 3 + \frac{3}{2} = 3 + 1\frac{1}{2} = 4\frac{1}{2}$$

$$2 \times 3 = 6$$

So, the result for the triple recipe is:

$5\,^1/_4$	cup	Flour
$3\,^3/_4$	tsp	Baking powder
$2\,^1/_4$	tsp	Salt
$1\,^1/_8$	cup	Sugar
$4\,^1/_2$	Tbsp	Butter
6	large	Eggs
$2\,^1/_4$	tsp	Vanilla extract
$1\,^1/_8$	cup	Sour cream

Mathematical Reasoning

Premise and Argument

A premise is a statement that precedes a conclusion, in an argument. It is the proposition, or assumption, of an argument. An argument will have two or more premises.

Example:

If it is hot, then I will go swimming. (Premise)
It is hot. (Premise)
Therefore, I will go swimming. (Conclusion)

Simple and Compound Statements

A **statement** in propositional logic is any sentence or expression that has a truth value—that is, that may in principle be considered true or false. "Hello!", for example, is not a statement; there's no sense in which it could be considered true or false. On the other hand, "$2 = 3$" *is* a statement, albeit a clearly false one. A **compound statement** is a statement that contains one or more other statements, combined or modified in some way. A **simple statement**, or a **proposition**, is a statement that cannot be broken down further into smaller statements.

For example, consider the statement, "If it rains tomorrow, then the streets will be flooded and traffic will be slow." This is a compound statement, because two smaller statements are embedded within it: "it rains tomorrow" and "the streets will be flooded and traffic will be slow." the former cannot be broken down further, and is therefore a simple statement, but the latter is another compound statement, because it includes two simple statements: "the streets will be flooded" and "traffic will be slow."

Common operations used to combine and modify simple statements into compound statements include conjunction, disjunction, negation, and implication.

Conjunction

Conjunction is an operation that combines two or more statements into a compound statement that is true if and only if all of the component statements are true. When the statements are written out, conjunction is marked by the word "and." For example, the statement "Roses are red and violets are blue" is a compound statement that is a conjunction of the two simple statements "roses are red" and "violets are blue."

Conjunction is represented by the operator $\wedge$. In the previous example, if proposition P is "roses are red" and proposition Q is "violets are blue," then the compound statement "roses are red and violets are blue" would be written as "$P \wedge Q$."

Disjunction

Disjunction is an operation that combines two or more statements into a compound statement that is true if and only if at least one of the component statements is true. When the statements are written out, conjunction is marked by the word "or." For example, the statement "I'll clean the closet today, or you'll clean it tomorrow" is a compound statement that is a disjunction of the simple statements "I'll clean the closet today" and "you'll clean the closet tomorrow."

Disjunction is represented by the operator $\vee$. In the previous example, if proposition P is "I'll clean the closet today" and proposition Q is "you'll clean the closet tomorrow," then the compound statement "I'll clean the closet today, or you'll clean it tomorrow" would be written as "$P \vee Q$."

Note that while in everyday language "or" implies exclusivity, as one or the other option but not both, in formal logic disjunction includes the possibility of both propositions being true. If I clean the closet today *and* you clean it tomorrow, then the sample statement "I'll clean the closet today, or you'll clean it tomorrow" is true.

Conditional and Biconditional Statements

A conditional statement, or **implication**, is a compound statement of the form "if P, then Q." for instance, the statement "if a snake has rattles, then it's venomous" is a conditional statement. It can also be written "P implies Q" ("that a snake has rattles implies that it's venomous") or "P only if Q" ("a snake has rattles only if it's venomous"). the conditional statement is true when both P and Q are true, and even when P is false, regardless of Q. In other words, the conditional statement is false only when P is true and Q is false. the conditional statement is written as "$P \rightarrow Q$." P is called the **premise** of the statement, and Q the **conclusion**.

A **biconditional statement** is a combination of two conditional statements: both "if P, then Q" and "if Q, then P." To state it more concisely, "P if and only if Q." an example is "A number is even if and only if it is divisible by 2." the biconditional statement is true when P and Q are either both true or both false; it is false if P is true and Q is false or vice versa. the biconditional statement is written "$P \leftrightarrow Q$."

Existential and Universal Quantifiers

A **quantifier** is a logical construct used in a compound statement to give information on the number of subjects for which a statement is true. The **existential quantifier** specifies that the statement is true for at least one subject. It is usually introduced as "there exists," such as "there exists a real number that is equal to its own square." The symbol ∃ is used to signify the existential quantifier. For example, the preceding statement could be written as "$\exists x \in \mathbb{R}\, x = x^2$." The **universal quantifier** specifies that the statement is true for *every* subject. It is usually said as "all" or "for all", such as "all real numbers are less than their own squares plus one." The symbol ∀ is used to signify the universal quantifier. For example, the preceding statement could be written as

$$\forall x \in \mathbb{R}\, x < x^2 + 1$$

Sometimes it is useful to specify that there exists *exactly* one subject that meets a given criterion. In other words, there exists a *unique* such subject. This can be signified by adding an exclamation mark after the existential quantifier: "$\exists!\, x \in \mathbb{R}\, |x| = 0$" means "there exists a unique real number that has an absolute value of zero."

Truth Tables

A truth table shows the truth value of one or more compound statements for each possible combination of truth values of the propositions within it. The truth table contains one column for each **proposition**, and one column for each of the **compound statements** to be analyzed. It has one row for each combination of **truth values** of the propositions. Since each proposition has two possible truth values, the number of possible combinations for N propositions is 2^N, so the truth table will have 2^N rows.

The table below is a simple truth table for some common compound statements involving two propositions.

P	Q	$P \wedge Q$	$P \vee Q$	$\neg P$	$\neg Q$	$P \rightarrow Q$	$Q \rightarrow P$	$P \leftrightarrow Q$
T	T	T	T	F	F	T	T	T
T	F	F	T	F	T	F	T	F
F	T	F	T	T	F	T	F	F
F	F	F	F	T	T	T	T	T

Truth tables are useful for comparing two compound statements to see if they are equivalent. They are also useful for analyzing whether complicated compound statements are true or false. A table can have a column for each of the increasingly complex compound statements that combine to form the total statement.

Truth Table to Validate the Rule of Detachment

The Rule of Detachment states that given the premises, $P \rightarrow Q$ and P, the valid conclusion is Q.

In other words, for every case where $(P \rightarrow Q) \wedge P$ is true, Q will also be true. The truth table below illustrates this fact:

P	Q	$P \rightarrow Q$	$(P \rightarrow Q) \wedge P$
T	T	T	T
T	F	F	F
F	T	T	F
F	F	T	F

Notice the first cell under $(P \rightarrow Q) \wedge P$ is true, while the first cell under Q is also true. Thus, for every case where $(P \rightarrow Q) \wedge P$ was true, Q was also true.

Truth Table to Validate the Chain Rule

The Chain Rule states that given the premises, $P \rightarrow Q$ and $Q \rightarrow R$, the valid conclusion is $P \rightarrow R$.

In other words, for every case where $(P \rightarrow Q) \wedge (Q \rightarrow R)$ is true, $P \rightarrow R$ will also be true. The truth table below illustrates this fact:

P	Q	R	$P \rightarrow Q$	$Q \rightarrow R$	$(P \rightarrow Q) \wedge (Q \rightarrow R)$	$P \rightarrow R$
T	T	T	T	T	T	T
T	T	F	T	F	F	F
T	F	T	F	T	F	T
T	F	F	F	T	F	F
F	T	T	T	T	T	T
F	T	F	T	F	F	T
F	F	T	T	T	T	T
F	F	F	T	T	T	T

Notice that for every case where $(P \rightarrow Q) \wedge (Q \rightarrow R)$ was true, $P \rightarrow R$ was also true.

For example, consider the premises below:

If I hike a mountain, I will not eat a sandwich.
If I do not eat a sandwich, I will drink some water.
I will not drink some water.

Write a valid conclusive statement. Explain how you arrived at your answer. Be specific in your explanation.

Valid conclusive statement: I will not hike a mountain.

Application of the chain rule and rule of contraposition give the valid conclusion of $\neg P$. According to the chain rule, given $P \rightarrow \neg Q$ and $\neg Q \rightarrow R$, then $P \rightarrow R$. According to the rule of contraposition, $P \rightarrow R$ and $\neg R$ yields $\neg P$. On a truth table, for every place where $(P \rightarrow R) \wedge \neg R$ is true, $\neg P$ is also true. Thus, this is a valid conclusive statement.

Negation

In propositional logic, negation refers to the inversion of the truth value of a statement. The **negation** of a statement is true if the original statement is false, and false if the original statement is true. Negation can be signified by the word "not." For instance, the negation of the statement "Bob's cat is black" is "Bob's cat is not black." the symbol for negation is $\neg$. So, if the proposition P is "Bob's cat is black," then $\neg P$ would be "Bob's cat is not black." Two negations cancel each other out: $\neg\neg P = P$, or "not not P equals P."

It's important to be careful when combining negation with **quantifiers**. The negation of "there exists a cow that has a blue horn" is not "there exists a cow that does not have a blue horn." Rather, the negation is "there does not exist a cow that has a blue horn." the statements $\neg\exists x\ P(x)$ and $\exists x\ \neg P(x)$ are not equivalent. the same is true for the universal quantifier: $\neg\forall x\ P(x)$ and $\forall x\ \neg P(x)$ do not mean the same thing. There is, however, a connection between the negated quantifiers: $\neg\exists x\ P(x)$ is equivalent to $\forall x\ \neg P(x)$, and $\exists x\ \neg P(x)$ is equivalent to $\neg\forall x\ P(x)$.

De Morgan's Laws

De Morgan's Laws are a set of useful relations connecting negation, conjunction, and disjunction. They can be stated briefly as "the negation of a conjunction is the disjunction of the negations" and "the negation of a disjunction is the conjunction of the negations." This can be written as:

$$\neg(P \wedge Q) \leftrightarrow (\neg P) \vee (\neg Q) \text{ and } \neg(P \vee Q) \leftrightarrow (\neg P) \wedge (\neg Q)$$

For instance, if proposition P is "$x > 3$" and proposition Q is "$y > 3$", then De Morgan's Laws state that "it is not true that both x and y are greater than 3" is equivalent to "either x is not greater than 3, or y is not greater than 3."

The validity of **De Morgan's Laws** can be shown with truth tables. Note that the columns highlighted in the same color match:

P	Q	$\neg P$	$\neg Q$	$(\neg P) \wedge (\neg Q)$	$(\neg P) \vee (\neg Q)$	$P \wedge Q$	$P \vee Q$	$\neg(P \wedge Q)$	$\neg(P \vee Q)$
T	T	F	F	F	F	T	T	F	F
T	F	F	T	F	T	F	T	T	F
F	T	T	F	F	T	F	T	T	F
F	F	T	T	T	T	F	F	T	T

Converse, Inverse, and Contrapositive of a Conditional Statement

The converse of a conditional statement is a conditional statement with the premise and conclusion interchanged. the converse of $P \to Q$ is $Q \to P$. The **inverse** has the premise and conclusion both negated. The inverse of $P \to Q$ is $\neg P \to \neg Q$. The **contrapositive** has the premise and conclusion both negated *and* interchanged. The contrapositive of $P \to Q$ is $\neg Q \to \neg P$.

For example, given the **conditional statement**, "If there is a key in the lock, then someone is home," the **converse** is "if someone is home, then there is a key in the lock," the **inverse** is "if there is not a key in the lock, then no one is home," and the **contrapositive** is "if no one is home, then there is not a key in the lock."

Note that the converse and inverse of a statement are *not* logically equivalent to the original statement. For instance, the statement "if $x = 4$, then $x > 2$" is true, but its converse "if $x > 2$, then $x = 4$" is not, because there are many numbers greater than 2, not just 4. A statement *is*, however, logically equivalent to its contrapositive—and the converse and inverse, while not equivalent to the original statement, are equivalent to each other. The following truth table summarizes the relationships:

P	Q	$\neg P$	$\neg Q$	$P \to Q$ (statement)	$Q \to P$ (converse)	$\neg P \to \neg Q$ (inverse)	$\neg Q \to \neg P$ (contrapositive)
T	T	F	F	T	T	T	T
T	F	F	T	F	T	T	F
F	T	T	F	T	F	F	T
F	F	T	T	T	T	T	T

Inductive Reasoning

Inductive reasoning is a method used to make a conjecture, based on patterns and observations. The conclusion of an inductive argument may be true or false.

Mathematical Example:

A cube has 6 faces, 8 vertices, and 12 edges. A square pyramid has 5 faces, 5 vertices, and 8 edges. A triangular prism has 5 faces, 6 vertices, and 9 edges. Thus, the sum of the numbers of faces and vertices, minus the number of edges, will always equal 2, for any solid.

Non-Mathematical Example:

Almost all summer days in Tucson are hot. It is a summer day in Tucson. Therefore, it will probably be hot.

Deductive Reasoning

Deductive reasoning is a method that proves a hypothesis or set of premises. The conclusion of a valid deductive argument will be true, given that the premises are true. Deductive reasoning utilizes logic to determine a conclusion. For instance, consider the following application of the chain rule:

If a ding is a dong, then a ping is a pong.	$p \rightarrow q$
If a ping is a pong, then a ring is a ting.	$q \rightarrow r$
A ding is a dong.	p
Therefore, a ring is a ting.	$\therefore r$

Formal Reasoning

Formal reasoning, in mathematics, involves justification using formal steps and processes to arrive at a conclusion. Formal reasoning is utilized when writing proofs and using logic. For example, when applying logic, validity of a conclusion is determined by truth tables. A set of premises will yield a given conclusion. This type of thinking is formal reasoning. Writing a geometric proof also employs formal reasoning. For example:

If a quadrilateral has four congruent sides, it is a rhombus.
If a shape is a rhombus, then the diagonals are perpendicular.
A quadrilateral has four congruent sides.
Therefore, the diagonals are perpendicular.

Informal Reasoning

Informal reasoning, in mathematics, uses patterns and observations to make conjectures. The conjecture may be true or false. Several, or even many, examples may show a certain pattern, shedding light on a possible conclusion. However, informal reasoning does not provide a justifiable conclusion. A conjecture may certainly be deemed as likely or probable. However, informal reasoning will not reveal a certain conclusion. Consider the following example:

Mathematical Idea – Given a sequence that starts with 1 and each term decreases by a factor of $\frac{1}{2}$, the limit of the sum of the sequence will be 2.

Informal Reasoning – The sum of 1 and $\frac{1}{2}$ is $1\frac{1}{2}$. The sum of 1, $\frac{1}{2}$, and $\frac{1}{4}$ is $1\frac{3}{4}$. The sum of 1, $\frac{1}{2}$, $\frac{1}{4}$, and $\frac{1}{8}$ is $1\frac{7}{8}$. Thus, it appears that as the sequence approaches infinity, the sum of the sequence approaches 2.

Proofs

A **proof** serves to show the deductive or inductive process that relates the steps leading from a hypothesis to a conclusion. A proof may be direct ($p \rightarrow q$), meaning that a conclusion is shown to be true, given a hypothesis. There are also proofs by contradiction ($p \land \sim q$), whereby the hypothesis is assumed to be true, and the negation of the conclusion is assumed to be true. (In other words, the statement is assumed to be false.) Proofs by contraposition ($\sim q \rightarrow \sim p$) show that the negation of the conclusion leads to the negation of the hypothesis. (In other words, the negation of the conclusion is assumed to be true, and it must be shown that the negation of the hypothesis is also true.) A mathematical induction proof seeks to show that $P(1)$ is true and that $P(k+1)$ is true, given that $P(k)$ is true. Direct proofs, proofs by contradiction, and proofs by contraposition use deductive methods, while a mathematical induction proof uses an inductive method.

Direct proofs are those that assume a statement to be true. The purpose of such a proof is to show that the conclusion is true, given that the hypothesis is true. A sample of a direct proof is shown below:

Prove "If m divides a and m divides b, then m divides $a + b$."

Proof:

- Assume m divides a and m divides b.
- Thus, a equals the product of m and some integer factor, p, by the definition of division, and b equals the product of m and some integer factor, q, by the definition of division. According to substitution, $a + b$ may be rewritten as $(m \times p) + (m \times q)$. Factoring out the m gives $m(p + q)$. Since m divides $p + q$, and $p + q$ is an integer, according to the closure property, we have shown that m divides $a + b$, by the definition of division.

Indirect proofs (or proofs by contradiction) are those that assume a statement to be false. The purpose of such a proof is to show that a hypothesis is false, given the negation of the conclusion, indicating that the conclusion must be true. A sample of an indirect proof is shown below:

Prove "If $3x + 7$ is odd, then x is even."

Proof:

- Assume $3x + 7$ is odd and x is odd.
- According to the definition of odd, $x = 2a + 1$, where a is an element of the integers.
- Thus, by substitution, $3x + 7 = 3(2a + 1) + 7$, which simplifies as $6a + 3 + 7$, or $6a + 10$, which may be rewritten as $2(3a + 5)$. Any even integer may be written as the product of 2 and some integer, k. Thus, we have shown the hypothesis to be false, meaning that the conditional statement must be true.

A **proof by contraposition** is one written in the form, $\sim Q \rightarrow \sim P$. In other words, a proof by contraposition seeks to show that the negation of Q will yield the negation of P. A sample of a proof by contraposition is shown below:

Prove "If $5x + 7$ is even, then x is odd."

Proof:

- Assume that if x is even, then $5x + 7$ is odd.
- Assume x is even.
- Thus, by the definition of an even integer, $x = 2a$.

By substitution, $5x + 7$ may be rewritten as $5(2a) + 7$, which simplifies as $10a + 7$. This expression cannot be written as the product of 2 and some factor, k. Thus, $5x + 7$ is odd, by definition of an odd integer. So, when $5x + 7$ is even, x is odd, according to contraposition.

A **proof by contradiction** is one written in the form, $p \wedge \sim q$. In other words, a proof by contradiction seeks to show the negation of q will result in a false hypothesis, indicating that the conclusion of the statement, as written, must be true. In other words, the conditional statement of $p \rightarrow q$ is true.

Mathematical Induction Proof Utilizing Inductive Reasoning

A mathematical induction proof utilizes inductive reasoning in its assumption that if $P(k)$ is true, then $P(k+1)$ is also true. The induction hypothesis is $P(k)$. This step utilizes inductive reasoning because an observation is used to make the conjecture that $P(k+1)$ is also true.

Example:

For all natural numbers, n, the sum is equal to $(n+1)\left(\frac{n}{2}\right)$.
Show that $P(1)$ is true.
$1 = (1+1)\left(\frac{1}{2}\right)$.
Assume P(k) is true.
$1 + 2 + 3 + 4 + \cdots + k = (k+1)\left(\frac{k}{2}\right)$.

This previous step is the inductive hypothesis. This hypothesis may be used to write the conjecture that $P(k+1)$ is also true: $(1 + 2 + 3 + 4 + \cdots + k) + (k+1) = [(k+1)+1]\left(\frac{k+1}{2}\right)$

$$(k+1)\left(\frac{k}{2}\right) + (k+1) = [(k+1)+1]\left(\frac{k}{2} + \frac{1}{2}\right)$$
$$(k+1)\left(\frac{k}{2}\right) + (k+1) = \left(\frac{k}{2}(k+1) + \frac{k}{2}\right) + \left(\frac{1}{2}(k+1) + \frac{1}{2}(1)\right)$$
$$(k+1)\left(\frac{k}{2}\right) + (k+1) = \frac{k}{2}(k+1) + \frac{k}{2} + \frac{k+1}{2} + \frac{1}{2}$$
$$(k+1)\left(\frac{k}{2}\right) + (k+1) = \frac{k}{2}(k+1) + \frac{2k+2}{2}$$
$$(k+1)\left(\frac{k}{2}\right) + (k+1) = \frac{k}{2}(k+1) + (k+1)$$

PRACTICE

P1. Given the following statements:

If I get a bonus, then I will go on vacation.
If I go on vacation, then I will visit Egypt.
I got a bonus.
Therefore, I will visit Egypt.

(a) Rewrite the statements in logical notation.

(b) Make a truth table for the scenario.

(c) Determine if the argument is logical.

(d) TRUE or FALSE: It would contradict this argument to visit Egypt and not have received a bonus.

P2. Given the following statements:

I will run a marathon in January if and only if the Cubs win the World Series.
I will not run a marathon in January.
Therefore, the Cubs did not win the World Series.

(a) Rewrite the statements in logical notation.

(b) Make a truth table for the scenario.

(c) Determine if the argument is logical.

(d) TRUE or FALSE: It is logically equivalent to the first premise above to say, "I will not run a marathon in January if and only if the Cubs do not win the World Series.

P3. Use proof by induction to demonstrate: "The sum of n odd natural numbers is equal to n^2."

P4. Use informal reasoning to justify the statement, "If n is a whole number, then $n^2 + n + 1$ is odd." Explain the reasoning steps used.

P5. Use formal reasoning to justify the statement, "If a divides b, a divides c, and a divides d, then a divides the sum of b, c, and d." Show the formal proof.

PRACTICE SOLUTIONS

P1. (a) Let us say "getting a bonus" $= B$, "going on vacation" $= V$, and "visiting Egypt" $= E$:

If I get a bonus, then I will go on vacation.	$B \rightarrow V$
If I go on vacation, then I will visit Egypt.	$V \rightarrow E$
I got a bonus.	B
Therefore, I will visit Egypt.	$\therefore E$

(b) The truth table for the scenario:

B	V	E	$B \to V$	$V \to E$	$(B \to V) \wedge (V \to E)$	$B \to E$
T	T	T	T	T	T	T
T	T	F	T	F	F	F
T	F	T	F	T	F	T
T	F	F	F	T	F	F
F	T	T	T	T	T	T
F	T	F	T	F	F	T
F	F	T	T	T	T	T
F	F	F	T	T	T	T

(c) This is an instance of the chain rule and is logically sound.

(d) FALSE: It would NOT contradict this argument to visit Egypt and not have received a bonus. Look at the rows of the truth table where $B = \text{F}$ and $E = \text{T}$, in these cases both statements hold:

B	V	E	$B \to V$	$V \to E$	$(B \to V) \wedge (V \to E)$	$B \to E$
F	T	T	T	T	T	T
F	F	T	T	T	T	T

P2. (a) Let us say "Cubs win" $= C$ and "running a marathon" $= M$:

I will run a marathon in January if and only if the Cubs win the World Series. $C \leftrightarrow M$
I will not run a marathon in January. $\neg M$
Therefore, the Cubs did not win the World Series. $\therefore \neg C$

(b) The truth table for the scenario:

C	M	$\neg C$	$\neg M$	$C \leftrightarrow M$	$C \leftrightarrow M \wedge \neg M$	$\neg M \to \neg C$
T	T	F	F	T	F	T
T	F	F	T	F	F	F
F	T	T	F	F	T	T
F	F	T	T	T	T	T

(c) Based on the truth table, it is clear that $C \leftrightarrow M \wedge \neg M$ is logically equivalent to $\neg C$.

(d) TRUE: The following truth table demonstrates the equivalence:

C	M	$\neg C$	$\neg M$	$C \leftrightarrow M$	$\neg M \leftrightarrow \neg C$
T	T	F	F	T	T
T	F	F	T	F	F
F	T	T	F	F	F
F	F	T	T	T	T

P3. Show that $P(1)$ is true.

$1 = 1^2$.

Assume $P(k)$ is true.

$1 + 3 + 5 + \cdots + (2k + 1) = k^2$.

We want to show that $1 + 3 + 5 + \cdots + (2(k+1)+1) = (k+1)^2$.

$$1 + 3 + 5 + \cdots + (2k+1) + [2k+1] = k^2 + [2k+1].$$

We can distribute 2 to each of the k terms:

$$(1+2) + (3+2) + (5+2) + \cdots + (2k+1+2) + [1] = k^2 + [2k+1].$$

$$3 + 5 + 7 + \cdots + \big((2k+2)+1\big) + [1] = k^2 + 2k + 1.$$

Rearrange and simplify:

$$1 + 3 + 5 + 7 + \cdots + (2(k+1)+1) = (k+1)^2.$$

$P(k+1)$ is true. Thus, according to mathematical induction,

$$1 + 3 + 5 + \cdots + (2n+1) = n^2.$$

P4. Using the sequence, 0, 1, 2, 3, 4, 5, 6, ... for *n*, evaluation of the expression, $n^2 + n + 1$, gives $0^2 + 0 + 1$, $1^2 + 1 + 1$, $2^2 + 2 + 1$, $3^2 + 3 + 1$, $4^2 + 4 + 1$, $5^2 + 5 + 1$, and $6^2 + 6 + 1$, or 1, 3, 7, 13, 21, 31, and 43, all of which are odd numbers. Thus, it appears that given any whole number, n, evaluation of the expression $n^2 + n + 1$ will yield an odd number.

P5. Direct Proof:

Assume *a* divides *b*, *a* divides *c*, and *a* divides *d*.

Given the definition of divides, *a* divides *b* indicates that there exists some integer, r, such that $b = a \times r$. Also, *a* divides *c* indicates that there exists some integer, *s*, such that $c = a \times s$. Finally, *a* divides *d* indicates that there exists some integer, *t*, such that $d = a \times t$. By substitution, the sum of *b*, *c*, and *d* may be written as $(a \times r) + (a \times s) + (a \times t)$. Factoring out an *a* gives $a(r + s + t)$. The factor $(r + s + t)$ is an integer, according to the closure property under addition. Thus, *a* divides the sum of *b*, *c*, and *d*.

Patterns, Algebraic Relationships, and Functions

Proportions and Ratios

Proportions

A proportion is a relationship between two quantities that dictates how one changes when the other changes. A **direct proportion** describes a relationship in which a quantity increases by a set amount for every increase in the other quantity, or decreases by that same amount for every decrease in the other quantity. Example: Assuming a constant driving speed, the time required for a car trip increases as the distance of the trip increases. The distance to be traveled and the time required to travel are directly proportional.

Inverse proportion is a relationship in which an increase in one quantity is accompanied by a decrease in the other, or vice versa. Example: the time required for a car trip decreases as the speed increases and increases as the speed decreases, so the time required is inversely proportional to the speed of the car.

Review Video: Proportions
Visit mometrix.com/academy and enter code: 505355

Ratios

A **ratio** is a comparison of two quantities in a particular order. Example: If there are 14 computers in a lab, and the class has 20 students, there is a student to computer ratio of 20 to 14, commonly written as 20:14. Ratios are normally reduced to their smallest whole number representation, so 20:14 would be reduced to 10:7 by dividing both sides by 2.

Review Video: Ratios
Visit mometrix.com/academy and enter code: 996914

Constant of Proportionality

When two quantities have a proportional relationship, there exists a **constant of proportionality** between the quantities; the product of this constant and one of the quantities is equal to the other quantity. For example, if one lemon costs $0.25, two lemons cost $0.50, and three lemons cost $0.75, there is a proportional relationship between the total cost of lemons and the number of lemons purchased. The constant of proportionality is the **unit price**, namely $0.25/lemon. Notice that the total price of lemons, t, can be found by multiplying the unit price of lemons, p, and the number of lemons, n: $t = pn$.

Work/Unit Rate

Unit rate expresses a quantity of one thing in terms of one unit of another. For example, if you travel 30 miles every two hours, a unit rate expresses this comparison in terms of one hour: in one hour you travel 15 miles, so your unit rate is 15 miles per hour. Other examples are how much one ounce of food costs (price per ounce) or figuring out how much one egg costs out of the dozen (price per 1 egg, instead of price per 12 eggs). The denominator of a unit rate is always 1. Unit rates are used to compare different situations to solve problems. For example, to make sure you get the best deal when deciding which kind of soda to buy, you can find the unit rate of each. If soda #1 costs $1.50 for a 1-liter bottle, and soda #2 costs $2.75 for a 2-liter bottle, it would be a better deal to buy soda #2, because its unit rate is only $1.375 per 1-liter, which is cheaper than soda #1. Unit rates can also help determine the length of time a given event will take. For example, if you can paint 2 rooms in 4.5 hours, you can determine how long it will take you to paint 5 rooms by solving for the unit rate per room and then multiplying that by 5.

Review Video: Rates and Unit Rates
Visit mometrix.com/academy and enter code: 185363

Slope

On a graph with two points, (x_1, y_1) and (x_2, y_2), the **slope** is found with the formula $m = \frac{y_2 - y_1}{x_2 - x_1}$; where $x_1 \neq x_2$ and m stands for slope. If the value of the slope is **positive**, the line has an *upward direction* from left to right. If the value of the slope is **negative**, the line has a *downward direction* from left to right. Consider the following example:

A new book goes on sale in bookstores and online stores. In the first month, 5,000 copies of the book are sold. Over time, the book continues to grow in popularity. The data for the number of copies sold is in the table below.

# of Months on Sale	1	2	3	4	5
# of Copies Sold (In Thousands)	5	10	15	20	25

So, the number of copies that are sold and the time that the book is on sale is a proportional relationship. In this example, an equation can be used to show the data: $y = 5x$, where x is the number of months that the book is on sale. Also, y is the number of copies sold. So the slope of the corresponding line is $\frac{\text{rise}}{\text{run}} = \frac{5}{1} = 5$.

Review Video: Finding the Slope of a Line
Visit mometrix.com/academy and enter code: 766664

Finding an Unknown in Equivalent Expressions

It is often necessary to apply information given about a rate or proportion to a new scenario. For example, if you know that Jedha can run a marathon (26 miles) in 3 hours, how long would it take her to run 10 miles at the same pace? Start by setting up equivalent expressions:

$$\frac{26\text{ mi}}{3\text{ hr}} = \frac{10\text{ mi}}{x\text{ hr}}$$

Now, cross multiply and solve for x:

$$\begin{aligned} 26x &= 30 \\ x &= \frac{30}{26} = \frac{15}{13} \\ x &\cong 1.15\text{ hrs } or \text{ 1 hr 9 min} \end{aligned}$$

So, at this pace, Jedha could run 10 miles in about 1.15 hours or about 1 hour and 9 minutes.

Review Video: Cross Multiply Fractions
Visit mometrix.com/academy and enter code: 893904

Practice

P1. Solve the following for x.

(a) $\frac{45}{12} = \frac{15}{x}$

(b) $\frac{0.50}{2} = \frac{1.50}{x}$

(c) $\frac{40}{8} = \frac{x}{24}$

P2. At a school, for every 20 female students there are 15 male students. This same student ratio happens to exist at another school. If there are 100 female students at the second school, how many male students are there?

P3. In a hospital emergency room, there are 4 nurses for every 12 patients. What is the ratio of nurses to patients? If the nurse-to-patient ratio remains constant, how many nurses must be present to care for 24 patients?

P4. In a bank, the banker-to-customer ratio is 1:2. If seven bankers are on duty, how many customers are currently in the bank?

P5. Janice made $40 during the first 5 hours she spent babysitting. She will continue to earn money at this rate until she finishes babysitting in 3 more hours. Find how much money Janice earns per hour and the total she earned babysitting.

P6. The McDonalds are taking a family road trip, driving 300 miles to their cabin. It took them 2 hours to drive the first 120 miles. They will drive at the same speed all the way to their cabin. Find the speed at which the McDonalds are driving and how much longer it will take them to get to their cabin.

P7. It takes Andy 10 minutes to read 6 pages of his book. He has already read 150 pages in his book that is 210 pages long. Find how long it takes Andy to read 1 page and also find how long it will take him to finish his book if he continues to read at the same speed.

Practice Solutions

P1. Cross multiply, then solve for x:

(a) $45x = 12 \times 15$

$45x = 180$

$x = \frac{180}{45} = 4$

(b) $0.5x = 1.5 \times 2$

$0.5x = 3$

$x = \frac{3}{0.5} = 6$

(c) $8x = 40 \times 24$

$8x = 960$

$x = \frac{960}{8} = 120$

P2. One way to find the number of male students is to set up and solve a proportion.

$$\frac{\text{number of female students}}{\text{number of male students}} = \frac{20}{15} = \frac{100}{\text{number of male students}}$$

Represent the unknown number of male students as the variable x: $\frac{20}{15} = \frac{100}{x}$

Cross multiply and then solve for x:

$$20x = 15 \times 100$$
$$x = \frac{1500}{20}$$
$$x = 75$$

P3. The ratio of nurses to patients can be written as 4 to 12, 4:12, or $\frac{4}{12}$. Because four and twelve have a common factor of four, the ratio should be reduced to 1:3, which means that there is one nurse present for every three patients. If this ratio remains constant, there must be eight nurses present to care for 24 patients.

P4. Use proportional reasoning or set up a proportion to solve. Because there are twice as many customers as bankers, there must be fourteen customers when seven bankers are on duty. Setting up and solving a proportion gives the same result:

$$\frac{\text{number of bankers}}{\text{number of customers}} = \frac{1}{2} = \frac{7}{\text{number of customers}}$$

Represent the unknown number of patients as the variable x: $\frac{1}{2} = \frac{7}{x}$.

To solve for x, cross multiply: $1 \times x = 7 \times 2$, so $x = 14$.

P5. Janice earns $8 per hour. This can be found by taking her initial amount earned, $40, and dividing it by the number of hours worked, 5. Since $\frac{40}{5} = 8$, Janice makes $8 in one hour. This can also be found by finding the unit rate, money earned per hour: $\frac{40}{5} = \frac{x}{1}$. Since cross multiplying yields $5x = 40$, and division by 5 shows that $x = 8$, Janice earns $8 per hour.

Janice will earn $64 babysitting in her 8 total hours (adding the first 5 hours to the remaining 3 gives the 8-hour total). Since Janice earns $8 per hour and she worked 8 hours, $\frac{\$8}{\text{hr}} \times 8 \text{ hrs} = \$64$. This can also be found by setting up a proportion comparing money earned to babysitting hours. Since she earns $40 for 5 hours and since the rate is constant, she will earn a proportional amount in 8 hours: $\frac{40}{5} = \frac{x}{8}$. Cross multiplying will yield $5x = 320$, and division by 5 shows that $x = 64$.

P6. The McDonalds are driving 60 miles per hour. This can be found by setting up a proportion to find the unit rate, the number of miles they drive per one hour: $\frac{120}{2} = \frac{x}{1}$. Cross multiplying yields $2x = 120$ and division by 2 shows that $x = 60$.

Since the McDonalds will drive this same speed, it will take them another 3 hours to get to their cabin. This can be found by first finding how many miles the McDonalds have left to drive, which is $300 - 120 = 180$. The McDonalds are driving at 60 miles per hour, so a proportion can be set up to determine how many hours it will take them to drive 180 miles: $\frac{180}{x} = \frac{60}{1}$. Cross multiplying yields

$60x = 180$, and division by 60 shows that $x = 3$. This can also be found by using the formula $D = r \times t$ (or distance = rate × time), where $180 = 60 \times t$, and division by 60 shows that $t = 3$.

P7. It takes Andy 10 minutes to read 6 pages, $\frac{10}{6} = 1\frac{2}{3}$ minutes, which is 1 minute and 40 seconds.

Next, determine how many pages Andy has left to read, $210 - 150 = 60$. Since it is now known that it takes him $1\frac{2}{3}$ minutes to read each page, that rate must be multiplied by however many pages he has left to read (60) to find the time he'll need: $60 \times 1\frac{2}{3} = 100$, so it will take him 100 minutes, or 1 hour and 40 minutes, to read the rest of his book.

Review Video: Proportions in the Real World
Visit mometrix.com/academy and enter code: 221143

Expressions

Terms and Coefficients

Mathematical expressions consist of a combination of one or more values arranged in terms that are added together. As such, an expression could be just a single number, including zero. A **variable term** is the product of a real number, also called a **coefficient**, and one or more variables, each of which may be raised to an exponent. Expressions may also include numbers without a variable, called **constants** or **constant terms**. The expression $6s^2$, for example, is a single term where the coefficient is the real number 6 and the variable term is s^2. Note that if a term is written as simply a variable to some exponent, like t^2, then the coefficient is 1, because $t^2 = 1t^2$.

Linear Expressions

A **single variable linear expression** is the sum of a single variable term, where the variable has no exponent, and a constant, which may be zero. For instance, the expression $2w + 7$ has $2w$ as the variable term and 7 as the constant term. It is important to realize that terms are separated by addition or subtraction. Since an expression is a sum of terms, expressions such as $5x - 3$ can be written as $5x + (-3)$ to emphasize that the constant term is negative. A real-world example of a single variable linear expression is the perimeter of a square, four times the side length, often expressed: $4s$.

In general, a **linear expression** is the sum of any number of variable terms so long as none of the variables have an exponent. For example, $3m + 8n - \frac{1}{4}p + 5.5q - 1$ is a linear expression, but $3y^3$ is not. In the same way, the expression for the perimeter of a general triangle, the sum of the side lengths $(a + b + c)$ is considered to be linear, but the expression for the area of a square, the side length squared (s^2) is not.

Equations

Linear Equations

Equations that can be written as $ax + b = 0$, where $a \neq 0$, are referred to as **one variable linear equations**. A solution to such an equation is called a **root**. In the case where we have the equation $5x + 10 = 0$, if we solve for x we get a solution of $x = -2$. In other words, the root of the equation is -2. This is found by first subtracting 10 from both sides, which gives $5x = -10$. Next, simply divide both sides by the coefficient of the variable, in this case 5, to get $x = -2$. This can be checked by plugging -2 back into the original equation $(5)(-2) + 10 = -10 + 10 = 0$.

The **solution set** is the set of all solutions of an equation. In our example, the solution set would simply be -2. If there were more solutions (there usually are in multivariable equations) then they would also be included in the solution set. When an equation has no true solutions, it is referred to as an **empty set**. Equations with identical solution sets are **equivalent equations**. An **identity** is a term whose value or determinant is equal to 1.

Linear equations can be written many ways. Below is a list of some forms linear equations can take:

- **Standard Form**: $Ax + By = C$; the slope is $\frac{-A}{B}$ and the y-intercept is $\frac{C}{B}$
- **Slope Intercept Form**: $y = mx + b$, where m is the slope and b is the y-intercept
- **Point-Slope Form**: $y - y_1 = m(x - x_1)$, where m is the slope and (x_1, y_1) is a point on the line
- **Two-Point Form**: $\frac{y-y_1}{x-x_1} = \frac{y_2-y_1}{x_2-x_1}$, where (x_1, y_1) and (x_2, y_2) are two points on the given line
- **Intercept Form**: $\frac{x}{x_1} + \frac{y}{y_1} = 1$, where $(x_1, 0)$ is the point at which a line intersects the x-axis, and $(0, y_1)$ is the point at which the same line intersects the y-axis

Review Video: Slope-Intercept and Point-Slope Forms
Visit mometrix.com/academy and enter code: 113216

Solving One-Variable Linear Equations

Multiply all terms by the lowest common denominator to eliminate any fractions. Look for addition or subtraction to undo so you can isolate the variable on one side of the equal sign. Divide both sides by the coefficient of the variable. When you have a value for the variable, substitute this value into the original equation to make sure you have a true equation. Consider the following example:

Kim's savings are represented by the table below. Represent her savings, using an equation.

X (Months)	Y (Total Savings)
2	$1300
5	$2050
9	$3050
11	$3550
16	$4800

The table shows a function with a constant rate of change, or slope, of 250. Given the points on the table, the slopes can be calculated as $(2050 - 1300)/(5 - 2)$, $(3050 - 2050)/(9 - 5)$, $(3550 - 3050)/(11 - 9)$, and $(4800 - 3550)/(16 - 11)$, each of which equals 250. Thus, the table shows a constant rate of change, indicating a linear function. The slope-intercept form of a linear equation is written as $y = mx + b$, where m represents the slope and b represents the y-intercept. Substituting the slope into this form gives $y = 250x + b$. Substituting corresponding x- and y-values from any point into this equation will give the y-intercept, or b. Using the point, (2, 1300), gives $1300 = 250(2) + b$, which simplifies as b = 800. Thus, her savings may be represented by the equation, $y = 250x + 800$.

Rules for Manipulating Equations

Like Terms

Like terms are terms in an equation that have the same variable, regardless of whether or not they also have the same coefficient. This includes terms that *lack* a variable; all constants (i.e. numbers without variables) are considered like terms. If the equation involves terms with a variable raised to different powers, the like terms are those that have the variable raised to the same power.

For example, consider the equation $x^2 + 3x + 2 = 2x^2 + x - 7 + 2x$. In this equation, 2 and -7 are like terms; they are both constants. $3x$, x, and $2x$ are like terms, they all include the variable x raised to the first power. x^2 and $2x^2$ are like terms, they both include the variable x, raised to the second power. $2x$ and $2x^2$ are not like terms; although they both involve the variable x, the variable is not raised to the same power in both terms. The fact that they have the same coefficient, 2, is not relevant.

Carrying Out the Same Operation on Both Sides of an Equation

When solving an equation, the general procedure is to carry out a series of operations on both sides of an equation, choosing operations that will tend to simplify the equation when doing so. The reason why the same operation must be carried out on both sides of the equation is because that leaves the meaning of the equation unchanged, and yields a result that is equivalent to the original equation. This would not be the case if we carried out an operation on one side of an equation and not the other. Consider what an equation means: it is a statement that two values or expressions are equal. If we carry out the same operation on both sides of the equation—add 3 to both sides, for example—then the two sides of the equation are changed in the same way, and so remain equal. If we do that to only one side of the equation—add 3 to one side but not the other—then that wouldn't be true; if we change one side of the equation but not the other then the two sides are no longer equal.

Advantage of Combining Like Terms

Combining like terms refers to adding or subtracting like terms—terms with the same variable—and therefore reducing sets of like terms to a single term. The main advantage of doing this is that it simplifies the equation. Often, combining like terms can be done as the first step in solving an equation, though it can also be done later, such as after distributing terms in a product.

For example, consider the equation $2(x + 3) + 3(2 + x + 3) = -4$. The 2 and the 3 in the second set of parentheses are like terms, and we can combine them, yielding $2(x + 3) + 3(x + 5) = -4$. Now we can carry out the multiplications implied by the parentheses, distributing the outer 2 and 3 accordingly: $2x + 6 + 3x + 15 = -4$. The $2x$ and the $3x$ are like terms, and we can add them together: $5x + 6 + 15 = -4$. Now, the constants 6, 15, and -4 are also like terms, and we can combine them as well: subtracting 6 and 15 from both sides of the equation, we get $5x = -4 - 6 - 15$, or $5x = -25$, which simplifies further to $x = -5$.

Canceling Terms on Opposite Sides of an Equation

Two terms on opposite sides of an equation can be canceled if and only if they *exactly* match each other. They must have the same variable raised to the same power and the same coefficient. For example, in the equation $3x + 2x^2 + 6 = 2x^2 - 6$, $2x^2$ appears on both sides of the equation and can be canceled, leaving $3x + 6 = -6$. The 6 on each side of the equation *cannot* be canceled, because it is added on one side of the equation and subtracted on the other. While they cannot be canceled, however, the 6 and -6 are like terms and can be combined, yielding $3x = -12$, which simplifies further to $x = -4$.

It's also important to note that the terms to be canceled must be independent terms and cannot be part of a larger term. For example, consider the equation $2(x + 6) = 3(x + 4) + 1$. We cannot cancel the x's, because even though they match each other they are part of the larger terms $2(x + 6)$ and $3(x + 4)$. We must first distribute the 2 and 3, yielding $2x + 12 = 3x + 12 + 1$. Now we see that the terms with the x's do not match, but the 12s do, and can be canceled, leaving $2x = 3x + 1$, which simplifies to $x = -1$.

Process for Manipulating Equations

Isolating Variables

To **isolate a variable** means to manipulate the equation so that the variable appears by itself on one side of the equation, and does not appear at all on the other side. Generally, an equation or inequality is considered to be solved once the variable is isolated and the other side of the equation or inequality is simplified as much as possible. In the case of a two-variable equation or inequality, only one variable needs to be isolated; it will not usually be possible to simultaneously isolate both variables.

For a linear equation—an equation in which the variable only appears raised to the first power—isolating a variable can be done by first moving all the terms with the variable to one side of the equation and all other terms to the other side. (*Moving* a term really means adding the inverse of the term to both sides; when a term is *moved* to the other side of the equation its sign is flipped.) Then combine like terms on each side. Finally, divide both sides by the coefficient of the variable, if applicable. The steps need not necessarily be done in this order, but this order will always work.

Equations with More Than One Solution

Some types of non-linear equations, such as equations involving squares of variables, may have more than one solution. For example, the equation $x^2 = 4$ has two solutions: 2 and –2. Equations with absolute values can also have multiple solutions: $|x| = 1$ has the solutions $x = 1$ and $x = -1$.

It is also possible for a linear equation to have more than one solution, but only if the equation is true regardless of the value of the variable. In this case, the equation is considered to have infinitely many solutions, because any possible value of the variable is a solution. We know a linear equation has infinitely many solutions if when we combine like terms the variables cancel, leaving a true statement. For example, consider the equation $2(3x + 5) = x + 5(x + 2)$. Distributing, we get $6x + 10 = x + 5x + 10$; combining like terms gives $6x + 10 = 6x + 10$, and the $6x$ terms cancel to leave $10 = 10$. This is clearly true, so the original equation is true for any value of x. We could also have canceled the 10s leaving $0 = 0$, but again this is clearly true—in general if both sides of the equation match exactly, it has infinitely many solutions.

Equations with No Solution

Some types of non-linear equations, such as equations involving squares of variables, may have no solution. For example, the equation $x^2 = -2$ has no solutions in the real numbers, because the square of any real number must be positive. Similarly, $|x| = -1$ has no solution, because the absolute value of a number is always positive.

It is also possible for an equation to have no solution even if does not involve any powers greater than one, absolute values, or other special functions. For example, the equation $2(x + 3) + x = 3x$ has no solution. We can see that if we try to solve it. First, we distribute, leaving $2x + 6 + x = 3x$. But now if we try to combine all the terms with the variable, we find that they cancel: we have $3x$ on the left and $3x$ on the right, canceling to leave us with $6 = 0$. This is clearly false. In general, whenever the variable terms in an equation cancel leaving different constants on both sides, it means that the equation has no solution. (If we are left with the *same* constant on both sides, the equation has infinitely many solutions instead.)

Features of Equations That Require Special Treatment

Linear Equations

A linear equation is an equation in which variables only appear by themselves; they are not multiplied together, not with exponents other than one, and not inside absolute value signs or any other functions. For example, the equation $x + 1 - 3x = 5 - x$ is a linear equation; while x appears multiple times, it never appears with an exponent other than one, or inside any function. The two-variable equation $2x - 3y = 5 + 2x$ is also a linear equation. In contrast, the equation $x^2 - 5 = 3x$ is *not* a linear equation, because it involves the term x^2. $\sqrt{x} = 5$ is not a linear equation, because it involves a square root. $(x - 1)^2 = 4$ is not a linear equation because even though there's no exponent on the x directly, it appears as part of an expression that is squared. The two-variable equation $x + xy - y = 5$ is not a linear equation because it includes the term xy, where two variables are multiplied together.

Linear equations can always be solved (or shown to have no solution) by combining like terms and performing simple operations on both sides of the equation. Some non-linear equations can be solved by similar methods, but others may require more advanced methods of solution, if they can be solved analytically at all.

Solving Equations Involving Roots

In an equation involving roots, the first step is to isolate the term with the root, if possible, and then raise both sides of the equation to the appropriate power to eliminate it. Consider an example equation, $2\sqrt{x + 1} - 1 = 3$. In this case, begin by adding 1 to both sides, yielding $2\sqrt{x + 1} = 4$, and then dividing both sides by 2, yielding $\sqrt{x + 1} = 2$. Now square both sides, yielding $x + 1 = 4$. Finally, subtracting 1 from both sides yields $x = 3$.

Squaring both sides of an equation may, however, yield a spurious solution—a solution to the squared equation that is *not* a solution of the original equation. It's therefore necessary to plug the solution back into the original equation to make sure it works. In this case, it does: $2\sqrt{3 + 1} - 1 = 2\sqrt{4} - 1 = 2(2) - 1 = 4 - 1 = 3$.

The same procedure applies for other roots as well. For example, given the equation $3 + \sqrt[3]{2x} = 5$, we can first subtract 3 from both sides, yielding $\sqrt[3]{2x} = 2$ and isolating the root. Raising both sides to the third power yields $2x = 2^3$, i.e. $2x = 8$. We can now divide both sides by 2 to get $x = 4$.

Solving Equations with Exponents

To solve an equation involving an exponent, the first step is to isolate the variable with the exponent. We can then take the appropriate root of both sides to eliminate the exponent. For instance, for the equation $2x^3 + 17 = 5x^3 - 7$, we can subtract $5x^3$ from both sides to get $-3x^3 + 17 = -7$, and then subtract 17 from both sides to get $-3x^3 = -24$. Finally, we can divide both sides by –3 to get $x^3 = 8$. Finally, we can take the cube root of both sides to get $x = \sqrt[3]{8} = 2$.

One important but often overlooked point is that equations with an exponent greater than 1 may have more than one answer. The solution to $x^2 = 9$ isn't simply $x = 3$; it's $x = \pm 3$ (that is, $x = 3$ or $x = -3$). For a slightly more complicated example, consider the equation $(x - 1)^2 - 1 = 3$. Adding 1 to both sides yields $(x - 1)^2 = 4$; taking the square root of both sides yields $x - 1 = 2$. We can then add 1 to both sides to get $x = 3$. However, there's a second solution. We also have the possibility that $x - 1 = -2$, in which case $x = -1$. Both $x = 3$ and $x = -1$ are valid solutions, as can be verified by substituting them both into the original equation.

Solving Equations with Absolute Values

When solving an equation with an absolute value, the first step is to isolate the absolute value term. We then consider two possibilities: when the expression inside the absolute value is positive or when it is negative. In the former case, the expression in the absolute value equals the expression on the other side of the equation; in the latter, it equals the additive inverse of that expression—the expression times negative one. We consider each case separately and finally check for spurious solutions.

For instance, consider solving $|2x - 1| + x = 5$ for x. We can first isolate the absolute value by moving the x to the other side: $|2x - 1| = -x + 5$. Now, we have two possibilities. First, that $2x - 1$ is positive, and hence $2x - 1 = -x + 5$. Rearranging and combining like terms yields $3x = 6$, and hence $x = 2$. The other possibility is that $2x - 1$ is negative, and hence $2x - 1 = -(-x + 5) = x - 5$. In this case, rearranging and combining like terms yields $x = -4$. Substituting $x = 2$ and $x = -4$ back into the original equation, we see that they are both valid solutions.

Note that the absolute value of a sum or difference applies to the sum or difference as a whole, not to the individual terms; in general, $|2x - 1|$ is not equal to $|2x + 1|$ or to $|2x| - 1$.

Review Video: Solving Absolute Value Inequalities
Visit mometrix.com/academy and enter code: 997008

Spurious Solutions

A **spurious solution** may arise when we square both sides of an equation as a step in solving it or under certain other operations on the equation. It is a solution to the squared or otherwise modified equation that is *not* a solution of the original equation. To identify a spurious solution, it's useful when you solve an equation involving roots or absolute values to plug the solution back into the original equation to make sure it's valid.

Choosing Which Variable to Isolate in Two-Variable Equations

Similar to methods for a one-variable equation, solving a two-variable equation involves isolating a variable: manipulating the equation so that a variable appears by itself on one side of the equation, and not at all on the other side. However, in a two-variable equation, you will usually only be able to isolate one of the variables; the other variable may appear on the other side along with constant terms, or with exponents or other functions.

Often one variable will be much more easily isolated than the other, and therefore that's the variable you should choose. If one variable appears with various exponents, and the other is only raised to the first power, the latter variable is the one to isolate: given the equation $a^2 + 2b = a^3 + b + 3$, the b only appears to the first power, whereas a appears squared and cubed, so b is the variable that can be solved for: combining like terms and isolating the b on the left side of the equation, we get $b = a^3 - a^2 + 3$. If both variables are equally easy to isolate, then it's best to isolate the independent variable, if one is defined; if the two variables are x and y, the convention is that y is the independent variable.

Practice

P1. Seeing the equation $2x + 4 = 4x + 7$, a student divides the first terms on each side by 2, yielding $x + 4 = 2x + 7$, and then combines like terms to get $x = -3$. However, this is incorrect, as can be seen by substituting -3 into the original equation. Explain what is wrong with the student's reasoning.

P2. Describe the steps necessary to solve the equation $2x + 1 - x = 4 + 3x + 7$.

P3. Describe the steps necessary to solve the equation $2(x+5) = 7(4-x)$.

P4. Find all real solutions to the equation $1 - \sqrt{x} = 2$.

P5. Find all real solutions to the equation $|x+1| = 2x + 5$.

P6. Solve for x: $-x + 2\sqrt{x+5} + 1 = 3$.

P7. Ray earns $10 an hour at his job. Write an equation for his earnings as a function of time spent working. Determine how long Ray has to work in order to earn $360.

P8. Simplify the following: $3x + 2 + 2y = 5y - 7 + |2x - 1|$

Practice Solutions

P1. As stated, it's easy to verify that the student's solution is incorrect: $2(-3) + 4 = -2$ and $4(-3) + 7 = -5$; clearly $-2 \neq -5$. The mistake was in the first step, which illustrates a common type of error in solving equations. The student tried to simplify the two variable terms by dividing them by 2. However, it's not valid to multiply or divide only one term on each side of an equation by a number; when multiplying or dividing, the operation must be applied to *every* term in the equation. So, dividing by 2 would yield not $x + 4 = 2x + 7$, but $x + 2 = 2x + \frac{7}{2}$. While this is now valid, that fraction is inconvenient to work with, so this may not be the best first step in solving the equation. Rather, it may have been better to first combine like terms. Subtracting $4x$ from both sides yields $-2x + 4 = 7$; subtracting 4 from both sides yields $-2x = 3$; *now* we can divide both sides by -2 to get $x = -\frac{3}{2}$.

P2. Our ultimate goal is to isolate the variable, x. To that end we first move all the terms containing x to the left side of the equation, and all the constant terms to the right side. Note that when we move a term to the other side of the equation its sign changes. We are therefore now left with $2x - x - 3x = 4 + 7 - 1$.

Next, we combine the like terms on each side of the equation, adding and subtracting the terms as appropriate. This leaves us with $-2x = 10$.

At this point, we're almost done; all that remains is to divide both sides by -2 to leave the x by itself. We now have our solution, $x = -5$. We can verify that this is a correct solution by substituting it back into the original equation.

P3. Generally, in equations that have a sum or difference of terms multiplied by another value or expression, the first step is to multiply those terms, distributing as necessary: $2(x+5) = 2(x) + 2(5) = 2x + 10$, and $7(4-x) = 7(4) - 7(x) = 28 - 7x$. So, the equation becomes $2x + 10 = 28 - 7x$. We can now add $7x$ to both sides to eliminate the variable from the right-hand side: $9x + 10 = 28$. Similarly, we can subtract 10 from both sides to move all the constants to the right: $9x = 18$. Finally, we can divide both sides by 9, yielding the final answer, $x = 2$.

P4. It's not hard to isolate the root: subtract one from both sides, yielding $-\sqrt{x} = 1$. Finally, multiply both sides by –1, yielding $\sqrt{x} = -1$. Squaring both sides of the equation yields $x = 1$. However, if we plug this back into the original equation, we get $1 - \sqrt{1} = 2$, which is false. Therefore $x = 1$ is a spurious solution, and the equation has no real solutions.

P5. This equation has two possibilities: $x + 1 = 2x + 5$, which simplifies to $x = -4$; or $x + 1 = -(2x + 5) = -2x - 5$, which simplifies to $x = -2$. However, if we try substituting both values back into the original equation, we see that only $x = -2$ yields a true statement. $x = -4$ is a spurious solution; $x = -2$ is the only valid solution to the equation.

P6. Start by isolating the term with the root. We can do that by moving the $-x$ and the 1 to the other side, yielding $2\sqrt{x + 5} = 3 + x - 1$, or $2\sqrt{x + 5} = x + 2$. Dividing both sides of the equation by 2 would give us a fractional term that could be messy to deal with, so we won't do that for now. Instead, we square both sides of the equation; note that on the left-hand side the 2 is outside the square root sign, so we have to square it. As a result, we get $4(x + 5) = (x + 2)^2$. Expanding both sides gives us $4x + 20 = x^2 + 4x + 4$. In this case, we see that we have $4x$ on both sides, so we can cancel the $4x$ (which is what allows us to solve this equation despite the different powers of x). We now have $20 = x^2 + 4$, or $x^2 = 16$. Since the variable is raised to an even power, we need to take the positive and negative roots, so $x = \pm 4$: that is, $x = 4$ or $x = -4$. Substituting both values into the original equation, we see that $x = 4$ satisfies the equation but $x = -4$ does not; hence $x = -4$ is a spurious solution, and the only solution to the equation is $x = 4$.

P7. The number of dollars that Ray earns is dependent on the number of hours he works, so earnings will be represented by the dependent variable *y* and hours worked will be represented by the independent variable *x*. He earns 10 dollars per hour worked, so his earnings can be calculated as $y = 10x$. To calculate the number of hours Ray must work in order to earn \$360, plug in 360 for *y* and solve for *x*:

$$360 = 10x$$
$$x = \frac{360}{10} = 36$$

P8. To simplify this equation, we must isolate one of its variables on one side of the equation. In this case, the x appears under an absolute value sign, which makes it difficult to isolate. The *y*, on the other hand, only appears without an exponent—the equation is linear in *y*. We will therefore choose to isolate the *y*. The first step, then, is to move all the terms with *y* to the left side of the equation, which we can do by subtracting 5*y* from both sides:

$$3x + 2 - 3y = -7 + |2x - 1|$$

We can then move all the terms that do *not* include *y* to the right side of the equation, by subtracting $3x$ and 2 from both sides of the equation:

$$-3y = -3x - 9 + |2x - 1|$$

Finally, we can isolate the *y* by dividing both sides by –3.

$$y = x + 3 - \frac{1}{3}|2x - 1|$$

This is as far as we can simplify the equation; we cannot combine the terms inside and outside the absolute value sign. We can therefore consider the equation to be solved.

Inequalities

Working with Inequalities

Commonly in algebra and other upper-level fields of math you find yourself working with mathematical expressions that do not equal each other. The statement comparing such expressions with symbols such as < (less than) or > (greater than) is called an *inequality*. An example of an inequality is $7x > 5$. To solve for x, simply divide both sides by 7 and the solution is shown to be $x > \frac{5}{7}$. Graphs of the solution set of inequalities are represented on a number line. Open circles are used to show that an expression approaches a number but is never quite equal to that number.

Review Video: Inequalities
Visit mometrix.com/academy and enter code: 347842

Conditional inequalities are those with certain values for the variable that will make the condition true and other values for the variable where the condition will be false. **Absolute inequalities** can have any real number as the value for the variable to make the condition true, while there is no real number value for the variable that will make the condition false. Solving inequalities is done by following the same rules for solving equations with the exception that when multiplying or dividing by a negative number the direction of the inequality sign must be flipped or reversed. **Double inequalities** are situations where two inequality statements apply to the same variable expression. An example of this is $-c < ax + b < c$.

Determining Solutions to Inequalities

To determine whether a coordinate is a solution of an inequality, you can substitute the values of the coordinate into the inequality, simplify, and check whether the resulting statement holds true. For instance, to determine whether $(-2,4)$ is a solution of the inequality $y \geq -2x + 3$, substitute the values into the inequality, $4 \geq -2(-2) + 3$. Simplify the right side of the inequality and the result is $4 \geq 7$, which is a false statement. Therefore, the coordinate is not a solution of the inequality. You can also use this method to determine which part of the graph of an inequality is shaded. The graph of $y \geq -2x + 3$ includes the solid line $y = -2x + 3$ and, since it excludes the point $(-2,4)$ to the left of the line, it is shaded to the right of the line.

Flipping Inequality Signs

When given an inequality, we can always turn the entire inequality around, swapping the two sides of the inequality and changing the inequality sign. For instance, $x + 2 > 2x - 3$ is equivalent to $2x - 3 < x + 2$. Aside from that, normally the inequality does not change if we carry out the same operation on both sides of the inequality. There is, however, one principal exception: if we *multiply* or *divide* both sides of the inequality by a *negative number*, the inequality is flipped. For example, if we take the inequality $-2x < 6$ and divide both sides by -2, the inequality flips and we are left with $x > -3$. This *only* applies to multiplication and division, and only with negative numbers. Multiplying or dividing both sides by a positive number, or adding or subtracting any number regardless of sign, does not flip the inequality.

Compound Inequalities

A **compound inequality** is an equality that consists of two inequalities combined with *and* or *or*. The two components of a proper compound inequality must be of opposite type: that is, one must be greater than (or greater than or equal to), the other less than (or less than or equal to). For instance, "$x + 1 < 2$ or $x + 1 > 3$" is a compound inequality, as is "$2x \geq 4$ and $2x \leq 6$." An *and* inequality can be written more compactly by having one inequality on each side of the common part: "$2x \geq 1$ and $2x \leq 6$," can also be written as $1 \leq 2x \leq 6$.

In order for the compound inequality to be meaningful, the two parts of an *and* inequality must overlap; otherwise no numbers satisfy the inequality. On the other hand, if the two parts of an *or* inequality overlap, then *all* numbers satisfy the inequality and as such the inequality is usually not meaningful.

Solving a compound inequality requires solving each part separately. For example, given the compound inequality "$x + 1 < 2$ or $x + 1 > 3$," the first inequality, $x + 1 < 2$, reduces to $x < 1$, and the second part, $x + 1 > 3$, reduces to $x > 2$, so the whole compound inequality can be written as "$x < 1$ or $x > 2$." Similarly, $1 \leq 2x \leq 6$ can be solved by dividing each term by 2, yielding $\frac{1}{2} \leq x \leq 3$.

Solving Inequalities Involving Absolute Values

To solve an inequality involving an absolute value, first isolate the term with the absolute value. Then proceed to treat the two cases separately as with an absolute value equation, but flipping the inequality in the case where the expression in the absolute value is negative (since that essentially involves multiplying both sides by -1.) The two cases are then combined into a compound inequality; if the absolute value is on the greater side of the inequality, then it is an *or* compound inequality, if on the lesser side, then it's an *and.*

Consider the inequality $2 + |x - 1| \geq 3$. We can isolate the absolute value term by subtracting 2 from both sides: $|x - 1| \geq 1$. Now, we're left with the two cases $x - 1 \geq 1$ or $x - 1 \leq -1$: note that in the latter, negative case, the inequality is flipped. $x - 1 \geq 1$ reduces to $x \geq 2$, and $x - 1 \leq -1$ reduces to $x \leq 0$. Since in the inequality $|x - 1| \geq 1$ the absolute value is on the greater side, the two cases combine into an *or* compound inequality, so the final, solved inequality is "$x \leq 0$ or $x \geq 2$."

Review Video: Solving Absolute Value Inequalities
Visit mometrix.com/academy and enter code: 997008

Solving Inequalities Involving Square Roots

Solving an inequality with a square root involves two parts. First, we solve the inequality as if it were an equation, isolating the square root and then squaring both sides of the equation. Second, we restrict the solution to the set of values of x for which the value inside the square root sign is non-negative.

For example, in the inequality, $\sqrt{x - 2} + 1 < 5$, we can isolate the square root by subtracting 1 from both sides, yielding $\sqrt{x - 2} < 4$. Squaring both sides of the inequality yields $x - 2 < 16$, so $x < 18$. Since we can't take the square root of a negative number, we also require the part inside the square root to be non-negative. In this case, that means $x - 2 \geq 0$. Adding 2 to both sides of the inequality yields $x \geq 2$. Our final answer is a compound inequality combining the two simple inequalities: $x \geq 2$ and $x < 18$, or $2 \leq x < 18$.

Note that we only get a compound inequality if the two simple inequalities are in opposite directions; otherwise we take the one that is more restrictive.

The same technique can be used for other even roots, such as fourth roots. It is *not*, however, used for cube roots or other odd roots—negative numbers *do* have cube roots, so the condition that the quantity inside the root sign cannot be negative does not apply.

Special Circumstances

Sometimes an inequality involving an absolute value or an even exponent is true for all values of x, and we don't need to do any further work to solve it. This is true if the inequality, once the absolute value or exponent term is isolated, says that term is greater than a negative number (or greater than or equal to zero). Since an absolute value or a number raised to an even exponent is *always* non-negative, this inequality is always true.

Graphical Solutions to Equations and Inequalities

When equations are shown graphically, they are usually shown on a **Cartesian coordinate plane**. The Cartesian coordinate plane consists of two number lines placed perpendicular to each other and intersecting at the zero point, also known as the origin. The horizontal number line is known as the x-axis, with positive values to the right of the origin, and negative values to the left of the origin. The vertical number line is known as the y-axis, with positive values above the origin, and negative values below the origin. Any point on the plane can be identified by an ordered pair in the form (x, y), called coordinates. The x-value of the coordinate is called the abscissa, and the y-value of the coordinate is called the ordinate. The two number lines divide the plane into **four quadrants**: I, II, III, and IV.

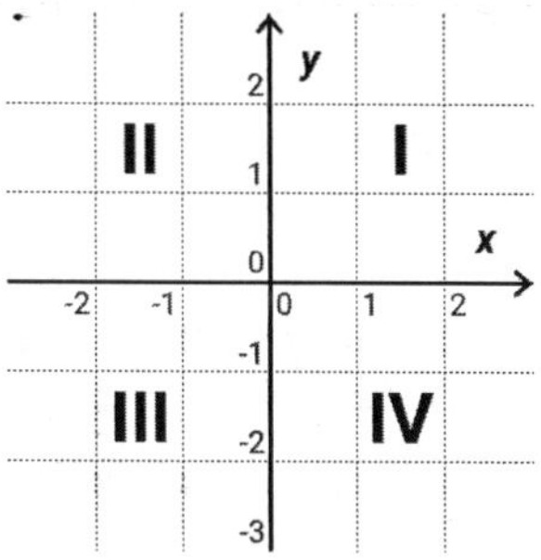

Note that in quadrant I $x > 0$ and $y > 0$, in quadrant II $x < 0$ and $y > 0$, in quadrant III $x < 0$ and $y < 0$, and in quadrant IV $x > 0$ and $y < 0$.

Recall that if the value of the slope of a line is positive, the line slopes upward from left to right. If the value of the slope is negative, the line slopes downward from left to right. If the y-coordinates are the same for two points on a line, the slope is 0 and the line is a **horizontal line**. If the x-coordinates are the same for two points on a line, there is no slope and the line is a **vertical line**. Two or more lines that have equivalent slopes are **parallel lines**. **Perpendicular lines** have slopes that are negative reciprocals of each other, such as $\frac{a}{b}$ and $\frac{-b}{a}$.

Graphing Simple Inequalities

To graph a simple inequality, we first mark on the number line the value that signifies the end point of the inequality. If the inequality is strict (involves a less than or greater than), we use a hollow circle; if it is not strict (less than or equal to or greater than or equal to), we use a solid circle. We then fill in the part of the number line that satisfies the inequality: to the left of the marked point for less than (or less than or equal to), to the right for greater than (or greater than or equal to).

For example, we would graph the inequality $x < 5$ by putting a hollow circle at 5 and filling in the part of the line to the left:

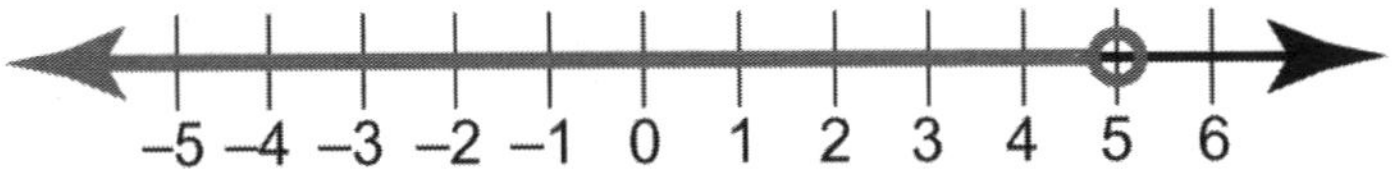

Graphing Compound Inequalities

To graph a compound inequality, we fill in both parts of the inequality for an *or* inequality, or the overlap between them for an *and* inequality. More specifically, we start by plotting the endpoints of each inequality on the number line. For an *or* inequality, we then fill in the appropriate side of the line for each inequality. Typically, the two component inequalities do not overlap, which means the shaded part is *outside* the two points. For an *and* inequality, we instead fill in the part of the line that meets both inequalities.

For the inequality "$x \leq -3$ or $x > 4$," we first put a solid circle at –3 and a hollow circle at 4. We then fill the parts of the line *outside* these circles:

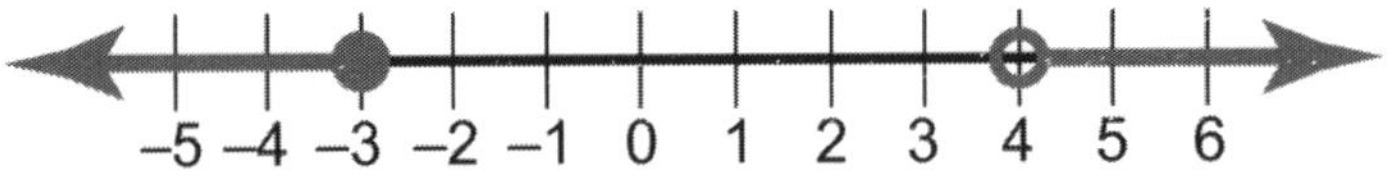

Graphing Inequalities Including Absolute Values

An inequality with an absolute value can be converted to a compound inequality. To graph the inequality, first convert it to a compound inequality, and then graph that normally. If the absolute value is on the greater side of the inequality, we end up with an *or* inequality; we plot the endpoints of the inequality on the number line and fill in the part of the line *outside* those points. If the absolute value is on the smaller side of the inequality, we end up with an *and* inequality; we plot the endpoints of the inequality on the number line and fill in the part of the line *between* those points.

For example, the inequality $|x + 1| \geq 4$ can be rewritten as $x \geq 3$ or $x \leq -5$. We place solid circles at the points 3 and -5 and fill in the part of the line *outside* them:

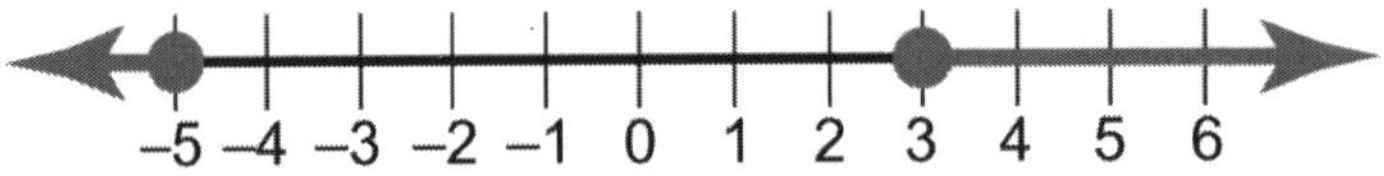

Graphing Equations in Two Variables

One way of graphing an equation in two variables is to plot enough points to get an idea for its shape and then draw the appropriate curve through those points. A point can be plotted by substituting in a value for one variable and solving for the other. If the equation is linear, we only need two points and can then draw a straight line between them.

For example, consider the equation $y = 2x - 1$. This is a linear equation—both variables only appear raised to the first power—so we only need two points. When $x = 0, y = 2(0) - 1 = -1$.

When $x = 2, y = 2(2) - 1 = 3$. We can therefore choose the points $(0, -1)$ and $(2, 3)$, and draw a line between them:

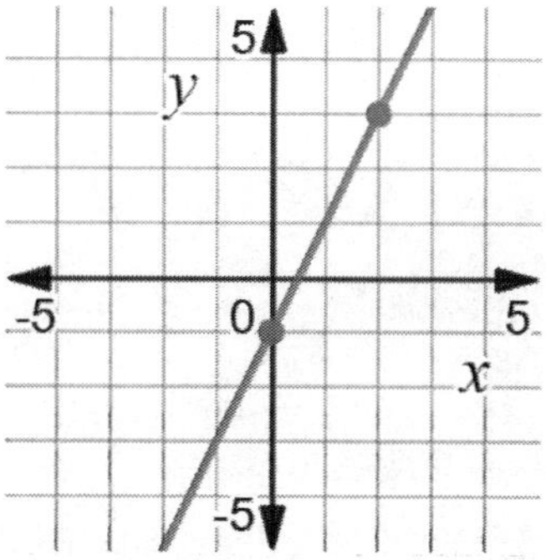

Graphing Inequalities in Two Variables

To graph an inequality in two variables, we first graph the border of the inequality. This means graphing the equation that we get if we replace the inequality sign with an equals sign. If the inequality is strict (> or <), we graph the border with a dashed or dotted line; if it is not strict (≥ or ≤), we use a solid line. We can then test any point not on the border to see if it satisfies the inequality. If it does, we shade in that side of the border; if not, we shade in the other side. As an example, consider $y > 2x + 2$. To graph this inequality, we first graph the border, $y = 2x + 2$. Since it is a strict inequality, we use a dashed line. Then, we choose a test point. This can be any point not on the border; in this case, we will choose the origin, (0,0). (This makes the calculation easy and is generally a good choice unless the border passes through the origin.) Putting this into the original inequality, we get $0 > 2(0) + 2$, i.e. $0 > 2$. This is *not* true, so we shade in the side of the border that does *not* include the point (0,0):

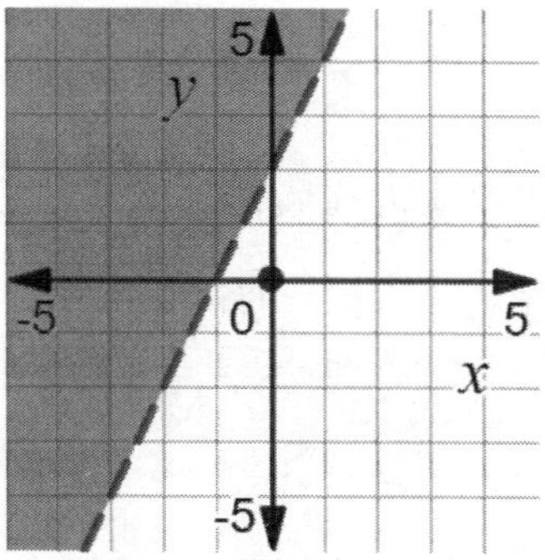

Graphing Compound Inequalities in Two Variables

One way to graph a compound inequality in two variables is to first graph each of the component inequalities. For an *and* inequality, we then shade in only the parts where the two graphs overlap; for an *or* inequality, we shade in any region that pertains to either of the individual inequalities.

Consider the graph of "$y \geq x - 1$ *and* $y \leq -x$":

We first shade in the individual inequalities:

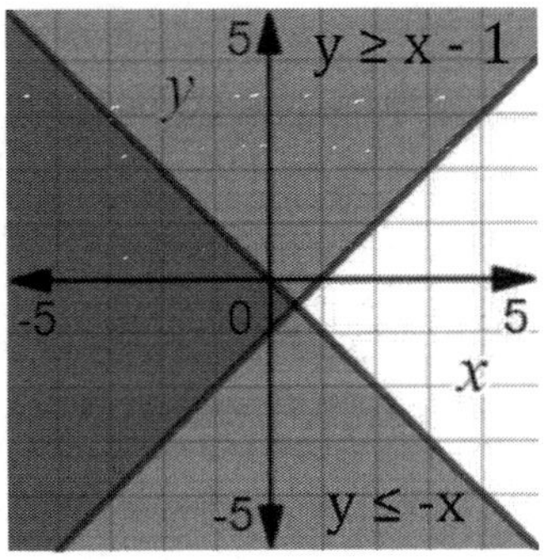

Now, since the compound inequality has an *and*, we only leave shaded the overlap—the part that pertains to *both* inequalities:

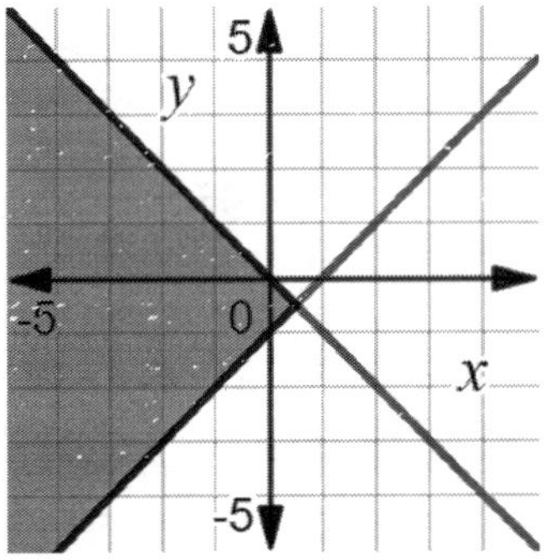

If instead the inequality had been "$y \geq x - 1$ *or* $y \leq -x$," our final graph would involve the *total* shaded area:

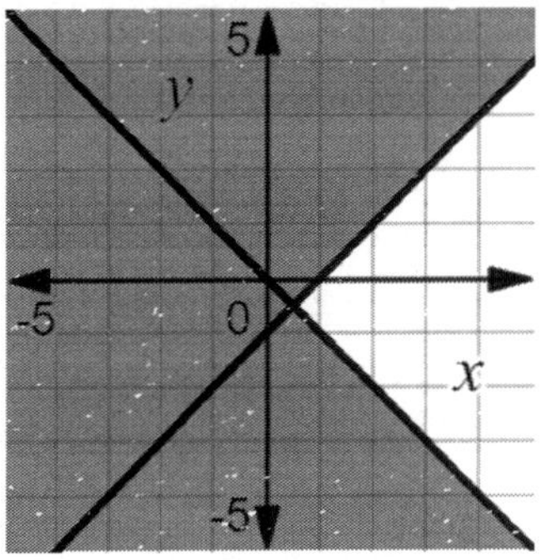

Practice

P1. Analyze the following inequalities:

(a) $2 - |x + 1| < 3$
(b) $2(x - 1)^2 + 7 \leq 1$

P2. Graph the following on a number line:

(a) $x \geq 3$
(b) $-2 \leq x \leq 6$
(c) $|x| < 2$

Practice Solutions

P1. (a) Subtracting 2 from both sides yields $-|x+1| < 1$; multiplying by -1 and flipping the inequality, since we're multiplying by a negative number, yields $|x+1| > -1$. But since the absolute value cannot be negative, it's *always* greater than -1, so this inequality is true for all values of x.

(b) Subtracting 7 from both sides yields $2(x-1)^2 \leq -6$; dividing by 2 yields $(x-1)^2 \leq -3$. But $(x-1)^2$ must be nonnegative, and hence cannot be less than or equal to -3; this inequality has no solution.

P2. (a) We would graph the inequality $x \geq 3$ by putting a solid circle at 3 and filling in the part of the line to the right:

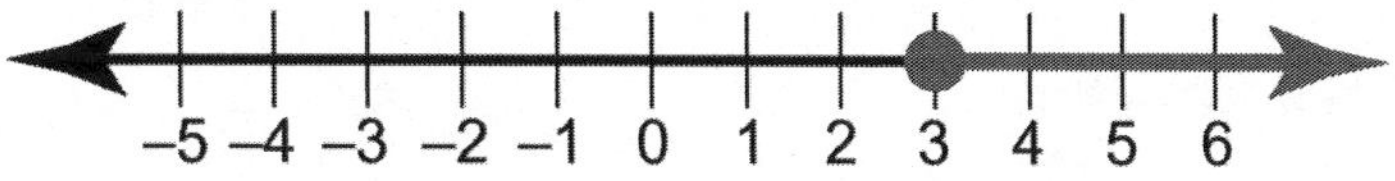

(b) The inequality $-2 \leq x \leq 6$ is equivalent to "$x \geq -2$ and $x \leq 6$." To plot this compound inequality, we first put solid circles at -2 and 6, and then fill in the part of the line *between* these circles:

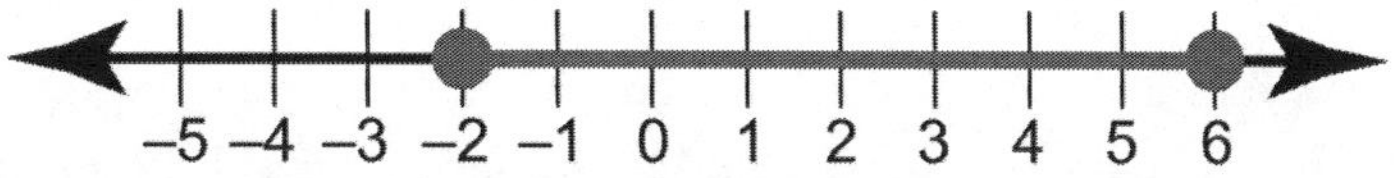

(c) The inequality $|x| < 2$ can be rewritten as "$x > -2$ and $x < 2$." We place hollow circles at the points -2 and 2 and fill in the part of the line between them:

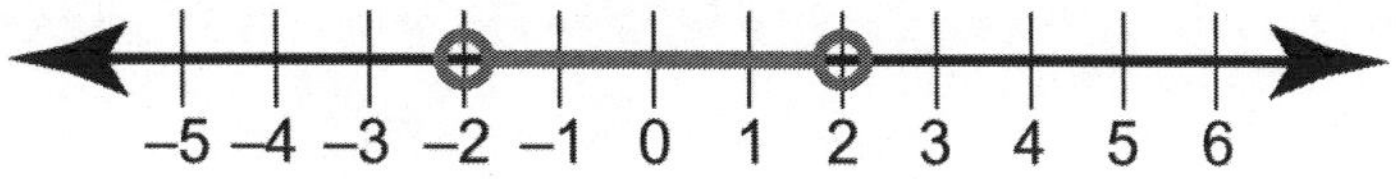

Systems of Equations

Solving Systems of Equations

A **system of equations** is a set of simultaneous equations that all use the same variables. A solution to a system of equations must be true for each equation in the system. **Consistent systems** are those with at least one solution. **Inconsistent systems** are systems of equations that have no solution.

Review Video: Systems of Equations
Visit mometrix.com/academy and enter code: 658153

Substitution

To solve a system of linear equations by **substitution**, start with the easier equation and solve for one of the variables. Express this variable in terms of the other variable. Substitute this expression in the other equation and solve for the other variable. The solution should be expressed in the form (x, y). Substitute the values into both of the original equations to check your answer. Consider the following system of equations:

$$\begin{aligned} x + 6y &= 15 \\ 3x - 12y &= 18 \end{aligned}$$

Solving the first equation for x: $x = 15 - 6y$

Substitute this value in place of x in the second equation, and solve for y:

$$\begin{aligned} 3(15 - 6y) - 12y &= 18 \\ 45 - 18y - 12y &= 18 \\ 30y &= 27 \\ y &= \frac{27}{30} = \frac{9}{10} = 0.9 \end{aligned}$$

Plug this value for y back into the first equation to solve for x:

$$x = 15 - 6(0.9) = 15 - 5.4 = 9.6$$

Check both equations if you have time:

$$\begin{aligned} 9.6 + 6(0.9) &= 15 \\ 9.6 + 5.4 &= 15 \\ 15 &= 15 \end{aligned} \qquad \begin{aligned} 3(9.6) - 12(0.9) &= 18 \\ 28.8 - 10.8 &= 18 \\ 18 &= 18 \end{aligned}$$

Therefore, the solution is (9.6, 0.9).

Elimination

To solve a system of equations using **elimination**, begin by rewriting both equations in standard form $Ax + By = C$. Check to see if the coefficients of one pair of like variables add to zero. If not, multiply one or both of the equations by a non-zero number to make one set of like variables add to zero. Add the two equations to solve for one of the variables. Substitute this value into one of the original equations to solve for the other variable. Check your work by substituting into the other equation. Now, let's look at solving the following system using the elimination method:

$$\begin{aligned} 5x + 6y &= 4 \\ x + 2y &= 4 \end{aligned}$$

If we multiply the second equation by -3, we can eliminate the y terms:

$$\begin{aligned} 5x + 6y &= 4 \\ -3x - 6y &= -12 \end{aligned}$$

Add the equations together and solve for x:

$$\begin{aligned} 2x &= -8 \\ x &= \frac{-8}{2} = -4 \end{aligned}$$

Plug the value for x back in to either of the original equations and solve for y:

$$-4 + 2y = 4$$
$$y = \frac{4+4}{2} = 4$$

Check both equations if you have time:

$$5(-4) + 6(4) = 4 \qquad -4 + 2(4) = 4$$
$$-20 + 24 = 4 \qquad -4 + 8 = 4$$
$$4 = 4 \qquad 4 = 4$$

Therefore, the solution is (-4,4).

Review Video: Substitution and Elimination for Solving Linear Systems
Visit mometrix.com/academy and enter code: 958611

GRAPHICALLY

To solve a system of linear equations **graphically**, plot both equations on the same graph. The solution of the equations is the point where both lines cross. If the lines do not cross (are parallel), then there is **no solution**.

For example, consider the following system of equations:

$$y = 2x + 7$$
$$y = -x + 1$$

Since these equations are given in slope-intercept form, they are easy to graph; the y intercepts of the lines are (0,7) and (0,1). The respective slopes are 2 and –1, thus the graphs look like this:

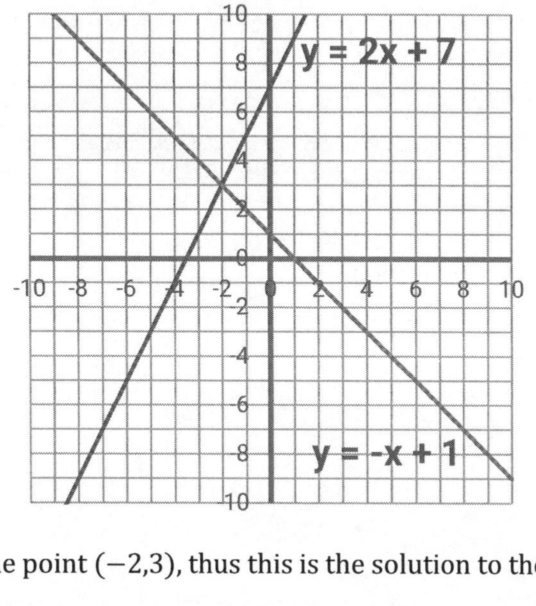

The two lines intersect at the point $(-2,3)$, thus this is the solution to the system of equations.

Solving a system graphically is generally only practical if both coordinates of the solution are integers; otherwise the intersection will lie between gridlines on the graph and the coordinates will be difficult or impossible to determine exactly. It also helps if, as in this example, the equations are in slope-intercept form or some other form that makes them easy to graph. Otherwise, another method of solution (by substitution or elimination) is likely to be more useful.

Solving Systems of Equations Using the Trace Feature

Using the trace feature on a calculator requires that you rewrite each equation, isolating the y-variable on one side of the equal sign. Enter both equations in the graphing calculator and plot the graphs simultaneously. Use the trace cursor to find where the two lines cross. Use the zoom feature if necessary to obtain more accurate results. Always check your answer by substituting into the original equations. The trace method is likely to be less accurate than other methods due to the resolution of graphing calculators but is a useful tool to provide an approximate answer.

Calculations Using Points

Sometimes you need to perform calculations using only points on a graph as input data. Using points, you can determine what the **midpoint** and **distance** are. If you know the equation for a line, you can calculate the distance between the line and the point.

To find the **midpoint** of two points (x_1, y_1) and (x_2, y_2), average the x-coordinates to get the x-coordinate of the midpoint, and average the y-coordinates to get the y-coordinate of the midpoint. The formula is: $\left(\frac{x_1+x_2}{2}, \frac{y_1+y_2}{2}\right)$.

The **distance** between two points is the same as the length of the hypotenuse of a right triangle with the two given points as endpoints, and the two sides of the right triangle parallel to the x-axis and y-axis, respectively. The length of the segment parallel to the x-axis is the difference between the x-coordinates of the two points. The length of the segment parallel to the y-axis is the difference between the y-coordinates of the two points. Use the Pythagorean theorem $a^2 + b^2 = c^2$ or $c = \sqrt{a^2 + b^2}$ to find the distance. The formula is $\mathrm{d} = \sqrt{(x_2 - x_1)^2 + (y_2 - y_1)^2}$.

When a line is in the format $Ax + By + C = 0$, where A, B, and C are coefficients, you can use a point (x_1, y_1) not on the line and apply the formula $d = \frac{|Ax_1+By_1+C|}{\sqrt{A^2+B^2}}$ to find the distance between the line and the point (x_1, y_1).

Review Video: Calculations Using Points on a Graph
Visit mometrix.com/academy and enter code: 883228

Practice

P1. Solve the following systems of equations:

(a) $3x + 4y = 9$
$-12x + 7y = 10$

(b) $-3x + 2y = -1$
$4x - 5y = 6$

P2. Find the distance and midpoint between points (2,4) and (8,6).

Practice Solutions

P1. (a) If we multiply the first equation by 4, we can eliminate the x terms:

$$12x + 16y = 36$$
$$-12x + 7y = 10$$

Add the equations together and solve for y:

$$23y = 46$$
$$y = 2$$

Plug the value for y back in to either of the original equations and solve for x:

$$3x + 4(2) = 9$$
$$x = \frac{9-8}{3} = \frac{1}{3}$$

The solution is $\left(\frac{1}{3}, 2\right)$

(b) Solving the first equation for y:

$$-3x + 2y = -1$$
$$2y = 3x - 1$$
$$y = \frac{3x-1}{2}$$

Substitute this expression in place of y in the second equation, and solve for x:

$$4x - 5\left(\frac{3x-1}{2}\right) = 6$$
$$4x - \frac{15x}{2} + \frac{5}{2} = 6$$
$$8x - 15x + 5 = 12$$
$$-7x = 7$$
$$x = -1$$

Plug the value for x back in to either of the original equations and solve for y:

$$-3(-1) + 2y = -1$$
$$3 + 2y = -1$$
$$2y = -4$$
$$y = -2$$

The solution is $(-1,-2)$

P2. Use the formulas for distance and midpoint:

$$\begin{aligned}\text{Distance} &= \sqrt{(x_2-x_1)^2+(y_2-y_1)^2}\\ &= \sqrt{(8-2)^2+(6-4)^2}\\ &= \sqrt{(6)^2+(2)^2}\\ &= \sqrt{36+4}\\ &= \sqrt{40} \text{ or } 2\sqrt{10}\end{aligned}$$

$$\begin{aligned}\text{Midpoint} &= \left(\frac{x_1+x_2}{2},\frac{y_1+y_2}{2}\right)\\ &= \left(\frac{2+8}{2},\frac{4+6}{2}\right)\\ &= \left(\frac{10}{2},\frac{10}{2}\right)\\ &= (5,5)\end{aligned}$$

Polynomial Algebra

Monomials and Polynomials

A **monomial** is a single variable or product of constants and variables, such as x, $2x$, or $\frac{2}{x}$. There will never be addition or subtraction symbols in a monomial. Like monomials have like variables, but they may have different coefficients. **Polynomials** are algebraic expressions that use addition and subtraction to combine two or more monomials. Two terms make a **binomial**, three terms make a **trinomial**, etc. The **degree of a monomial** is the sum of the exponents of the variables. The **degree of a polynomial** is the highest degree of any individual term.

Review Video: Polynomials
Visit mometrix.com/academy and enter code: 305005

Simplifying Polynomials

Simplifying polynomials requires combining like terms. The like terms in a polynomial expression are those that have the same variable raised to the same power. It is often helpful to connect the like terms with arrows or lines in order to separate them from the other monomials. Once you have determined the like terms, you can rearrange the polynomial by placing them together. Remember to include the sign that is in front of each term. Once the like terms are placed together, you can apply each operation and simplify. When adding and subtracting polynomials, only add and subtract the **coefficient**, or the number part; the variable and exponent stay the same.

The FOIL Method

In general, multiplying polynomials is done by multiplying each term in one polynomial by each term in the other and adding the results. In the specific case for multiplying binomials, there is a useful acronym, FOIL, that can help you make sure to cover each combination of terms. The **FOIL method** for $(Ax+By)(Cx+Dy)$ would be:

F	Multiply the *first* terms of each binomial	$(\overbrace{Ax}^{first}+By)(\overbrace{Cx}^{first}+Dy)$	ACx^2
O	Multiply the *outer* terms	$(\overbrace{Ax}^{outer}+By)(Cx+\overbrace{Dy}^{outer})$	$ADxy$
I	Multiply the *inner* terms	$(Ax+\overbrace{By}^{inner})(\overbrace{Cx}^{inner}+Dy)$	$BCxy$
L	Multiply the *last* terms of each binomial	$(Ax+\overbrace{By}^{last})(Cx+\overbrace{Dy}^{last})$	BDy^2

Then, add up the result of each and combine like terms: $ACx^2 + (AD + BC)xy + BDy^2$.

For example, using the FOIL method on binomials $(x + 2)$ and $(x - 3)$:

$$\begin{array}{llcl}
\text{First:} & (\boxed{x} + 2)(\boxed{x} + (-3)) & \rightarrow & (x)(x) = x^2 \\
\text{Outer:} & (\boxed{x} + 2)(x + \boxed{(-3)}) & \rightarrow & (x)(-3) = -3x \\
\text{Inner:} & (x + \boxed{2})(\boxed{x} + (-3)) & \rightarrow & (2)(x) = 2x \\
\text{Last:} & (x + \boxed{2})(x + \boxed{(-3)}) & \rightarrow & (2)(-3) = -6
\end{array}$$

This results in: $(x^2) + (-3x) + (2x) + (-6)$

Combine like terms: $x^2 + (-3 + 2)x + (-6) = x^2 - x - 6$

Review Video: Multiplying Terms Using the FOIL Method
Visit mometrix.com/academy and enter code: 854792

Dividing Polynomials

Use long division to divide a polynomial by either a monomial or another polynomial of equal or lesser degree.

When **dividing by a monomial**, divide each term of the polynomial by the monomial.

When **dividing by a polynomial**, begin by arranging the terms of each polynomial in order of one variable. You may arrange in ascending or descending order, but be consistent with both polynomials. To get the first term of the quotient, divide the first term of the dividend by the first term of the divisor. Multiply the first term of the quotient by the entire divisor and subtract that product from the dividend. Repeat for the second and successive terms until you either get a remainder of zero or a remainder whose degree is less than the degree of the divisor. If the quotient has a remainder, write the answer as a mixed expression in the form:

$$\text{quotient} + \frac{\text{remainder}}{\text{divisor}}$$

For example, we can evaluate the following expression in the same way as long division:

$$\frac{x^3 - 3x^2 - 2x + 5}{x - 5}$$

$$\begin{array}{r|l}
 & \quad\quad\;\; x^2 + 2x + 8 \\
x - 5 & x^3 - 3x^2 - 2x + 5 \\
 & \underline{x^3 - 5x^2} \\
 & \quad\quad 2x^2 - 2x \\
 & \quad\quad \underline{2x^2 - 10x} \\
 & \quad\quad\quad\quad 8x + 5 \\
 & \quad\quad\quad\quad \underline{8x + 40} \\
 & \quad\quad\quad\quad\quad 45
\end{array}$$

$$\frac{x^3 - 3x^2 - 2x + 5}{x - 5} = x^2 + 2x + 8 + \frac{45}{x - 5}$$

When **factoring** a polynomial, first check for a common monomial factor, that is, look to see if each coefficient has a common factor or if each term has an x in it. If the factor is a trinomial but not a perfect trinomial square, look for a factorable form, such as one of these:

$$x^2 + (a + b)x + ab = (x + a)(x + b)$$
$$(ac)x^2 + (ad + bc)x + bd = (ax + b)(cx + d)$$

For factors with four terms, look for groups to factor. Once you have found the factors, write the original polynomial as the product of all the factors. Make sure all of the polynomial factors are prime. Monomial factors may be *prime* or *composite*. Check your work by multiplying the factors to make sure you get the original polynomial.

Below are patterns of some special products to remember to help make factoring easier:

- Perfect trinomial squares: $x^2 + 2xy + y^2 = (x + y)^2$ or $x^2 - 2xy + y^2 = (x - y)^2$
- Difference between two squares: $x^2 - y^2 = (x + y)(x - y)$
- Sum of two cubes: $x^3 + y^3 = (x + y)(x^2 - xy + y^2)$
    - Note: the second factor is *not* the same as a perfect trinomial square, so do not try to factor it further.
- Difference between two cubes: $x^3 - y^3 = (x - y)(x^2 + xy + y^2)$
    - Again, the second factor is *not* the same as a perfect trinomial square.
- Perfect cubes: $x^3 + 3x^2y + 3xy^2 + y^3 = (x + y)^3$ and $x^3 - 3x^2y + 3xy^2 - y^3 = (x - y)^3$

Rational Expressions

Rational expressions are fractions with polynomials in both the numerator and the denominator; the value of the polynomial in the denominator cannot be equal to zero. Be sure to keep track of values that make the denominator of the original expression zero as the final result inherits the same restrictions. For example, a denominator of $x - 3$ indicates that the expression is not defined when $x = 3$ and, as such, regardless of any operations done to the expression, it remains undefined there.

To **add or subtract** rational expressions, first find the common denominator, then rewrite each fraction as an equivalent fraction with the common denominator. Finally, add or subtract the numerators to get the numerator of the answer, and keep the common denominator as the denominator of the answer.

When **multiplying** rational expressions, factor each polynomial and cancel like factors (a factor which appears in both the numerator and the denominator). Then, multiply all remaining factors in the numerator to get the numerator of the product, and multiply the remaining factors in the denominator to get the denominator of the product. Remember: cancel entire factors, not individual terms.

To **divide** rational expressions, take the reciprocal of the divisor (the rational expression you are dividing by) and multiply by the dividend.

Review Video: Rational Expressions
Visit mometrix.com/academy and enter code: 415183

SIMPLIFYING RATIONAL EXPRESSIONS

To simplify a rational expression, factor the numerator and denominator completely. Factors that are the same and appear in the numerator and denominator have a ratio of 1. For example, look at the following expression:

$$\frac{x-1}{1-x^2}$$

The denominator, $(1-x^2)$, is a difference of squares. It can be factored as $(1-x)(1+x)$. The factor $1-x$ and the numerator $x-1$ are opposites and have a ratio of –1. Rewrite the numerator as $-1(1-x)$. So, the rational expression can be simplified as follows:

$$\frac{x-1}{1-x^2}=\frac{-1(1-x)}{(1-x)(1+x)}=\frac{-1}{1+x}$$

Note that since the original expression is only defined for $x \neq \{-1, 1\}$, the simplified expression has the same restrictions.

Review Video: Reducing Rational Expressions
Visit mometrix.com/academy and enter code: 788868

PRACTICE

P1. Expand the following polynomials:

(a) $(x+3)(x-7)(2x)$

(b) $(x+2)^2(x-2)^2$

(c) $(x^2+5x+5)(3x-1)$

P2. Evaluate the following rational expressions:

(a) $\frac{x^3-2x^2-5x+6}{3x+6}$

(b) $\frac{x^2+4x+4}{4-x^2}$

PRACTICE SOLUTIONS

P1. (a) Apply the FOIL method and the distributive property of multiplication:

$$\begin{aligned}(x+3)(x-7)(2x) &= (x^2-7x+3x-21)(2x)\\ &= (x^2-4x-21)(2x)\\ &= 2x^3-8x^2-42x\end{aligned}$$

(b) Note the difference of squares form:

$$\begin{aligned}(x+2)^2(x-2)^2 &= (x+2)(x+2)(x-2)(x-2)\\ &= [(x+2)(x-2)][(x+2)(x-2)]\\ &= (x^2-4)(x^2-4)\\ &= x^4-8x^2+16\end{aligned}$$

(c) Multiply each pair of monomials and combine like terms:

$$(x^2 + 5x + 5)(3x - 1) = 3x^3 + 15x^2 + 15x - x^2 - 5x - 5$$
$$= 3x^3 + 14x^2 + 10x - 5$$

P2. (a) Rather than trying to factor the fourth-degree polynomial, we can use long division:

$$\frac{x^3 - 2x^2 - 5x + 6}{3x + 6} = \frac{x^3 - 2x^2 - 5x + 6}{3(x + 2)}$$

$$\begin{array}{r|l} & x^2 \quad -4x \quad +3 \\ \hline x + 2 & x^3 - 2x^2 - 5x + 6 \\ & x^3 + 2x^2 \\ \hline & \quad -4x^2 - 5x \\ & \quad -4x^2 - 8x \\ \hline & \qquad 3x + 6 \\ & \qquad 3x + 6 \\ \hline & \qquad\quad 0 \end{array}$$

$$\frac{x^3 - 2x^2 - 5x + 6}{3(x + 2)} = \frac{x^2 - 4x + 3}{3}$$

Note that since the original expression is only defined for $x \neq \{-2\}$, the simplified expression has the same restrictions.

(b) The denominator, $(4 - x^2)$, is a difference of squares. It can be factored as $(2 - x)(2 + x)$. The numerator, $(x^2 + 4x + 4)$, is a perfect square. It can be factored as $(x + 2)(x + 2)$. So, the rational expression can be simplified as follows:

$$\frac{x^2 + 4x + 4}{4 - x^2} = \frac{(x + 2)(x + 2)}{(2 - x)(2 + x)} = \frac{(x + 2)}{(2 - x)}$$

Note that since the original expression is only defined for $x \neq \{-2, 2\}$, the simplified expression has the same restrictions.

Quadratics

Solving Quadratic Equations

Quadratic equations are a special set of trinomials of the form $y = ax^2 + bx + c$ that occur commonly in math and real-world applications. The **roots** of a quadratic equation are the solutions that satisfy the equation when $y = 0$; in other words, where the graph touches the x-axis. There are several ways to determine these solutions including using the quadratic formula, factoring, completing the square, and graphing the function.

> **Review Video: Changing Constants in Graphs of Functions: Quadratic Equations**
> Visit mometrix.com/academy and enter code: 476276

Quadratic Formula

The **quadratic formula** is used to solve quadratic equations when other methods are more difficult. To use the quadratic formula to solve a quadratic equation, begin by rewriting the equation in standard form $ax^2 + bx + c = 0$, where a, b, and c are coefficients. Once you have identified the values of the coefficients, substitute those values into the quadratic formula

$$x = \frac{-b \pm \sqrt{b^2 - 4ac}}{2a}$$

Evaluate the equation and simplify the expression. Again, check each root by substituting into the original equation. In the quadratic formula, the portion of the formula under the radical $(b^2 - 4ac)$ is called the **discriminant**. If the discriminant is zero, there is only one root: $-\frac{b}{2a}$. If the discriminant is positive, there are two different real roots. If the discriminant is negative, there are no real roots; you will instead find complex roots. Often these solutions don't make sense in context and are ignored.

Review Video: Using the Quadratic Formula
Visit mometrix.com/academy and enter code: 163102

FACTORING

To solve a quadratic equation by factoring, begin by rewriting the equation in standard form, $x^2 + bx + c = 0$. Remember that the goal of factoring is to find numbers f and g such that $(x + f)(x + g) = x^2 + (f + g)x + fg$, in other words $(f + g) = b$ and $fg = c$. This can be a really useful method when b and c are integers. Determine the factors of c and look for pairs that could sum to b.

For example, consider finding the roots of $x^2 + 6x - 16 = 0$. The factors of -16 include, -4 and 4, -8 and 2, -2 and 8, -1 and 16, and 1 and -16. The factors that sum to 6 are -2 and 8. Write these factors as the product of two binomials, $0 = (x - 2)(x + 8)$. Finally, since these binomials multiply together to equal zero, set them each equal to zero and solve each for x. This results in $x - 2 = 0$, which simplifies to $x = 2$ and $x + 8 = 0$, which simplifies to $x = -8$. Therefore, the roots of the equation are 2 and -8.

Review Video: Factoring Quadratic Equations
Visit mometrix.com/academy and enter code: 336566

COMPLETING THE SQUARE

One way to find the roots of a quadratic equation is to find a way to manipulate it such that it follows the form of a perfect square $(x^2 + 2px + p^2)$ by adding and subtracting a constant. This process is called **completing the square**. In other words, if you are given a quadratic that is not a perfect square, $x^2 + bx + c = 0$, you can find a constant d that could be added in to make it a perfect square:

$$x^2 + bx + c + (d - d) = 0;\ \{\text{Let } b = 2p \text{ and } c + d = p^2\}$$
$$\text{then: } x^2 + 2px + p^2 - d = 0 \text{ and } d = \frac{b^2}{4} - c$$

Once you have completed the square you can find the roots of the resulting equation:

$$\begin{aligned} x^2 + 2px + p^2 - d &= 0 \\ (x + p)^2 &= d \\ x + p &= \pm\sqrt{d} \\ x &= -p \pm \sqrt{d} \end{aligned}$$

It is worth noting that substituting the original expressions into this solution gives the same result as the quadratic formula where $a = 1$:

$$x = -p \pm \sqrt{d} = -\frac{b}{2} \pm \sqrt{\frac{b^2}{4} - c} = -\frac{b}{2} \pm \frac{\sqrt{b^2 - 4c}}{2} = \frac{-b \pm \sqrt{b^2 - 4c}}{2}$$

Completing the square can be seen as arranging block representations of each of the terms to be as close to a square as possible and then filling in the gaps. For example, consider the quadratic expression $x^2 + 6x + 2$:

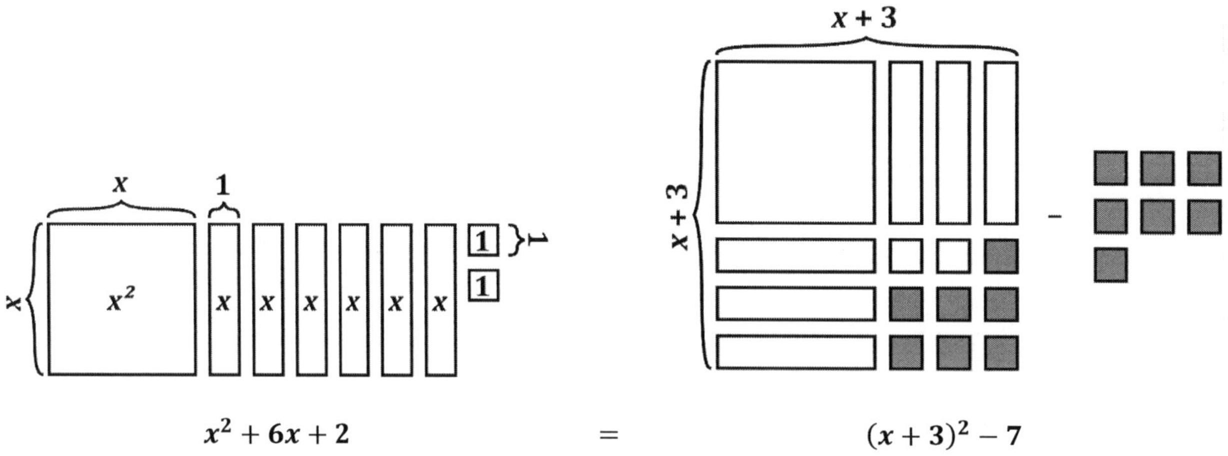

USING GIVEN ROOTS TO FIND QUADRATIC EQUATION

One way to find the roots of a quadratic equation is to factor the equation and use the **zero product property**, setting each factor of the equation equal to zero to find the corresponding root. We can use this technique in reverse to find an equation given its roots. Each root corresponds to a linear equation which in turn corresponds to a factor of the quadratic equation.

For example, we can find a quadratic equation whose roots are $x = 2$ and $x = -1$. The root $x = 2$ corresponds to the equation $x - 2 = 0$, and the root $x = -1$ corresponds to the equation $x + 1 = 0$.

These two equations correspond to the factors $(x - 2)$ and $(x + 1)$, from which we can derive the equation $(x - 2)(x + 1) = 0$, or $x^2 - x - 2 = 0$.

Any integer multiple of this entire equation will also yield the same roots, as the integer will simply cancel out when the equation is factored. For example, $2x^2 - 2x - 4 = 0$ factors as $2(x - 2)(x + 1) = 0$.

SOLVING A SYSTEM OF EQUATIONS CONSISTING OF A LINEAR EQUATION AND A QUADRATIC EQUATION

ALGEBRAICALLY

Generally, the simplest way to solve a system of equations consisting of a linear equation and a quadratic equation algebraically is through the method of substitution. One possible strategy is to solve the linear equation for y and then substitute that expression into the quadratic equation. After expansion and combining like terms, this will result in a new quadratic equation for x, which, like all quadratic equations, may have zero, one, or two solutions. Plugging each solution for x back into one of the original equations will then produce the corresponding value of y.

For example, consider the following system of equations:

$$x + y = 1$$
$$y = (x + 3)^2 - 2$$

We can solve the linear equation for y to yield $y = -x + 1$. Substituting this expression into the quadratic equation produces $-x + 1 = (x + 3)^2 - 2$. We can simplify this equation:

$$\begin{aligned} -x + 1 &= (x + 3)^2 - 2 \\ -x + 1 &= x^2 + 6x + 9 - 2 \\ -x + 1 &= x^2 + 6x + 7 \\ 0 &= x^2 + 7x + 6 \end{aligned}$$

This quadratic equation can be factored as $(x + 1)(x + 6) = 0$. It therefore has two solutions: $x_1 = -1$ and $x_2 = -6$. Plugging each of these back into the original linear equation yields $y_1 = -x_1 + 1 = -(-1) + 1 = 2$ and $y_2 = -x_2 + 1 = -(-6) + 1 = 7$. Thus, this system of equations has two solutions, $(-1,2)$ and $(-6,7)$.

It may help to check your work by putting each x and y value back into the original equations and verifying that they do provide a solution.

GRAPHICALLY

To solve a system of equations consisting of a linear equation and a quadratic equation graphically, plot both equations on the same graph. The linear equation will, of course, produce a straight line, while the quadratic equation will produce a parabola. These two graphs will intersect at zero, one, or two points; each point of intersection is a solution of the system.

For example, consider the following system of equations:

$$y = -2x + 2$$
$$y = -2x^2 + 4x + 2$$

The linear equation describes a line with a y-intercept of $(0,2)$ and a slope of -2.

To graph the quadratic equation, we can first find the vertex of the parabola: the x-coordinate of the vertex is $h = -\frac{b}{2a} = -\frac{4}{2(-2)} = 1$, and the y coordinate is $k = -2(1)^2 + 4(1) + 2 = 4$. Thus, the vertex lies at $(1,4)$. To get a feel for the rest of the parabola, we can plug in a few more values of x to find more points; by putting in $x = 2$ and $x = 3$ in the quadratic equation, we find that the points

(2,2) and $(3,-4)$ lie on the parabola; by symmetry, so must $(0,2)$ and $(-1,-4)$. We can now plot both equations:

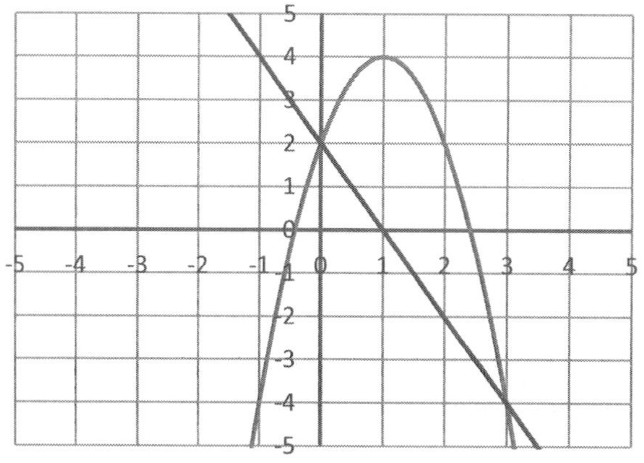

These two curves intersect at the points (0,2) and $(3,-4)$, thus these are the solutions of the equation.

PRACTICE

P1. Find the roots of $y = 2x^2 + 8x + 4$.

P2. Find a quadratic equation with roots $x = 4$ and $x = -6$.

PRACTICE SOLUTIONS

P1. First, substitute 0 in for y in the quadratic equation: $0 = 2x^2 + 8x + 4$

Next, try to factor the quadratic equation. Since $a \neq 1$, list the factors of ac, or 8:

$$(1,8), (-1,-8), (2,4), (-2,-4)$$

Look for the factors of ac that add up to b, or 8. Since none do, the equation cannot be factored with whole numbers. Substitute the values of a, b, and c into the quadratic formula, $x = \frac{-b \pm \sqrt{b^2-4ac}}{2a}$:

$$x = \frac{-8 \pm \sqrt{8^2 - 4(2)(4)}}{2(2)}$$

Use the order of operations to simplify:

$$x = \frac{-8 \pm \sqrt{64 - 32}}{4}$$
$$x = \frac{-8 \pm \sqrt{32}}{4}$$

Reduce and simplify:

$$x = \frac{-8 \pm \sqrt{(16)(2)}}{4}$$
$$x = \frac{-8 \pm 4\sqrt{2}}{4}$$
$$x = -2 \pm \sqrt{2}$$
$$x = (-2 + \sqrt{2}) \text{ and } (-2 - \sqrt{2})$$

P2. The root $x = 4$ corresponds to the equation $x - 4 = 0$, and the root $x = -6$ corresponds to the equation $x + 6 = 0$. These two equations correspond to the factors $(x - 4)$ and $(x + 6)$, from which we can derive the equation $(x - 4)(x + 6) = 0$, or $x^2 + 2x - 24 = 0$.

Basic Functions

Function and Relation

When expressing functional relationships, the **variables** x and y are typically used. These values are often written as the **coordinates** (x, y). The x-value is the independent variable and the y-value is the dependent variable. A **relation** is a set of data in which there is not a unique y-value for each x-value in the dataset. This means that there can be two of the same x-values assigned to different y-values. A relation is simply a relationship between the x- and y-values in each coordinate but does not apply to the relationship between the values of x and y in the data set. A **function** is a relation where one quantity depends on the other. For example, the amount of money that you make depends on the number of hours that you work. In a function, each x-value in the data set has one unique y-value because the y-value depends on the x-value.

Review Video: Definition of a Function
Visit mometrix.com/academy and enter code: 784611

Functions

A function has exactly one value of **output variable** (dependent variable) for each value of the **input variable** (independent variable). The set of all values for the input variable (here assumed to be x) is the domain of the function, and the set of all corresponding values of the output variable (here assumed to be y) is the range of the function. When looking at a graph of an equation, the easiest way to determine if the equation is a function or not is to conduct the vertical line test. If a vertical line drawn through any value of x crosses the graph in more than one place, the equation is not a function.

Finding the Domain and Range of a Function

The **domain** of a function $f(x)$ is the set of all input values for which the function is defined. The **range** of a function $f(x)$ is the set of all possible output values of the function—that is, of every possible value of $f(x)$, for any value of x in the function's domain. For a function expressed in a table, every input-output pair is given explicitly. To find the domain, we just list all the x values and to find the range, we just list all the values of $f(x)$. Consider the following example:

x	-1	4	2	1	0	3	8	6
$f(x)$	3	0	3	−1	−1	2	4	6

In this case, the domain would be {-1, 4, 2, 1, 0, 3, 8, 6}, or, putting them in ascending order, {-1, 0, 1, 2, 3, 4, 6, 8}. (Putting the values in ascending order isn't strictly necessary, but generally makes the set easier to read.) The range would be {3, 0, 3, −1, −1, 2, 4, 6}. Note that some of these values appear more than once. This is entirely permissible for a function; while each value of x must be matched to a unique value of $f(x)$, the converse is not true. We don't need to list each value more than once, so eliminating duplicates, the range is {3, 0, −1, 2, 4, 6}, or, putting them in ascending order, {−1, 0, 2, 3, 4, 6}.

Note that by definition of a function, no input value can be matched to more than one output value. It is good to double-check to make sure that the data given follows this and is therefore actually a function.

Review Video: Domain and Range
Visit mometrix.com/academy and enter code: 778133

Determining a Function

You can determine whether an equation is a **function** by substituting different values into the equation for x. You can display and organize these numbers in a data table. A **data table** contains the values for x and y, which you can also list as coordinates. In order for a function to exist, the table cannot contain any repeating x-values that correspond with different y-values. If each x-coordinate has a unique y-coordinate, the table contains a function. However, there can be repeating y-values that correspond with different x-values. An example of this is when the function contains an exponent. For example, if $x^2 = y$, $2^2 = 4$, and $(-2)^2 = 4$.

Review Video: Basics of Functions
Visit mometrix.com/academy and enter code: 822500

Writing a Function Rule Using a Table

If given a set of data, place the corresponding x- and y-values into a table and analyze the relationship between them. Consider what you can do to each x-value to obtain the corresponding y-value. Try adding or subtracting different numbers to and from x and then try multiplying or dividing different numbers to and from x. If none of these **operations** give you the y-value, try combining the operations. Once you find a rule that works for one pair, make sure to try it with each additional set of ordered pairs in the table. If the same operation or combination of operations satisfies each set of coordinates, then the table contains a function. The rule is then used to write the equation of the function in "$y =$" form.

Direct and Inverse Variations of Variables

Variables that vary directly are those that either both increase at the same rate or both decrease at the same rate. For example, in the functions $y = kx$ or $y = kx^n$, where k and n are positive, the value of y increases as the value of x increases and decreases as the value of x decreases.

Variables that vary inversely are those where one increases while the other decreases. For example, in the functions $y = \frac{k}{x}$ or $y = \frac{k}{x^n}$ where k and n are positive, the value of y increases as the value of x decreases and decreases as the value of x increases.

In both cases, k is the constant of variation.

PROPERTIES OF FUNCTIONS

There are many different ways to classify functions based on their structure or behavior. Important features of functions include:

- **End behavior**: the behavior of the function at extreme values ($f(x)$ as $x \to \pm\infty$)
- **y-intercept**: the value of the function at $f(0)$
- **Roots**: the values of x where the function equals zero ($f(x) = 0$)
- **Extrema**: minimum or maximum values of the function or where the function changes direction ($f(x) \geq k$ or $f(x) \leq k$)

CLASSIFICATION OF FUNCTIONS

An **invertible function** is defined as a function, $f(x)$, for which there is another function, $f^{-1}(x)$, such that $f^{-1}(f(x)) = x$. For example, if $f(x) = 3x - 2$ the inverse function, $f^{-1}(x)$, can be found:

$$x = 3(f^{-1}(x)) - 2$$
$$\frac{x+2}{3} = f^{-1}(x)$$

$$f^{-1}(f(x)) = \frac{3x - 2 + 2}{3} = \frac{3x}{3} = x$$

Note that $f^{-1}(x)$ is a valid function over all values of x.

In a **one-to-one function**, each value of x has exactly one value for y on the coordinate plane (this is the definition of a function) and each value of y has exactly one value for x. While the vertical line test will determine if a graph is that of a function, the horizontal line test will determine if a function is a one-to-one function. If a horizontal line drawn at any value of y intersects the graph in more than one place, the graph is not that of a one-to-one function. Do not make the mistake of using the horizontal line test exclusively in determining if a graph is that of a one-to-one function. A one-to-one function must pass both the vertical line test and the horizontal line test. As such, one-to-one functions are invertible functions.

A **many-to-one function** is a function whereby the relation is a function, but the inverse of the function is not a function. In other words, each element in the domain is mapped to one and only one element in the range. However, one or more elements in the range may be mapped to the same element in the domain. A graph of a many-to-one function would pass the vertical line test, but not the horizontal line test. This is why many-to-one functions are not invertible.

A **monotone function** is a function whose graph either constantly increases or constantly decreases. Examples include the functions $f(x) = x$, $f(x) = -x$, or $f(x) = x^3$.

An **even function** has a graph that is symmetric with respect to the y-axis and satisfies the equation $f(x) = f(-x)$. Examples include the functions $f(x) = x^2$ and $f(x) = ax^n$, where a is any real number and n is a positive even integer.

An **odd function** has a graph that is symmetric with respect to the origin and satisfies the equation $f(x) = -f(-x)$. Examples include the functions $f(x) = x^3$ and $f(x) = ax^n$, where a is any real number and n is a positive odd integer.

Constant functions are given by the equation $f(x) = b$, where b is a real number. There is no independent variable present in the equation, so the function has a constant value for all x. The graph of a constant function is a horizontal line of slope 0 that is positioned b units from the x-axis. If b is positive, the line is above the x-axis; if b is negative, the line is below the x-axis.

Identity functions are identified by the equation $f(x) = x$, where every value of the function is equal to its corresponding value of x. The only zero is the point $(0, 0)$. The graph is a line with a slope of 1.

In **linear functions**, the value of the function changes in direct proportion to x. The rate of change, represented by the slope on its graph, is constant throughout. The standard form of a linear equation is $ax + cy = d$, where a, c, and d are real numbers. As a function, this equation is commonly in the form $y = mx + b$ or $f(x) = mx + b$ where $m = -\frac{a}{c}$ and $b = \frac{d}{c}$. This is known as the slope-intercept form, because the coefficients give the slope of the graphed function (m) and its y-intercept (b). Solve the equation $mx + b = 0$ for x to get $x = -\frac{b}{m}$, which is the only zero of the function. The domain and range are both the set of all real numbers.

Algebraic functions are those that exclusively use polynomials and roots. These would include polynomial functions, rational functions, square root functions, and all combinations of these functions, such as polynomials as the radicand. These combinations may be joined by addition, subtraction, multiplication, or division, but may not include variables as exponents.

Absolute Value Functions

An **absolute value function** is in the format $f(x) = |ax + b|$. Like other functions, the domain is the set of all real numbers. However, because absolute value indicates positive numbers, the range is limited to positive real numbers. To find the zero of an absolute value function, set the portion inside the absolute value sign equal to zero and solve for x. An absolute value function is also known as a piecewise function because it must be solved in pieces—one for if the value inside the absolute value sign is positive, and one for if the value is negative. The function can be expressed as

$$f(x) = \begin{cases} ax + b \text{ if } ax + b \geq 0 \\ -(ax + b) \text{ if } ax + b < 0 \end{cases}$$

This will allow for an accurate statement of the range. The graph of an example absolute value function, $f(x) = |2x - 1|$, is below:

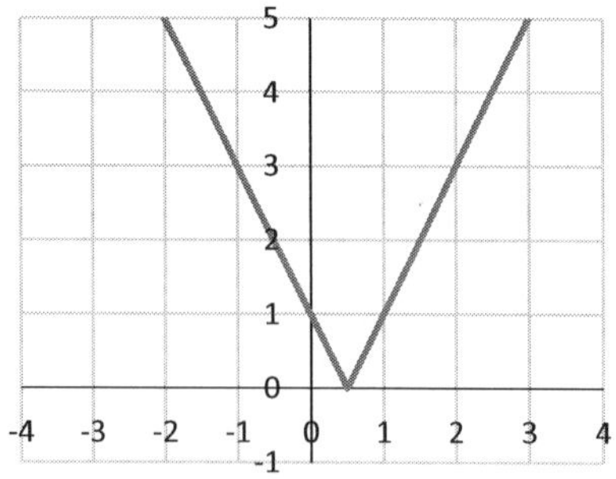

Piecewise Functions

A **piecewise function** is a function that has different definitions on two or more different intervals. The following, for instance, is one example of a piecewise-defined function:

$$f(x) = \begin{cases} x^2, & x < 0 \\ x, & 0 \leq x \leq 2 \\ (x-2)^2, & x > 2 \end{cases}$$

To graph this function, you would simply graph each part separately in the appropriate domain. The final graph would look like this:

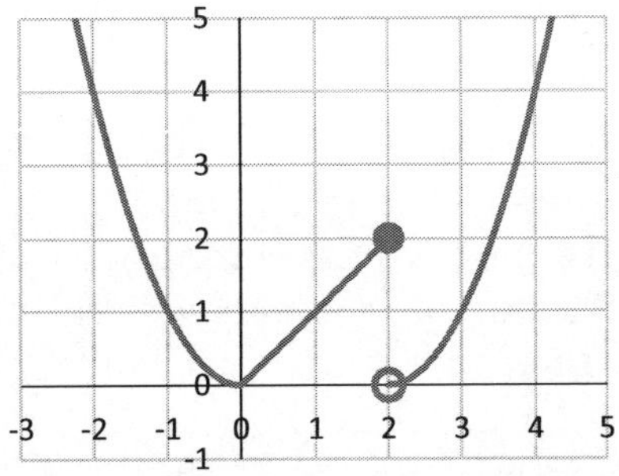

Note the filled and hollow dots at the discontinuity at $x = 2$. This is important to show which side of the graph that point corresponds to. Because $f(x) = x$ on the closed interval $0 \leq x \leq 2$, $f(2) = 2$. The point $(2, 2)$ is therefore marked with a filled circle, and the point $(2,0)$, which is the endpoint of the rightmost $(x - 2)^2$ part of the graph but *not actually part of the function*, is marked with a hollow dot to indicate this.

Quadratic Functions

A **quadratic function** is a function in the form $y = ax^2 + bx + c$, where a does not equal 0. While a linear function forms a line, a quadratic function forms a **parabola**, which is a u-shaped figure that either opens upward or downward. A parabola that opens upward is said to be a **positive quadratic function,** and a parabola that opens downward is said to be a **negative quadratic function**. The shape of a parabola can differ, depending on the values of a, b, and c. All parabolas contain a **vertex**, which is the highest possible point, the **maximum**, or the lowest possible point, the **minimum**. This is the point where the graph begins moving in the opposite direction. A quadratic function can have zero, one, or two solutions, and therefore zero, one, or two x-intercepts. Recall that the x-intercepts are referred to as the zeros, or roots, of a function. A quadratic function will have only one y-intercept. Understanding the basic components of a quadratic function can give you an idea of the shape of its graph.

Example graph of a positive quadratic function, $x^2 + 2x - 3$:

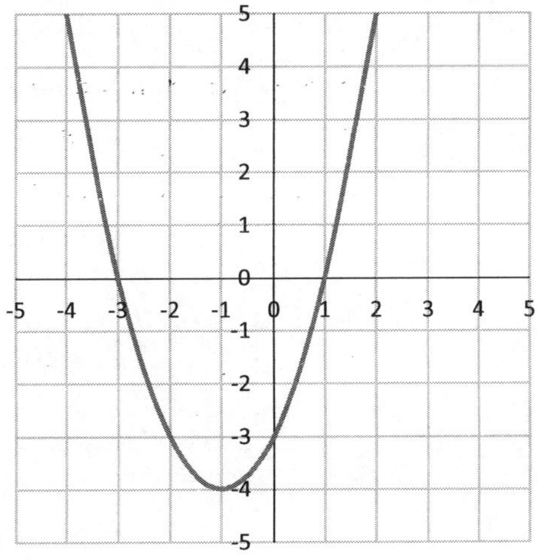

POLYNOMIAL FUNCTIONS

A **polynomial function** is a function with multiple terms and multiple powers of *x*, such as:

$$f(x) = a_n x^n + a_{n-1} x^{n-1} + a_{n-2} x^{n-2} + \cdots + a_1 x + a_0$$

where n is a non-negative integer that is the highest exponent in the polynomial and $a_n \neq 0$. The domain of a polynomial function is the set of all real numbers. If the greatest exponent in the polynomial is even, the polynomial is said to be of even degree and the range is the set of real numbers that satisfy the function. If the greatest exponent in the polynomial is odd, the polynomial is said to be odd and the range, like the domain, is the set of all real numbers.

Review Video: Simplifying Rational Polynomial Functions
Visit mometrix.com/academy and enter code: 351038

RATIONAL FUNCTIONS

A **rational function** is a function that can be constructed as a ratio of two polynomial expressions: $f(x) = \frac{p(x)}{q(x)}$, where $p(x)$ and $q(x)$ are both polynomial expressions and $q(x) \neq 0$. The domain is the set of all real numbers, except any values for which $q(x) = 0$. The range is the set of real numbers that satisfies the function when the domain is applied. When you graph a rational function, you will have vertical asymptotes wherever $q(x) = 0$. If the polynomial in the numerator is of lesser degree than the polynomial in the denominator, the *x*-axis will also be a horizontal asymptote. If the numerator and denominator have equal degrees, there will be a horizontal asymptote not on the *x*-axis. If the degree of the numerator is exactly one greater than the degree of the denominator, the graph will have an oblique, or diagonal, asymptote. The asymptote will be along the line $y = \frac{p_n}{q_{n-1}} x + \frac{p_{n-1}}{q_{n-1}}$, where p_n and q_{n-1} are the coefficients of the highest degree terms in their respective polynomials.

SQUARE ROOT FUNCTIONS

A **square root function** is a function that contains a radical and is in the format $f(x) = \sqrt{ax + b}$. The domain is the set of all real numbers that yields a positive radicand or a radicand equal to zero. Because square root values are assumed to be positive unless otherwise identified, the range is all real numbers from zero to infinity. To find the zero of a square root function, set the radicand equal to zero and solve for *x*. The graph of a square root function is always to the right of the zero and always above the *x*-axis.

Example graph of a square root function, $f(x) = \sqrt{2x + 1}$:

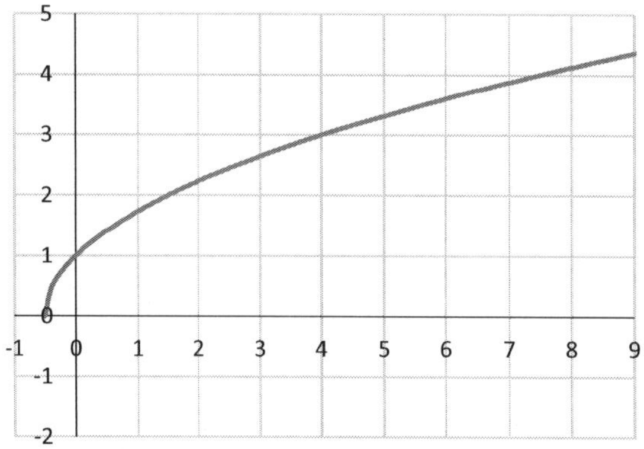

PRACTICE

P1. Martin needs a 20% medicine solution. The pharmacy has a 5% solution and a 30% solution. He needs 50 mL of the solution. If the pharmacist must mix the two solutions, how many milliliters of 5% solution and 30% solution should be used?

P2. Describe two different strategies for solving the following problem:

> Kevin can mow the yard in 4 hours. Mandy can mow the same yard in 5 hours. If they work together, how long will it take them to mow the yard?

P3. A car, traveling at 65 miles per hour, leaves Flagstaff and heads east on I-40. Another car, traveling at 75 miles per hour, leaves Flagstaff 2 hours later, from the same starting point and also heads east on I-40. Determine how many hours it will take the second car to catch the first car by:

(a) Using a table.

(b) Using algebra.

PRACTICE SOLUTIONS

P1. To solve this problem, a table may be created to represent the variables, percentages, and total amount of solution. Such a table is shown below:

	mL solution	% medicine	Total mL medicine
5% solution	x	0.05	$0.05x$
30% solution	y	0.30	$0.30y$
Mixture	$x + y = 50$	0.20	$(0.20)(50) = 10$

The variable x may be rewritten as $50 - y$, so the equation $0.05(50 - y) + 0.30y = 10$ may be written and solved for y. Doing so gives $y = 30$. So, 30 mL of 30% solution are needed. Evaluating the expression, $50 - y$ for an x-value of 20, shows that 20 mL of 5% solution are needed.

P2. Two possible strategies both involve the use of rational equations to solve. The first strategy involves representing the fractional part of the yard mowed by each person in one hour and setting this sum equal to the ratio of 1 to the total time needed. The appropriate equation is $1/4 + 1/5 = 1/t$, which simplifies as $9/20 = 1/t$, and finally as $t = 20/9$. So the time it will take them to mow the yard, when working together, is a little more than 2.2 hours.

A second strategy involves representing the time needed for each person as two fractions and setting the sum equal to 1 (representing 1 yard). The appropriate equation is $t/4 + t/5 = 1$, which simplifies as $9t/20 = 1$, and finally as $t = 20/9$. This strategy also shows the total time to be a little more than 2.2 hours.

P3. (a) One strategy might involve creating a table of values for the number of hours and distances for each car. The table may be examined to find the same distance traveled and the corresponding number of hours taken. Such a table is shown below:

Car A		Car B	
x (hours)	y (distance)	x (hours)	y (distance)
0	0	0	
1	65	1	
2	130	2	0
3	195	3	75
4	260	4	150
5	325	5	225
6	390	6	300
7	455	7	375
8	520	8	450
9	585	9	525
10	650	10	600
11	715	11	675
12	780	12	750
13	845	13	825
14	910	14	900
15	975	15	975

The table shows that after 15 hours, the distance traveled is the same. Thus, the second car catches up with the first car after a distance of 975 miles and 15 hours.

(b) A second strategy might involve setting up and solving an algebraic equation. This situation may be modeled as $65x = 75(x - 2)$. This equation sets the distances traveled by each car equal to one another. Solving for x gives $x = 15$. Thus, once again, the second car will catch up with the first car after 15 hours.

Advanced Functions

Step Functions

The double brackets indicate a step function. For a step function, the value inside the double brackets is rounded down to the nearest integer. The graph of the function $f_0(x) = [\![x]\!]$ appears on the left graph. In comparison $f(x) = 2\left[\!\left[\frac{1}{3}(x - 1)\right]\!\right]$ is on the right graph. The coefficient of 2 shows that it's stretched vertically by a factor of 2 (so there's a vertical distance of 2 units between successive "steps"). The coefficient of $\frac{1}{3}$ in front of the x shows that it's stretched horizontally by a factor of 3 (so each "step" is three units long), and the $x - 1$ shows that it's displaced one unit to the right.

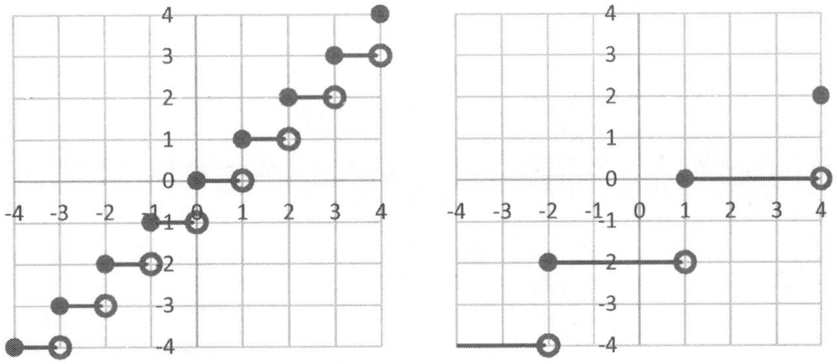

TRANSCENDENTAL FUNCTIONS

Transcendental functions are all functions that are non-algebraic. Any function that includes logarithms, trigonometric functions, variables as exponents, or any combination that includes any of these is not algebraic in nature, even if the function includes polynomials or roots.

EXPONENTIAL FUNCTIONS

Exponential functions are equations that have the format $y = b^x$, where base $b > 0$ and $b \neq 1$. The exponential function can also be written $f(x) = b^x$. Recall the properties of exponents, like the product of terms with the same base is equal to the base raised to the sum of the exponents ($a^x \times a^y = a^{x+y}$) and a term with an exponent that is raised to an exponent is equal to the base of the original term raised to the product of the exponents: ($(a^x)^y = a^{xy}$). The graph of an example exponential function, $f(x) = 2^x$, is below:

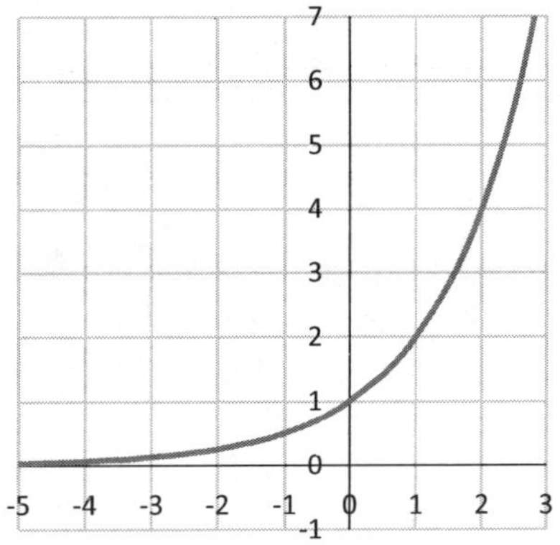

Note in the graph that the y-value approaches zero to the left and infinity to the right. One of the key features of an exponential function is that there will be one end that goes off to infinity and another that asymptotically approaches a lower bound. Common forms of exponential functions include:

Geometric sequences: $a_n = a_1 \times r^{n-1}$, where a_n is the value of the nth term, a_1 is the initial value, r is the common ratio, and n is the number of terms. Note that $a_1 \times r^{1-1} = a_1 \times r^0 = a_1 \times 1 = a_1$.

Population growth: $f(t) = ae^{rt}$, where $f(t)$ is the population at time $t \geq 0$, a is the initial population, e is the mathematical constant known as Euler's number, and r is the growth rate.

Compound interest: $f(t) = P\left(1 + \frac{r}{n}\right)^{nt}$, where $f(t)$ is the account value at a certain number of time periods $t \geq 0$, P is the initial principle balance, r is the interest rate, and n is the number of times the interest is applied per time period.

General exponential growth or decay: $f(t) = a(1 + r)^t$, where $f(t)$ is the future count, a is the current or initial count, r is the growth or decay rate, and t is the time.

For example, suppose the initial population of a town was 1,200 people. The population growth is 5%. The current population is 2,400. To find out how much time has passed since the town was founded, we can use the following function:

$$2400 = 1200e^{0.05t}.$$

The general form for population growth may be represented as $f(t) = ae^{rt}$, where $f(t)$ represents the current population, a represents the initial population, r represents the growth rate, and t represents the time. Thus, substituting the initial population, current population, and rate into this form gives the equation above.

The number of years that have passed were found by first dividing both sides of the equation by 1,200. Doing so gives $2 = e^{0.05t}$. Taking the natural logarithm of both sides gives $\ln(2) = ln(e^{0.05t})$. Applying the power property of logarithms, the equation may be rewritten as $\ln(2) = 0.05t \times \ln(e)$, which simplifies as $\ln(2) = 0.05t$. Dividing both sides of this equation by 0.05 gives $t \approx 13.86$. Thus, approximately 13.86 years passed.

Review Video: Biology Application - Exponential Growth Function
Visit mometrix.com/academy and enter code: 336069

Logarithmic Functions

Logarithmic functions are equations that have the format $y = \log_b x$ or $f(x) = \log_b x$. The base b may be any number except one; however, the most common bases for logarithms are base 10 and base e. The log base e is the natural logarithm, or *ln*, expressed by the function $f(x) = \ln x$.

Any logarithm that does not have an assigned value of b is assumed to be base 10: $\log x = \log_{10} x$. Exponential functions and logarithmic functions are related in that one is the inverse of the other. If $f(x) = b^x$, then $f^{-1}(x) = \log_b x$. This can perhaps be expressed more clearly by the two equations: $y = b^x$ and $x = \log_b y$.

The following properties apply to logarithmic expressions:

Property	Description
$\log_b 1 = 0$	The log of 1 is equal to 0 for any base
$\log_b b = 1$	The log of the base is equal to 1
$\log_b b^p = p$	The log of the base raised to a power is equal to that power
$\log_b MN = \log_b M + \log_b N$	The log of a product is the sum of the log of each factor
$\log_b \frac{M}{N} = \log_b M - \log_b N$	The log of a quotient is equal to the log of the dividend minus the log of the divisor
$\log_b M^p = p \log_b M$	The log of a value raised to a power is equal to the power times the log of the value

The graph of an example logarithmic function, $f(x) = \log_2(x + 2)$, is below:

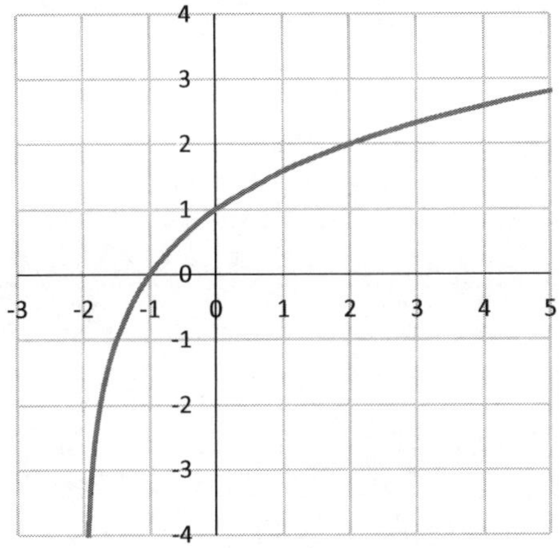

Trigonometric Functions

Trigonometric functions are periodic, meaning that they repeat the same form over and over. The basic trigonometric functions are sine (abbreviated 'sin'), cosine (abbreviated 'cos'), and tangent (abbreviated 'tan'). The simplest way to think of them is as describing the ratio of the side lengths of a right triangle in relation to the angles of the triangle.

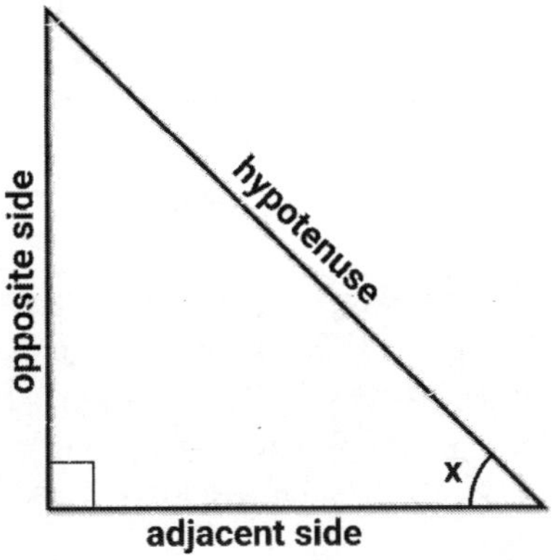

$$\sin x = \frac{\text{opposite side}}{\text{hypotenuse}}$$

$$\cos x = \frac{\text{adjacent side}}{\text{hypotenuse}}$$

$$\tan x = \frac{\text{opposite side}}{\text{adjacent side}}$$

Using sine as an example, trigonometric functions take the form $f(x) = A\sin(Bx + C) + D$, where the **amplitude** is simply equal to A. The **period** is the distance between successive peaks or troughs, essentially the length of the repeated pattern. In this form, the period is equal to $^{2\pi}/_{B}$. As for C, this is the **phase shift** or the horizontal shift of the function. The last term, D, is the vertical shift and determines the **midline** as $y = D$.

For instance, consider the function $f(x) = 2 + \frac{3}{2}\sin\left(\pi x + \frac{\pi}{2}\right)$. Here $A = \frac{3}{2}$, $B = \pi$, $C = \frac{\pi}{2}$, and $D = 2$, so the midline is at $y = 2$, the amplitude is $\frac{3}{2}$, and the period is $^{2\pi}/_{\pi} = 2$. To graph this function, we center the sine wave on the midline and extend it to a height above and below the midline equal to the amplitude—so this graph would have a minimum value of $2 - \frac{3}{2} = \frac{1}{2}$ and a maximum of $2 + \frac{3}{2} = \frac{7}{2}$. So, the function would be graphed as follows:

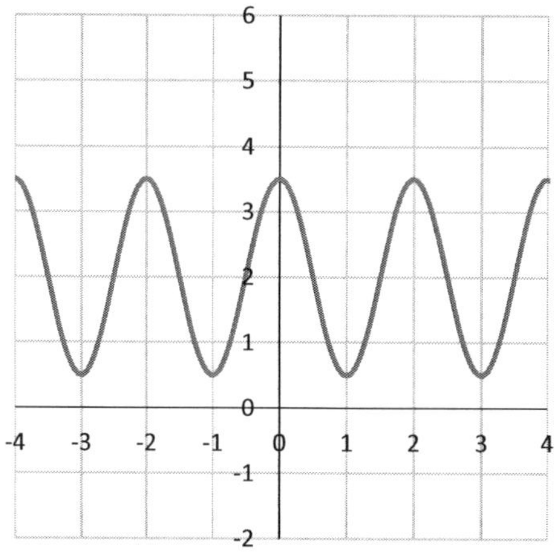

Manipulation of Functions

Translation occurs when values are added to or subtracted from the x or y values. If a constant is added to the y portion of each point, the graph shifts up. If a constant is subtracted from the y portion of each point, the graph shifts down. This is represented by the expression $f(x) \pm k$, where k is a constant. If a constant is added to the x portion of each point, the graph shifts left. If a constant is subtracted from the x portion of each point, the graph shifts right. This is represented by the expression $f(x \pm k)$, where k is a constant.

Stretching, compression, and reflection occur when different parts of a function are multiplied by different groups of constants. If the function as a whole is multiplied by a real number constant greater than 1, $(k \times f(x))$, the graph is stretched vertically. If k in the previous equation is greater than zero but less than 1, the graph is compressed vertically. If k is less than zero, the graph is reflected about the x-axis, in addition to being either stretched or compressed vertically if k is less than or greater than -1, respectively. If instead, just the x-term is multiplied by a constant greater than 1 $(f(k \times x))$, the graph is compressed horizontally. If k in the previous equation is greater than zero but less than 1, the graph is stretched horizontally. If k is less than zero, the graph is reflected about the y-axis, in addition to being either stretched or compressed horizontally if k is greater than or less than -1, respectively.

Algebraic Theorems

According to the **fundamental theorem of algebra**, every non-constant, single-variable polynomial has exactly as many roots as the polynomial's highest exponent. For example, if x^4 is the largest exponent of a term, the polynomial will have exactly 4 roots. However, some of these roots may have multiplicity or be non-real numbers. For instance, in the polynomial function $f(x) = x^4 - 4x + 3$, the only real roots are 1 and -1. The root 1 has multiplicity of 2 and there is one non-real root $(-1 - \sqrt{2}i)$.

The **remainder theorem** is useful for determining the remainder when a polynomial is divided by a binomial. The remainder theorem states that if a polynomial function $f(x)$ is divided by a binomial $x - a$, where a is a real number, the remainder of the division will be the value of $f(a)$. If $f(a) = 0$, then a is a root of the polynomial.

The **factor theorem** is related to the remainder theorem and states that if $f(a) = 0$ then $(x - a)$ is a factor of the function.

According to the **rational root theorem,** any rational root of a polynomial function $f(x) = a_n x^n + a_{n-1}x^{n-1} + \cdots + a_1 x + a_0$ with integer coefficients will, when reduced to its lowest terms, be a positive or negative fraction such that the numerator is a factor of a_0 and the denominator is a factor of a_n. For instance, if the polynomial function $f(x) = x^3 + 3x^2 - 4$ has any rational roots, the numerators of those roots can only be factors of 4 (1, 2, 4), and the denominators can only be factors of 1 (1). The function in this example has roots of 1 $\left(\text{or } \frac{1}{1}\right)$ and -2 $\left(\text{or } -\frac{2}{1}\right)$.

APPLYING THE BASIC OPERATIONS TO FUNCTIONS

For each of the basic operations, we will use these functions as examples: $f(x) = x^2$ and $g(x) = x$.

To find the sum of two functions f and g, assuming the domains are compatible, simply add the two functions together: $(f + g)(x) = f(x) + g(x) = x^2 + x$

To find the difference of two functions f and g, assuming the domains are compatible, simply subtract the second function from the first: $(f - g)(x) = f(x) - g(x) = x^2 - x$.

To find the product of two functions f and g, assuming the domains are compatible, multiply the two functions together: $(f \times g)(x) = f(x) \times g(x) = x^2 \times x = x^3$.

To find the quotient of two functions f and g, assuming the domains are compatible, divide the first function by the second: $\frac{f}{g}(x) = \frac{f(x)}{g(x)} = \frac{x^2}{x} = x\, ; x \neq 0$.

The example given in each case is fairly simple, but on a given problem, if you are looking only for the value of the sum, difference, product, or quotient of two functions at a particular x-value, it may be simpler to solve the functions individually and then perform the given operation using those values.

The composite of two functions f and g, written as $(f \circ g)(x)$ simply means that the output of the second function is used as the input of the first. This can also be written as $f\big(g(x)\big)$. In general, this can be solved by substituting $g(x)$ for all instances of x in $f(x)$ and simplifying. Using the example functions $f(x) = x^2 - x + 2$ and $g(x) = x + 1$, we can find that $(f \circ g)(x)$ or $f\big(g(x)\big)$ is equal to $f(x + 1) = (x + 1)^2 - (x + 1) + 2$, which simplifies to $x^2 + x + 2$.

It is important to note that $(f \circ g)(x)$ is not necessarily the same as $(g \circ f)(x)$. The process is not always commutative like addition or multiplication expressions. It *can* be commutative, but most often this is not the case.

PRACTICE

P1. A professor wishes to invest \$20,000 in a CD that compounds annually. The interest rate at his bank is 1.9%. How many years will it take for his account to reach \$50,000?

P2. Suppose a new strain of bacteria, after x days, shows a growth rate of 10%. The current count for the new bacteria strain is 100. How many days will pass before the count reaches 1 million bacteria?

P3. Each of the following functions cross the x- and y-axes at the same points. Identify the most likely function type of each graph

(a)

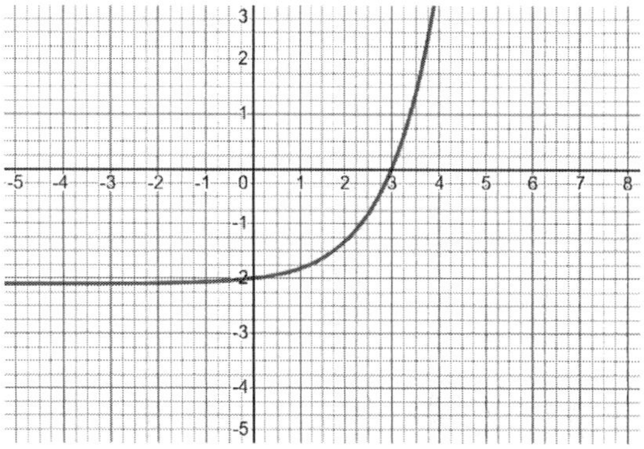

(b)

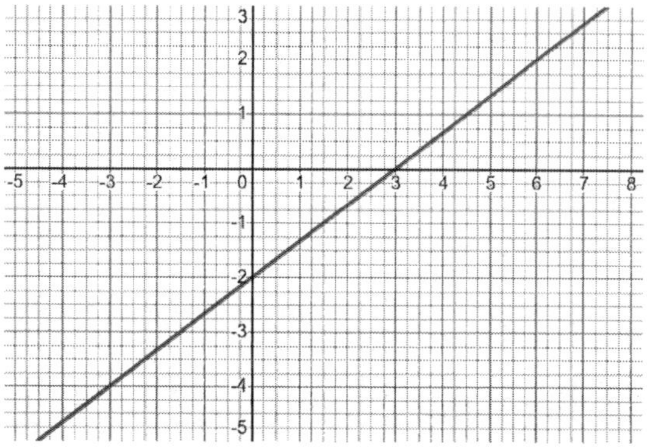

(c)

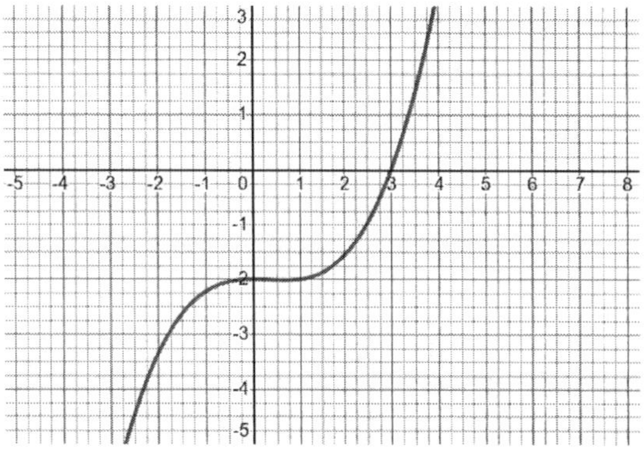

(d)

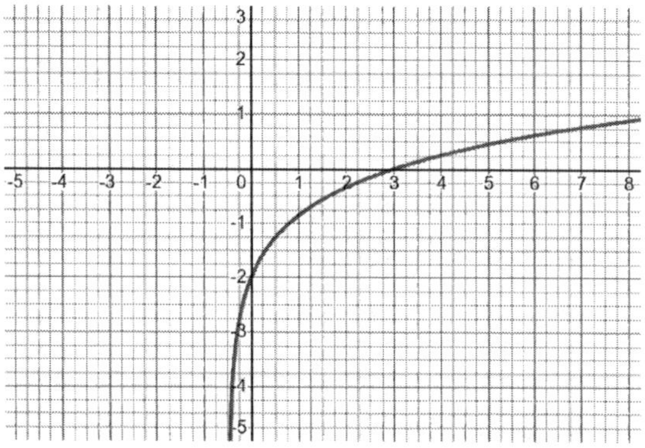

P4. Given the functions $f(x) = -3x + 3$, $g(x) = e^x + 3$, and $h(x) = x^2 - 2x + 1$, perform the following operations and write out the resulting function:

(a) Shift $g(x)$ 4 units to the left and 1 unit up, then compress the new function by a factor of $1/2$

(b) $\frac{f(x)}{h(x)}$

(c) $h(g(x))$

(d) $\frac{f(x)+h(x)}{x-1}$

Practice Solutions

P1. In order to solve this problem, the compound interest formula should be evaluated for a future value of \$50,000, principal of \$20,000, rate of 0.019, and number of years of t. The exponential equation may then be solved by taking the logarithm of both sides. The process is shown below:

$$50{,}000 = 20{,}000\left(1 + \frac{0.019}{1}\right)^t$$

Dividing both sides of the equation by 20,000 gives $2.5 = 1.019^t$. Taking the logarithm of both sides gives $\log(2.5) = t\log(1.019)$. Dividing both sides of this equation by $\log(1.019)$ gives $t \approx 48.68$. Thus, after approximately 49 years, the professor's account will reach \$50,000.

P2. The problem may be solved by writing and solving an exponential growth function, in the form, $f(x) = a(1+r)^x$, where $f(x)$ represents the future count, a represents the current count, r represents the growth rate, and x represents the time. Once the function is evaluated for a future count of 1,000,000, a current count of 100, and a growth rate of 0.10, the exponential equation may be solved by taking the logarithm of both sides.

The problem may be modeled with the equation $1{,}000{,}000 = 100 \times (1.10)^x$. Dividing both sides of the equation by 100 gives $10{,}000 = 1.10^x$. Taking the logarithm of both sides gives $\log(10{,}000) = x\log(1.10)$. Dividing both sides of this equation by $\log(1.10)$ gives $x \approx 96.6$. Thus, after approximately 97 days, the bacteria count will reach 1 million.

P3. (a) Exponential function – positive, increasing slope

(b) Linear function – positive, continuous slope.

(c) Polynomial function (odd degree) – positive, changing slope. Note that the graph goes off to infinity in opposite quadrants I and III, thus it is an odd degree.

(d) Logarithmic function – positive, decreasing slope

P4. (a) Shifting $g(x)$ to the left 4 units is the same as $g(x+4)$ and shifting the function up one unit is $g(x)+1$. Combining these and multiplying by ½ results in the following:

$$\begin{aligned}\frac{1}{2}\big(g(x+4)+1\big) &= \frac{1}{2}\big((e^{x+4}+3)+1\big)\\ &= \frac{e^{x+4}}{2}+2\end{aligned}$$

(b) Factor $h(x)$, noting that it is a perfect square, and be sure to note the constraint on x due to the original denominator of the rational expression:

$$\frac{f(x)}{h(x)} = \frac{-3x+3}{x^2-2x+1} = \frac{-3(x-1)}{(x-1)(x-1)} = \frac{-3}{(x-1)};x \neq 1$$

(c) Evaluate the composition as follows:

$$\begin{aligned}h\big(g(x)\big) &= (e^x+3)^2 - 2(e^x+3)+1\\ &= (e^x)^2+6e^x+9-2e^x-6+1\\ &= e^{2x}+4e^x+4\\ &= (e^x+2)^2\end{aligned}$$

(d) Note the constraint on x due to the original denominator of the rational expression:

$$\begin{aligned}\frac{f(x)+h(x)}{x-1} &= \frac{(-3x+3)+(x^2-2x+1)}{x-1}\\ &= \frac{-3(x-1)+(x-1)(x-1)}{x-1}\\ &= -3+(x-1)\\ &= x-4; x \neq 1\end{aligned}$$

Sequences

SEQUENCES

A **sequence** is a set of numbers that continues on in a defined pattern. The function that defines a sequence has a domain composed of the set of positive integers. Each member of the sequence is an element, or individual term. Each element is identified by the notation a_n, where a is the term of the sequence, and n is the integer identifying which term in the sequence a is. There are two different ways to represent a sequence that contains the element a_n. The first is the simple notation $\{a_n\}$. The expanded notation of a sequence is $a_1, a_2, a_3, \ldots a_n, \ldots$. Notice that the expanded form does not end with the nth term. There is no indication that the nth term is the last term in the sequence, only that the nth term is an element of the sequence.

ARITHMETIC SEQUENCES

An **arithmetic sequence**, or arithmetic progression, is a special kind of sequence in which each term has a specific quantity, called the common difference, that is added to the previous term. The common difference may be positive or negative. The general form of an arithmetic sequence containing n terms is $a_1, a_1 + d, a_1 + 2d, \ldots, a_1 + (n-1)d$, where d is the common difference. The formula for the general term of an arithmetic sequence is $a_n = a_1 + (n-1)d$, where a_n is the term you are looking for and d is the common difference. To find the sum of the first n terms of an arithmetic sequence, use the formula $s_n = \frac{n}{2}(a_1 + a_n)$.

Review Video: Arithmetic Sequence
Visit mometrix.com/academy and enter code: 676885

MONOTONIC SEQUENCES

A **monotonic sequence** is a sequence that is either nonincreasing or nondecreasing. A **nonincreasing** sequence is one whose terms either get progressively smaller in value or remain the same—a sequence that is bounded above. This means that all elements of the sequence must be less than a given real number. A **nondecreasing** sequence is one whose terms either get progressively larger in value or remain the same—a sequence that is bounded below. This means that all elements of the sequence must be greater than a given real number.

RECURSIVE SEQUENCES

When one element of a sequence is defined in terms of a previous element or elements of the sequence, the sequence is a **recursive sequence**. For example, given the recursive definition $a_1 = 1; a_2 = 1; a_n = a_{n-1} + a_{n-2}$ for all $n > 2$, you get the sequence 1, 1, 2, 3, 5, 8, …. This particular sequence is known as the Fibonacci sequence, and is defined as the numbers zero and one, and a continuing sequence of numbers, with each number in the sequence equal to the sum of the two previous numbers. It is important to note that the Fibonacci sequence can also be defined as the first two terms being equal to one, with the remaining terms equal to the sum of the previous two terms. Both definitions are considered correct in mathematics. Make sure you know which definition you are working with when dealing with Fibonacci numbers.

Sometimes one term of a sequence with a recursive definition can be found without knowing the previous terms of the sequence. This case is known as a **closed-form** expression for a recursive definition. In this case, an alternate formula will apply to the sequence to generate the same sequence of numbers. However, not all sequences based on recursive definitions will have a closed-form expression. Some sequences will require the use of the recursive definition.

Golden Ratio and Fibonacci Sequence

The golden ratio is approximately 1.6180339887498948482... and is often represented by the Greek letter phi, Φ. The exact value of Φ is $(1+\sqrt{5})/2$ and it is one of the solutions to $x - \frac{1}{x} = 1$. The golden ratio is represented within the Fibonacci sequence, since the ratio of a term to the previous term approaches Φ as the sequence approaches infinity:

n	a_n	a_{n-1}	$\frac{a_n}{a_{n-1}}$
3	2	1	2
4	3	2	1.5
5	5	3	$1.\overline{6}$
6	8	5	1.6
7	13	8	1.625
8	21	13	$1.\overline{615384}$
9	34	21	$1.\overline{619047}$
⋮	⋮	⋮	⋮
20	6765	4181	1.618033963

Geometric Sequences

Any function with the set of all natural numbers as the domain is also called a sequence. An element of a sequence is denoted by the symbol a_n, which represents the nth element of sequence a. Sequences may be arithmetic or geometric and may be defined by a recursive definition, closed-form expression or both. Arithmetic and geometric sequences both have recursive definitions based on the first term of the sequence, as well as both having formulas to find the sum of the first n terms in the sequence, assuming you know what the first term is. The sum of all the terms in a sequence is called a **series**. Consider the following example of a geometric sequence: Andy opens a savings account with $10. During each subsequent week, he plans to double the amount deposited during the previous week.

Sequence: 10, 20, 40, 80, 160, ...

Function: $a_n = 10 \times 2^{n-1}$

The sequence is a geometric sequence, with a common ratio of 2. All geometric sequences represent exponential functions. The nth term in any geometric sequence is represented by the general form, $a_n = a_1 \times r^{n-1}$, where a_n represents the value of the nth term, a_1 represents the value of the initial term, r represents the common ratio, and n represents the number of terms. Thus, substituting the initial value of 10 and common ratio of 2 gives the function, $a_n = 10 \times 2^{n-1}$.

Limit of a Sequence

Some sequences will have a **limit**, or a value the sequence approaches or sometimes even reaches but never passes. A sequence that has a limit is known as a convergent sequence because all the values of the sequence seemingly converge at that point. Sequences that do not converge at a particular limit are divergent sequences. The easiest way to determine whether a sequence converges or diverges is to find the limit of the sequence. If the limit is a real number, the sequence is a convergent sequence. If the limit is infinity, the sequence is a divergent sequence.

Remember the following rules for finding limits:

- $\lim_{n\to\infty} k = k$, for all real numbers k
- $\lim_{n\to\infty} \frac{1}{n} = 0$
- $\lim_{n\to\infty} n = \infty$
- $\lim_{n\to\infty} \frac{k}{n^p} = 0$, for all real numbers k and positive rational numbers p
- The limit of the sums of two sequences is equal to the sum of the limits of the two sequences: $\lim_{n\to\infty}(a_n + b_n) = \lim_{n\to\infty} a_n + \lim_{n\to\infty} b_n$.
- The limit of the difference between two sequences is equal to the difference between the limits of the two sequences: $\lim_{n\to\infty}(a_n - b_n) = \lim_{n\to\infty} a_n - \lim_{n\to\infty} b_n$
- The limit of the product of two sequences is equal to the product of the limits of the two sequences: $\lim_{n\to\infty}(a_n \times b_n) = \lim_{n\to\infty} a_n \times \lim_{n\to\infty} b_n$
- The limit of the quotient of two sequences is equal to the quotient of the limits of the two sequences, with some exceptions: $\lim_{n\to\infty}\left(\frac{a_n}{b_n}\right) = \frac{\lim_{n\to\infty} a_n}{\lim_{n\to\infty} b_n}$. In the quotient formula, it is important to consider that $b_n \neq 0$ and $\lim_{n\to\infty} b_n \neq 0$.
- The limit of a sequence multiplied by a scalar is equal to the scalar multiplied by the limit of the sequence: $\lim_{n\to\infty} ka_n = k \lim_{n\to\infty} a_n$, where k is any real number.

Infinite Series

An **infinite series**, also referred to as just a series, is a series of partial sums of a defined sequence. Each infinite sequence represents an infinite series according to the equation $\sum_{n=1}^{\infty} a_n = a_1 + a_2 + a_3 + \cdots + a_n + \cdots$. This notation can be shortened to $\sum_{n=1}^{\infty} a_n$ or $\sum a_n$. Every series is a sequence of partial sums, where the first partial sum is equal to the first element of the series, the second partial sum is equal to the sum of the first two elements of the series, and the nth partial sum is equal to the sum of the first n elements of the series.

Every infinite sequence of partial sums (infinite series) either converges or diverges. Like the test for convergence in a sequence, finding the limit of the sequence of partial sums will indicate whether it is a converging series or a diverging series. If there exists a real number S such that $\lim_{n\to\infty} S_n = S$, where S_n is the sequence of partial sums, then the series converges. If the limit equals infinity, then the series diverges. If $\lim_{n\to\infty} S_n = S$ and S is a real number, then S is also the convergence value of the series.

To find the sum as n approaches infinity for the sum of two convergent series, find the sum as n approaches infinity for each individual series and add the results.

$$\sum_{n=1}^{\infty}(a_n + b_n) = \sum_{n=1}^{\infty} a_n + \sum_{n=1}^{\infty} b_n$$

To find the sum as n approaches infinity for the difference between two convergent series, find the sum as n approaches infinity for each individual series and subtract the results.

$$\sum_{n=1}^{\infty}(a_n - b_n) = \sum_{n=1}^{\infty} a_n - \sum_{n=1}^{\infty} b_n$$

To find the sum as n approaches infinity for the product of a constant, also called a scalar, and a convergent series, find the sum as n approaches infinity for the series and multiply the result by the scalar.

$$\sum_{n=1}^{\infty} ka_n = k\sum_{n=1}^{\infty} a_n$$

The **n^{th} term test for divergence** involves taking the limit of the nth term of a sequence and determining whether or not the limit is equal to zero. If the limit of the nth term is not equal to zero, then the series is a diverging series. This test only works to prove divergence, however. If the nth term is equal to zero, the test is inconclusive.

PRACTICE

P1. Suppose Rachel has $4,500 in her account in month 1. With each passing month, her account is one-half of what it was during the previous month. What would be a formula for the value of her account in any future month?

P2. Determine if the following geometric sequences converge or diverge:

(a) $a_n = 500(3^{n-1})$; where $n = 1,2,3, \ldots$

(b) $a_n = 5(1^{n-1})$; where $n = 1,2,3, \ldots$

(c) $a_n = 50((-1)^{n-1})$; where $n = 1,2,3, \ldots$

(d) $a_n = 5000\left(\left(\frac{1}{5}\right)^{n-1}\right)$; where $n = 1,2,3, \ldots$

P3. Determine a recursive expression for the following sequences:

(a) $3, 7, 19, 55, 163, \ldots$

(b) $8, 6, 5, 4.5, 4.25, \ldots$

PRACTICE SOLUTIONS

P1. The sequence: 4500, 2250, 1125, 562.50, 281.25, ... is geometric, since there is a common ratio of $\frac{1}{2}$. Thus, this sequence represents an exponential function. All geometric sequences represent exponential functions. Recall the general form of a geometric sequence is $a_n = a_1 \times r^{n-1}$, and substituting the initial value of 4500 and common ratio of $\frac{1}{2}$ gives $a_n = 4500 \times \left(\frac{1}{2}\right)^{n-1}$.

P2. (a) $\lim_{n\to\infty} a_n \to 500(3^{\infty-1}) \to 500(\infty) \to \infty$. This sequence diverges.

(b) $\lim_{n\to\infty} a_n \to 5(1^{\infty-1}) \to 5(1) \to 5$. This sequence converges.

(c) $\lim_{n\to\infty} a_n \to 50((-1)^{\infty-1}) \to 50((-1)^{\infty}) \to undefined$. Since -1 raised to an integer power is either -1 or +1 this sequence just oscilates and does not converge. However, it is bounded above and below, so it does not diverge either.

(d) $\lim_{n\to\infty} a_n \to 5000\left(\left(\frac{1}{5}\right)^{\infty-1}\right) \to 500(0) \to 0$. This sequence converges.

P3. (a) Use a table to determine the pattern:

n	1	2	3	4	5
a_n	3	7	19	55	163
$d_n = a_n - a_{n-1}$	-	4	12	36	108
$r_n = \frac{d_n}{d_{n-1}}$	-	-	3	3	3

Since the difference between successive terms is increasing at a uniform rate, we can use that to the guess at a sequence: $a_n = 3a_{n-1} + d$. Substitute the first terms to find *d*:

$$7 = 3(3) + d$$
$$-2 = d$$

Thus, the recursive form would be $a_n = 3a_{n-1} - 2$

(b) Use a table to determine the pattern:

n	1	2	3	4	5
a_n	8	6	5	4.5	4.25
$d_n = a_n - a_{n-1}$	-	2	1	0.5	0.25
$r_n = \frac{d_n}{d_{n-1}}$	-	-	$\frac{1}{2}$	$\frac{1}{2}$	$\frac{1}{2}$

Since the difference between successive terms is increasing at a uniform rate, we can use that to the guess at a sequence: $a_n = \frac{a_{n-1}}{2} + d$. Substitute the first terms to find *d*:

$$6 = \frac{8}{2} + d$$
$$2 = d$$

Thus, the recursive form would be $a_n = \frac{a_{n-1}}{2} + 2$

Factorials

Factorials

The **factorial** is a function that can be performed on any **non-negative integer**. It is represented by the ! sign written after the integer on which it is being performed. The factorial of an integer is the product of all positive integers less than or equal to the number. For example, 4! (read "4 factorial") is calculated as $4 \times 3 \times 2 \times 1 = 24$.

Since 0 is not itself a positive integer, nor does it have any positive integers less than it, 0! cannot be calculated using this method. Instead, 0! is defined by convention to equal 1. This makes sense if you consider the pattern of descending factorials:

$$5! = 120$$
$$4! = \frac{5!}{5} = \frac{120}{5} = 24$$
$$3! = \frac{4!}{4} = \frac{24}{4} = 6$$
$$2! = \frac{3!}{3} = \frac{6}{3} = 2$$
$$1! = \frac{2!}{2} = \frac{2}{2} = 1$$
$$0! = \frac{1!}{1} = \frac{1}{1} = 1$$

PERMUTATIONS

For any given set of data, the individual elements in the set may be arranged in different groups containing different numbers of elements arranged in different orders. For example, given the set of integers from one to three, inclusive, the elements of the set are 1, 2, and 3: written as {1, 2, 3}. They may be arranged as follows: 1, 2, 3, 12, 21, 13, 31, 23, 32, 123, 132, 213, 231, 312, and 321. These ordered sequences of elements from the given set of data are called **permutations**. It is important to note that in permutations, the order of the elements in the sequence is important. The sequence 123 is not the same as the sequence 213. Also, no element in the given set may be used more times as an element in a permutation than it appears as an element in the original set. For example, 223 is not a permutation in the above example because the number 2 only appears one time in the given set.

To find the number of permutations of *r* items from a set of *n* items, use the formula ${}_nP_r = \frac{n!}{(n-r)!}$. When using this formula, each element of *r* must be unique. Also, this assumes that different arrangements of the same set of elements yields different outcomes. For example, 123 is not the same as 321; order is important.

A special case arises while finding the number of possible permutations of *n* items from a set of *n* items. Because $n = r$, the equation for the number of permutations becomes simply $P = n!$ The same result is true for $r = n - 1$. Both of these cases are a result of the fact that 0! and 1! are both equal to 1.

If a set contains one or more groups of **indistinguishable or interchangeable elements** (e.g., the set {1, 2, 3, 3}, which has a group of two indistinguishable 3's), there is a different formula for finding distinct permutations of all *n* elements. Use the formula $P = \frac{n!}{m_1!m_2!...m_k!}$, where *P* is the number of permutations, *n* is the total number of elements in the set, and m_1 through m_k are the number of identical elements in each group (e.g., for the set {1, 1, 2, 2, 2, 3, 3}, $m_1 = 2$, $m_2 = 3$, and $m_3 = 2$). It is important to note that each repeated number is counted as its own element for the purpose of defining *n* (e.g., for the set {1, 1, 2, 2, 2, 3, 3}, $n = 7$, not 3).

To find the number of possible permutations of **any number of elements** in a set of unique elements, you must apply the permutation formulas multiple times. For example, to find the total number of possible permutations of the set {1, 2, 3} first apply the permutation formula for situations where $n = r$ as follows: $P = n! = 3! = 6$. This gives the number of permutations of the three elements when all three elements are used. To find the number of permutations when only two of the three elements are used, use the formula ${}_nP_r = \frac{n!}{(n-r)!}$, where n is 3 and r is 2.

$${}_nP_r = \frac{n!}{(n-r)!} \Rightarrow {}_3P_2 = \frac{3!}{(3-2)!} = \frac{6}{1} = 6$$

To find the number of permutations when one element is used, use the formula ${}_nP_r = \frac{n!}{(n-r)!}$, where n is 3 and r is 1.

$${}_nP_r = \frac{n!}{(n-r)!} \Rightarrow {}_3P_1 = \frac{3!}{(3-1)!} = \frac{3!}{2!} = \frac{6}{2} = 3$$

Find the sum of the three formulas: $6 + 6 + 3 = 15$ total possible permutations.

Alternatively, the general formula for total possible permutations can be written as follows:

$$P_T = \sum_{i=1}^{n} \frac{n!}{(i-1)!}$$

Combinations

Combinations are essentially defined as permutations where the order in which the elements appear does not matter. Going back to the earlier example of the set {1, 2, 3}, the possible combinations that can be made from that set are 1, 2, 3, 12, 13, 23, and 123.

In a set containing n elements, the number of combinations of r items from the set can be found using the formula ${}_nC_r = \frac{n!}{r!(n-r)!}$. Notice the similarity to the formula for permutations. In effect, you are dividing the number of permutations by $r!$ to get the number of combinations, and the formula may be written ${}_nC_r = \frac{{}_nP_r}{r!}$. When finding the number of combinations, it is important to remember that the elements in the set must be unique (i.e., there must not be any duplicate items), and that no item may be used more than once in any given sequence.

Review Video: Probability - Permutation and Combination
Visit mometrix.com/academy and enter code: 907664

Practice

P1. Ichiro has 4 shirts, 1 jacket, and 5 different pairs of pants that he packed for his work trip. If wearing a jacket is optional, how many outfit combinations can he make?

P2. Determine the number of permutations and combinations of the following:

(a) Choose 3 from the set: $\{4, 5, 6, 7\}$

(b) Choose 2 from the set: $\{a, b, c, d, e\}$

(c) Choose 4 from the set: $\{a, h, m, t\}$

PRACTICE SOLUTIONS

P1. To start with, each shirt can be matched with each pair of pants, so that would be $4 \times 5 = 20$ combinations. Since the jacket is optional each of the 20 can be either with or without the jacket, i.e. $20 \times 2 = 40$. There are 40 distinct combinations he could wear.

P2. (a) ${}_nP_r = \frac{n!}{(n-r)!} = \frac{4!}{(4-3)!} = \frac{4\times3\times2\times1}{1} = 24$; ${}_nC_r = \frac{n!}{(n-r)!r!} = \frac{4!}{(4-3)!3!} = \frac{4\times3\times2\times1}{3\times2\times1} = 4$

(b) ${}_nP_r = \frac{n!}{(n-r)!} = \frac{5!}{(5-2)!} = \frac{5\times4\times3\times2\times1}{3\times2\times1} = 20$; ${}_nC_r = \frac{n!}{(n-r)!r!} = \frac{5!}{(5-2)!2!} = \frac{5\times4\times3\times2\times1}{(3\times2\times1)\times(2\times1)} = 10$

(c) ${}_nP_r = \frac{n!}{(n-r)!} = \frac{4!}{(4-4)!} = \frac{4\times3\times2\times1}{1} = 24$; ${}_nC_r = \frac{n!}{(n-r)!r!} = \frac{4!}{(4-4)!4!} = \frac{4\times3\times2\times1}{1\times(4\times3\times2\times1)} = 1$

Linear Algebra

MATRIX BASICS

A **matrix** (plural: matrices) is a rectangular array of numbers or variables, often called **elements**, which are arranged in columns and rows. A matrix is generally represented by a capital letter, with its elements represented by the corresponding lowercase letter with two subscripts indicating the row and column of the element. For example, n_{ab} represents the element in row a column b of matrix N.

$$N = \begin{bmatrix} n_{11} & n_{12} & n_{13} \\ n_{21} & n_{22} & n_{23} \end{bmatrix}$$

A matrix can be described in terms of the number of rows and columns it contains in the format $a \times b$, where a is the number of rows and b is the number of columns. The matrix shown above is a 2×3 matrix. Any $a \times b$ matrix where $a = b$ is a square matrix. A **vector** is a matrix that has exactly one column (**column vector**) or exactly one row (**row vector**).

The **main diagonal** of a matrix is the set of elements on the diagonal from the top left to the bottom right of a matrix. Because of the way it is defined, only square matrices will have a main diagonal. For the matrix shown below, the main diagonal consists of the elements $n_{11}, n_{22}, n_{33}, n_{44}$.

$$\begin{bmatrix} n_{11} & n_{12} & n_{13} & n_{14} \\ n_{21} & n_{22} & n_{23} & n_{24} \\ n_{31} & n_{32} & n_{33} & n_{34} \\ n_{41} & n_{42} & n_{43} & n_{44} \end{bmatrix}$$

A 3×4 matrix such as the one shown below would not have a main diagonal because there is no straight line of elements between the top left corner and the bottom right corner that joins the elements.

$$\begin{bmatrix} n_{11} & n_{12} & n_{13} & n_{14} \\ n_{21} & n_{22} & n_{23} & n_{24} \\ n_{31} & n_{32} & n_{33} & n_{34} \end{bmatrix}$$

A **diagonal matrix** is a square matrix that has a zero for every element in the matrix except the elements on the main diagonal. All the elements on the main diagonal must be nonzero numbers.

$$\begin{bmatrix} n_{11} & 0 & 0 & 0 \\ 0 & n_{22} & 0 & 0 \\ 0 & 0 & n_{33} & 0 \\ 0 & 0 & 0 & n_{44} \end{bmatrix}$$

If every element on the main diagonal of a diagonal matrix is equal to one, the matrix is called an **identity matrix**. The identity matrix is often represented by the letter *I*.

$$I = \begin{bmatrix} 1 & 0 & 0 & 0 \\ 0 & 1 & 0 & 0 \\ 0 & 0 & 1 & 0 \\ 0 & 0 & 0 & 1 \end{bmatrix}$$

A **zero matrix** is a matrix that has zero as the value for every element in the matrix.

$$\begin{bmatrix} 0 & 0 & 0 & 0 \\ 0 & 0 & 0 & 0 \\ 0 & 0 & 0 & 0 \\ 0 & 0 & 0 & 0 \end{bmatrix}$$

The zero matrix is the *identity for matrix addition*. Do not confuse the zero matrix with the identity matrix.

The **negative of a matrix** is also known as the additive inverse of a matrix. If matrix *N* is the given matrix, then matrix –*N* is its negative. This means that every element n_{ab} is equal to $-n_{ab}$ in the negative. To find the negative of a given matrix, change the sign of every element in the matrix and keep all elements in their original corresponding positions in the matrix.

If two matrices have the same order and all corresponding elements in the two matrices are the same, then the two matrices are **equal matrices**.

A matrix *N* may be **transposed** to matrix N^T by changing all rows into columns and changing all columns into rows. The easiest way to accomplish this is to swap the positions of the row and column notations for each element. For example, suppose the element in the second row of the third column of matrix *N* is $n_{23} = 6$. In the transposed matrix N^T, the transposed element would be $n_{32} = 6$, and it would be placed in the third row of the second column.

$$N = \begin{bmatrix} 1 & 2 & 3 \\ 4 & 5 & 6 \end{bmatrix};\ N^T = \begin{bmatrix} 1 & 4 \\ 2 & 5 \\ 3 & 6 \end{bmatrix}$$

To quickly transpose a matrix by hand, begin with the first column and rewrite a new matrix with those same elements in the same order in the first row. Write the elements from the second column of the original matrix in the second row of the transposed matrix. Continue this process until all columns have been completed. If the original matrix is identical to the transposed matrix, the matrices are symmetric.

The **determinant** of a matrix is a scalar value that is calculated by taking into account all the elements of a square matrix. A determinant only exists for square matrices. Finding the determinant of a 2×2 matrix is as simple as remembering a simple equation. For a 2×2 matrix

$M = \begin{bmatrix} m_{11} & m_{12} \\ m_{21} & m_{22} \end{bmatrix}$, the determinant is obtained by the equation $|M| = m_{11}m_{22} - m_{12}m_{21}$. Anything larger than 2×2 requires multiple steps. Take matrix $N = \begin{bmatrix} a & b & c \\ d & e & f \\ g & h & j \end{bmatrix}$. The determinant of N is calculated as $|N| = a\begin{vmatrix} e & f \\ h & j \end{vmatrix} - b\begin{vmatrix} d & f \\ g & j \end{vmatrix} + c\begin{vmatrix} d & e \\ g & h \end{vmatrix}$ or $|N| = a(ej - fh) - b(dj - fg) + c(dh - eg)$.

There is a shortcut for 3×3 matrices: add the products of each unique set of elements diagonally left-to-right and subtract the products of each unique set of elements diagonally right-to-left. In matrix N, the left-to-right diagonal elements are (a, e, j), (b, f, g), and (c, d, h). The right-to-left diagonal elements are (a, f, h), (b, d, j), and (c, e, g). $\det(N) = aej + bfg + cdh - afh - bdj - ceg$.

Calculating the determinants of matrices larger than 3×3 is rarely, if ever, done by hand.

The **inverse** of a matrix M is the matrix that, when multiplied by matrix M, yields a product that is the identity matrix. Multiplication of matrices will be explained in greater detail shortly. Not all matrices have inverses. Only a square matrix whose determinant is not zero has an inverse. If a matrix has an inverse, that inverse is unique to that matrix. For any matrix M that has an inverse, the inverse is represented by the symbol M^{-1}. To calculate the inverse of a 2×2 square matrix, use the following pattern:

$$M = \begin{bmatrix} m_{11} & m_{12} \\ m_{21} & m_{22} \end{bmatrix}; \; M^{-1} = \begin{bmatrix} \frac{m_{22}}{|M|} & \frac{-m_{12}}{|M|} \\ \frac{-m_{21}}{|M|} & \frac{m_{11}}{|M|} \end{bmatrix}$$

Another way to find the inverse of a matrix by hand is use an augmented matrix and elementary row operations. An **augmented matrix** is formed by appending the entries from one matrix onto the end of another. For example, given a 2×2 invertible matrix $N = \begin{bmatrix} a & b \\ c & d \end{bmatrix}$, you can find the inverse N^{-1} by creating an augmented matrix by appending a 2×2 identity matrix: $\left[\begin{array}{cc|cc} a & b & 1 & 0 \\ c & d & 0 & 1 \end{array}\right]$. To find the inverse of the original 2×2 matrix, perform elementary row operations to convert the original matrix on the left to an identity matrix: $\left[\begin{array}{cc|cc} 1 & 0 & e & f \\ 0 & 1 & g & h \end{array}\right]$. For instance, the first step might be to multiply the second row by $\frac{b}{d}$ and then subtract it from the first row to make its second column a zero. The end result is that the 2×2 section on the right will become the inverse of the original matrix: $N^{-1} = \begin{bmatrix} e & f \\ g & h \end{bmatrix}$.

ELEMENTARY ROW OPERATIONS

Elementary row operations include multiplying a row by a non-zero scalar, adding scalar multiples of two rows, and switching rows. These operations can be done using matrix multiplication with specialized transformation matrices. **Row switching** is achieved by swapping the corresponding rows in the identity matrix. For example, consider switching row 2 and row 3 in a 3×3 matrix:

$$M_{R_2 \leftrightarrow R_3} = \begin{bmatrix} 1 & 0 & 0 \\ 0 & 0 & 1 \\ 0 & 1 & 0 \end{bmatrix}$$

The transformation matrix for **row multiplication** is also based on the identity matrix with the scalar multiplication factor in place of the 1 in the corresponding row. Multiplying row 1 by -4 in a 3×3 matrix:

$$M_{-4R_1 \to R_1} = \begin{bmatrix} -4 & 0 & 0 \\ 0 & 1 & 0 \\ 0 & 0 & 1 \end{bmatrix}$$

The transformation matrix for **row addition** consists of the identity matrix with a 1 in the element corresponding to the two rows being added in the column where you want the result to go. Adding row 2 to row 1 in a 3×3 matrix:

$$M_{R_1 + R_2 \to R_1} = \begin{bmatrix} 1 & 0 & 0 \\ 1 & 1 & 0 \\ 0 & 0 & 1 \end{bmatrix}$$

Basic Operations with Matrices

There are two categories of basic operations with regard to matrices: operations between a matrix and a scalar, and operations between two matrices.

Scalar Operations

A scalar being added to a matrix is treated as though it were being added to each element of the matrix:

$$M + \mathrm{k} = \begin{bmatrix} m_{11} + k & m_{12} + k \\ m_{21} + k & m_{22} + k \end{bmatrix}$$

The same is true for the other three operations.

Subtraction:

$$M - k = \begin{bmatrix} m_{11} - k & m_{12} - k \\ m_{21} - k & m_{22} - k \end{bmatrix}$$

Multiplication:

$$M \times k = \begin{bmatrix} m_{11} \times k & m_{12} \times k \\ m_{21} \times k & m_{22} \times k \end{bmatrix}$$

Division:

$$M \div \mathrm{k} = \begin{bmatrix} m_{11} \div k & m_{12} \div k \\ m_{21} \div k & m_{22} \div k \end{bmatrix}$$

Matrix Addition and Subtraction

All four of the basic operations can be used with operations between matrices (although division is usually discarded in favor of multiplication by the inverse), but there are restrictions on the situations in which they can be used. Matrices that meet all the qualifications for a given operation are called **conformable matrices**. However, conformability is specific to the operation; two matrices that are conformable for addition are not necessarily conformable for multiplication.

For two matrices to be conformable for addition or subtraction, they must be of the same dimension; otherwise the operation is not defined. If matrix M is a 3×2 matrix and matrix N is a 2×3 matrix, the operations $M + N$ and $M - N$ are meaningless. If matrices M and N are the same size, the operation is as simple as adding or subtracting all of the corresponding elements:

$$\begin{bmatrix} m_{11} & m_{12} \\ m_{21} & m_{22} \end{bmatrix} + \begin{bmatrix} n_{11} & n_{12} \\ n_{21} & n_{22} \end{bmatrix} = \begin{bmatrix} m_{11} + n_{11} & m_{12} + n_{12} \\ m_{21} + n_{21} & m_{22} + n_{22} \end{bmatrix}$$

$$\begin{bmatrix} m_{11} & m_{12} \\ m_{21} & m_{22} \end{bmatrix} - \begin{bmatrix} n_{11} & n_{12} \\ n_{21} & n_{22} \end{bmatrix} = \begin{bmatrix} m_{11} - n_{11} & m_{12} - n_{12} \\ m_{21} - n_{21} & m_{22} - n_{22} \end{bmatrix}$$

The result of addition or subtraction is a matrix of the same dimension as the two original matrices involved in the operation.

MATRIX MULTIPLICATION

The first thing it is necessary to understand about matrix multiplication is that it is not commutative. In scalar multiplication, the operation is commutative, meaning that $a \times b = b \times a$. For matrix multiplication, this is not the case: $A \times B \neq B \times A$. The terminology must be specific when describing matrix multiplication. The operation $A \times B$ can be described as A multiplied (or **post-multiplied**) by B, or B **pre-multiplied** by A.

For two matrices to be conformable for multiplication, they need not be of the same dimension, but specific dimensions must correspond. Taking the example of two matrices M and N to be multiplied $M \times N$, matrix M must have the same number of columns as matrix N has rows. Put another way, if matrix M has the dimensions $a \times b$ and matrix N has the dimensions $c \times d$, b must equal c if the two matrices are to be conformable for this multiplication. The matrix that results from the multiplication will have the dimensions $a \times d$. If a and d are both equal to 1, the product is simply a scalar. Square matrices of the same dimensions are always conformable for multiplication, and their product is always a matrix of the same size.

The simplest type of matrix multiplication is a 1×2 matrix (a row vector) times a 2×1 matrix (a column vector). These will multiply in the following way:

$$\begin{bmatrix} m_{11} & m_{12} \end{bmatrix} \times \begin{bmatrix} n_{11} \\ n_{21} \end{bmatrix} = m_{11}n_{11} + m_{12}n_{21}$$

The two matrices are conformable for multiplication because matrix M has the same number of columns as matrix N has rows. Because the other dimensions are both 1, the result is a scalar. Expanding our matrices to 1×3 and 3×1, the process is the same:

$$\begin{bmatrix} m_{11} & m_{12} & m_{13} \end{bmatrix} \times \begin{bmatrix} n_{11} \\ n_{21} \\ n_{31} \end{bmatrix} = m_{11}n_{11} + m_{12}n_{21} + m_{13}n_{31}$$

Once again, the result is a scalar. This type of basic matrix multiplication is the building block for the multiplication of larger matrices.

To multiply larger matrices, treat each **row from the first matrix** and each **column from the second matrix** as individual vectors and follow the pattern for multiplying vectors. The scalar value found from multiplying the first-row vector by the first column vector is placed in the first row, first column of the new matrix. The scalar value found from multiplying the second-row vector by the first column vector is placed in the second row, first column of the new matrix. Continue this pattern until each row of the first matrix has been multiplied by each column of the second vector.

Below is an example of the multiplication of a 3×2 matrix and a 2×3 matrix.

$$\begin{bmatrix} m_{11} & m_{12} \\ m_{21} & m_{22} \\ m_{31} & m_{32} \end{bmatrix} \times \begin{bmatrix} n_{11} & n_{12} & n_{13} \\ n_{21} & n_{22} & n_{23} \end{bmatrix} = \begin{bmatrix} m_{11}n_{11} + m_{12}n_{21} & m_{11}n_{12} + m_{12}n_{22} & m_{11}n_{13} + m_{12}n_{23} \\ m_{21}n_{11} + m_{22}n_{21} & m_{21}n_{12} + m_{22}n_{22} & m_{21}n_{13} + m_{22}n_{23} \\ m_{31}n_{11} + m_{32}n_{21} & m_{31}n_{12} + m_{32}n_{22} & m_{31}n_{13} + m_{32}n_{23} \end{bmatrix}$$

This process starts by taking the first column of the second matrix and running it through each row of the first matrix. Removing all but the first M row and first N column, we would see only the following:

$$[m_{11}\ m_{12}] \times \begin{bmatrix} n_{11} \\ n_{21} \end{bmatrix} = m_{11}n_{11} + m_{12}n_{21}$$

The first product would then be $m_{11}n_{11} + m_{12}n_{21}$. This process will be continued for each column of the N matrix to find the first full row of the product matrix, as shown below.

$$[m_{11}n_{11} + m_{12}n_{21} \quad m_{11}n_{12} + m_{12}n_{22} \quad m_{11}n_{13} + m_{12}n_{23}]$$

After completing the first row, the next step would be to simply move to the second row of the M matrix and repeat the process until all of the rows have been finished. The result is a 3 × 3 matrix.

$$\begin{bmatrix} m_{11} & m_{12} \\ m_{21} & m_{22} \\ m_{31} & m_{32} \end{bmatrix} \times \begin{bmatrix} n_{11} & n_{12} & n_{13} \\ n_{21} & n_{22} & n_{23} \end{bmatrix} = \begin{bmatrix} m_{11}n_{11} + m_{12}n_{21} & m_{11}n_{12} + m_{12}n_{22} & m_{11}n_{13} + m_{12}n_{23} \\ m_{21}n_{11} + m_{22}n_{21} & m_{21}n_{12} + m_{22}n_{22} & m_{21}n_{13} + m_{22}n_{23} \\ m_{31}n_{11} + m_{32}n_{21} & m_{31}n_{12} + m_{32}n_{22} & m_{31}n_{13} + m_{32}n_{23} \end{bmatrix}$$

If the operation were done in reverse ($N \times M$), the result would be a 2 × 2 matrix.

$$\begin{bmatrix} n_{11} & n_{12} & n_{13} \\ n_{21} & n_{22} & n_{23} \end{bmatrix} \times \begin{bmatrix} m_{11} & m_{12} \\ m_{21} & m_{22} \\ m_{31} & m_{32} \end{bmatrix} = \begin{bmatrix} m_{11}n_{11} + m_{21}n_{12} + m_{31}n_{13} & m_{12}n_{11} + m_{22}n_{12} + m_{32}n_{13} \\ m_{11}n_{21} + m_{21}n_{22} + m_{31}n_{23} & m_{12}n_{21} + m_{22}n_{22} + m_{32}n_{23} \end{bmatrix}$$

Solving Systems of Equations

Matrices can be used to represent the coefficients of a system of linear equations and can be very useful in solving those systems. Take for instance three equations with three variables where all a, b, c, and d are known constants:

$$a_1x + b_1y + c_1z = d_1$$
$$a_2x + b_2y + c_2z = d_2$$
$$a_3x + b_3y + c_3z = d_3$$

To solve this system, define three matrices:

$$A = \begin{bmatrix} a_1 & b_1 & c_1 \\ a_2 & b_2 & c_2 \\ a_3 & b_3 & c_3 \end{bmatrix};\ D = \begin{bmatrix} d_1 \\ d_2 \\ d_3 \end{bmatrix};\ X = \begin{bmatrix} x \\ y \\ z \end{bmatrix}$$

The three equations in our system can be fully represented by a single matrix equation:

$$AX = D$$

We know that the identity matrix times X is equal to X, and we know that any matrix multiplied by its inverse is equal to the identity matrix.

$$A^{-1}AX = IX = X; \text{thus } X = A^{-1}D$$

Our goal then is to find the inverse of A, or A^{-1}. Once we have that, we can pre-multiply matrix D by A^{-1} (post-multiplying here is an undefined operation) to find matrix X.

Review Video: Comparison of Methods for Solving Systems
Visit mometrix.com/academy and enter code: 281590

Systems of equations can also be solved using the transformation of an augmented matrix in a process similar to that for finding a matrix inverse. Begin by arranging each equation of the system in the following format:

$$a_1x + b_1y + c_1z = d_1$$
$$a_2x + b_2y + c_2z = d_2$$
$$a_3x + b_3y + c_3z = d_3$$

Define matrices A and D and combine them into augmented matrix A_a:

$$A = \begin{bmatrix} a_1 & b_1 & c_1 \\ a_2 & b_2 & c_2 \\ a_3 & b_3 & c_3 \end{bmatrix}; D = \begin{bmatrix} d_1 \\ d_2 \\ d_3 \end{bmatrix}; A_a = \begin{bmatrix} a_1 & b_1 & c_1 & d_1 \\ a_2 & b_2 & c_2 & d_2 \\ a_3 & b_3 & c_3 & d_3 \end{bmatrix}$$

To solve the augmented matrix and the system of equations, use elementary row operations to form an identity matrix in the first 3×3 section. When this is complete, the values in the last column are the solutions to the system of equations:

$$\begin{bmatrix} 1 & 0 & 0 & x \\ 0 & 1 & 0 & y \\ 0 & 0 & 1 & z \end{bmatrix}$$

If an identity matrix is not possible, the system of equations has no unique solution. Sometimes only a partial solution will be possible. The following are partial solutions you may find:

$\begin{bmatrix} 1 & 0 & k_1 & x_0 \\ 0 & 1 & k_2 & y_0 \\ 0 & 0 & 0 & 0 \end{bmatrix}$ gives the non-unique solution $x = x_0 - k_1z;\ y = y_0 - k_2z$

$\begin{bmatrix} 1 & j_1 & k_1 & x_0 \\ 0 & 0 & 0 & 0 \\ 0 & 0 & 0 & 0 \end{bmatrix}$ gives the non-unique solution $x = x_0 - j_1y - k_1z$

This process can be used to solve systems of equations with any number of variables, but three is the upper limit for practical purposes. Anything more ought to be done with a graphing calculator.

Reduced Row-Echelon Forms

When a system of equations has a solution, finding the transformation of the augmented matrix will result in one of three reduced row-echelon forms. Only one of these forms will give a unique solution to the system of equations, however. The following examples show the solutions indicated by particular results:

$\begin{bmatrix} 1 & 0 & 0 & x_0 \\ 0 & 1 & 0 & y_0 \\ 0 & 0 & 1 & z_0 \end{bmatrix}$ gives the unique solution $x = x_0;\ y = y_0;\ z = z_0$

$\begin{bmatrix} 1 & 0 & k_1 & x_0 \\ 0 & 1 & k_2 & y_0 \\ 0 & 0 & 0 & 0 \end{bmatrix}$ gives a non-unique solution $x = x_0 - k_1z;\ y = y_0 - k_2z$

$\begin{bmatrix} 1 & j_1 & k_1 & x_0 \\ 0 & 0 & 0 & 0 \\ 0 & 0 & 0 & 0 \end{bmatrix}$ gives a non-unique solution $x = x_0 - j_1y - k_1z$

Geometric Transformations

The four *geometric transformations* are **translations**, **reflections**, **rotations**, and **dilations**. When geometric transformations are expressed as matrices, the process of performing the transformations is simplified. For calculations of the geometric transformations of a planar figure, make a $2 \times n$ matrix, where n is the number of vertices in the planar figure. Each column represents the rectangular coordinates of one vertex of the figure, with the top row containing the values of the x-coordinates and the bottom row containing the values of the y-coordinates. For example, given a planar triangular figure with coordinates (x_1, y_1), (x_2, y_2), and (x_3, y_3), the corresponding matrix is $\begin{bmatrix} x_1 & x_2 & x_3 \\ y_1 & y_2 & y_3 \end{bmatrix}$. You can then perform the necessary transformations on this matrix to determine the coordinates of the resulting figure.

Translation

A **translation** moves a figure along the x-axis, the y-axis, or both axes without changing the size or shape of the figure. To calculate the new coordinates of a planar figure following a translation, set up a matrix of the coordinates and a matrix of the translation values and add the two matrices.

$$\begin{bmatrix} h & h & h \\ v & v & v \end{bmatrix} + \begin{bmatrix} x_1 & x_2 & x_3 \\ y_1 & y_2 & y_3 \end{bmatrix} = \begin{bmatrix} h + x_1 & h + x_2 & h + x_3 \\ v + y_1 & v + y_2 & v + y_3 \end{bmatrix}$$

where h is the number of units the figure is moved along the x-axis (horizontally) and v is the number of units the figure is moved along the y-axis (vertically).

Reflection

To find the **reflection** of a planar figure over the x-axis, set up a matrix of the coordinates of the vertices and pre-multiply the matrix by the 2×2 matrix $\begin{bmatrix} 1 & 0 \\ 0 & -1 \end{bmatrix}$ so that $\begin{bmatrix} 1 & 0 \\ 0 & -1 \end{bmatrix} \begin{bmatrix} x_1 & x_2 & x_3 \\ y_1 & y_2 & y_3 \end{bmatrix} = \begin{bmatrix} x_1 & x_2 & x_3 \\ -y_1 & -y_2 & -y_3 \end{bmatrix}$. To find the reflection of a planar figure over the y-axis, set up a matrix of the coordinates of the vertices and pre-multiply the matrix by the 2×2 matrix $\begin{bmatrix} -1 & 0 \\ 0 & 1 \end{bmatrix}$ so that $\begin{bmatrix} -1 & 0 \\ 0 & 1 \end{bmatrix} \begin{bmatrix} x_1 & x_2 & x_3 \\ y_1 & y_2 & y_3 \end{bmatrix} = \begin{bmatrix} -x_1 & -x_2 & -x_3 \\ y_1 & y_2 & y_3 \end{bmatrix}$. To find the reflection of a planar figure over the line $y = x$, set up a matrix of the coordinates of the vertices and pre-multiply the matrix by the 2×2 matrix $\begin{bmatrix} 0 & 1 \\ 1 & 0 \end{bmatrix}$ so that $\begin{bmatrix} 0 & 1 \\ 1 & 0 \end{bmatrix} \begin{bmatrix} x_1 & x_2 & x_3 \\ y_1 & y_2 & y_3 \end{bmatrix} = \begin{bmatrix} y_1 & y_2 & y_3 \\ x_1 & x_2 & x_3 \end{bmatrix}$. Remember that the order of multiplication is important when multiplying matrices. The commutative property does not apply.

Rotation

To find the coordinates of the figure formed by rotating a planar figure about the origin θ degrees in a counterclockwise direction, set up a matrix of the coordinates of the vertices and pre-multiply the matrix by the 2×2 matrix $\begin{bmatrix} \cos\theta & \sin\theta \\ -\sin\theta & \cos\theta \end{bmatrix}$. For example, if you want to rotate a figure 90° clockwise around the origin, you would have to convert the degree measure to 270° counterclockwise and solve the 2×2 matrix you have set as the pre-multiplier: $\begin{bmatrix} \cos 270° & \sin 270° \\ -\sin 270° & \cos 270° \end{bmatrix} = \begin{bmatrix} 0 & -1 \\ 1 & 0 \end{bmatrix}$. Use this as the pre-multiplier for the matrix $\begin{bmatrix} x_1 & x_2 & x_3 \\ y_1 & y_2 & y_3 \end{bmatrix}$ and solve to find the new coordinates.

Dilation

To find the **dilation** of a planar figure by a scale factor of k, set up a matrix of the coordinates of the vertices of the planar figure and pre-multiply the matrix by the 2×2 matrix $\begin{bmatrix} k & 0 \\ 0 & k \end{bmatrix}$ so that $\begin{bmatrix} k & 0 \\ 0 & k \end{bmatrix}\begin{bmatrix} x_1 & x_2 & x_3 \\ y_1 & y_2 & y_3 \end{bmatrix} = \begin{bmatrix} kx_1 & kx_2 & kx_3 \\ ky_1 & ky_2 & ky_3 \end{bmatrix}$. This is effectively the same as multiplying the matrix by the scalar k, but the matrix equation would still be necessary if the figure were being dilated by different factors in vertical and horizontal directions. The scale factor k will be greater than 1 if the figure is being enlarged, and between 0 and 1 if the figure is being shrunk. Again, remember that when multiplying matrices, the order of the matrices is important. The commutative property does not apply, and the matrix with the coordinates of the figure must be the second matrix.

Practice

P1. A sporting-goods store sells baseballs, volleyballs, and basketballs.

Baseballs	\$3 each
Volleyballs	\$8 each
Basketballs	\$15 each

Here are the same store's sales numbers for one weekend:

	Baseballs	Volleyballs	Basketballs
Friday	5	4	4
Saturday	7	3	10
Sunday	4	3	6

Find the total sales for each day by multiplying matrices.

P2. Given the following matrices, perform the operations if possible:

$$A = \begin{bmatrix} 3 & 5 \\ -4 & -2 \end{bmatrix}, \quad B = \begin{bmatrix} -4 & -9 \\ 1 & 1 \\ 8 & -2 \end{bmatrix}, \quad C = \begin{bmatrix} -3 & 6 & -9 \\ 1 & 2 & 5 \end{bmatrix}, \quad D = \begin{bmatrix} -1 \\ -5 \\ -2 \end{bmatrix}$$

(a) $\det A$

(b) AB

(c) AC

(d) $\det(CD)$

(e) BA

(f) $BACD$

P3. Solve the following system of equations using an augmented matrix and elementary row operations:

$$4x + 6y + 5z = 1$$

$$-2x - 5y = z$$

$$x + -3y + 5z = 1$$

PRACTICE SOLUTIONS

P1. The first table can be represented by the following column-vector: $\begin{bmatrix} 3 \\ 8 \\ 15 \end{bmatrix}$

And the second table can be represented by this matrix: $\begin{bmatrix} 5 & 4 & 4 \\ 7 & 3 & 10 \\ 4 & 3 & 6 \end{bmatrix}$

Multiplying the second matrix by the first will result in a column vector showing the total sales for each day:

$$\begin{bmatrix} 5 & 4 & 4 \\ 7 & 3 & 10 \\ 4 & 3 & 6 \end{bmatrix} \times \begin{bmatrix} 3 \\ 8 \\ 15 \end{bmatrix} = \begin{bmatrix} 3 \times 5 + 8 \times 4 + 15 \times 4 \\ 3 \times 7 + 8 \times 3 + 15 \times 10 \\ 3 \times 4 + 8 \times 3 + 15 \times 6 \end{bmatrix} = \begin{bmatrix} 15 + 32 + 60 \\ 21 + 24 + 150 \\ 12 + 24 + 90 \end{bmatrix} = \begin{bmatrix} 107 \\ 195 \\ 126 \end{bmatrix}$$

From this, we can see that Friday's sales were \$107, Saturday's sales were \$195, and Sunday's sales were \$126.

P2. (a) $\det\left(\begin{bmatrix} 3 & 5 \\ -4 & -2 \end{bmatrix}\right) = 3(-2) - 5(-4) = -6 + 20 = 14$

(b) $AB = \begin{bmatrix} 3 & 5 \\ -4 & -2 \end{bmatrix} \times \begin{bmatrix} -4 & -9 \\ 1 & 1 \\ 8 & -2 \end{bmatrix} = undefined$, since columns in $A \neq$ rows in B

(c) $$AC = \begin{bmatrix} 3 & 5 \\ -4 & -2 \end{bmatrix} \times \begin{bmatrix} -3 & 6 & -9 \\ 1 & 2 & 5 \end{bmatrix} = \begin{bmatrix} 3(-3) + 5(1) & 3(6) + 5(2) & 3(-9) + 5(5) \\ -4(-3) + -2(1) & -4(6) + -2(2) & -4(-9) + -2(5) \end{bmatrix}$$

$$= \begin{bmatrix} -4 & 28 & -2 \\ 10 & -28 & 26 \end{bmatrix}$$

(d) $$CD = \begin{bmatrix} -3 & 6 & -9 \\ 1 & 2 & 5 \end{bmatrix} \times \begin{bmatrix} -1 \\ -5 \\ -2 \end{bmatrix} = \begin{bmatrix} -3(-1) + 6(-5) + -9(-2) \\ 1(-1) + 2(-5) + 5(-2) \end{bmatrix} = \begin{bmatrix} -9 \\ -21 \end{bmatrix}$$

The determinant is not defined for a non-square matrix. $\det(CD) = undefined$

(e) $$BA = \begin{bmatrix} -4 & -9 \\ 1 & 1 \\ 8 & -2 \end{bmatrix} \times \begin{bmatrix} 3 & 5 \\ -4 & -2 \end{bmatrix} = \begin{bmatrix} -4(3) + -9(-4) & -4(5) + -9(-2) \\ 1(3) + 1(-4) & 1(5) + 1(-2) \\ 8(3) + -2(-4) & 8(5) + -2(-2) \end{bmatrix} = \begin{bmatrix} 24 & -2 \\ -1 & 3 \\ 32 & 44 \end{bmatrix}$$

(f) $$BACD = BA \times CD = \begin{bmatrix} 24 & -2 \\ -1 & 3 \\ 32 & 44 \end{bmatrix} \times \begin{bmatrix} -9 \\ -21 \end{bmatrix} = \begin{bmatrix} 24(-9) + -2(-21) \\ -1(-9) + 3(-21) \\ 32(-9) + 44(-21) \end{bmatrix} = \begin{bmatrix} -174 \\ -54 \\ -1212 \end{bmatrix}$$

Recall that for matrix multiplication the order of terms matters, but not the grouping. That means $BACD = BA \times CD = B\big(A(CD)\big) = (BAC)D$ or any grouping that maintains the order will give the same result.

P3. Begin by setting up the augmented matrix: $\begin{bmatrix} 4 & 6 & 5 & 1 \\ -2 & -5 & -1 & 0 \\ 1 & -3 & 5 & 1 \end{bmatrix}$

Using elementary row operations, there are many ways to arrive at the answer. Here is one way (note that the row operations refer to the values in the row from the previous matrix):

$$\begin{matrix} 2R_2 \to R_2 \\ -4R_3 \to R_3 \end{matrix} = \begin{bmatrix} 4 & 6 & 5 & 1 \\ -4 & -10 & -2 & 0 \\ -4 & 12 & -20 & -4 \end{bmatrix}, \quad \begin{matrix} R_2 + R_1 \to R_2 \\ R_3 + R_1 \to R_3 \end{matrix} = \begin{bmatrix} 4 & 6 & 5 & 1 \\ 0 & -4 & 3 & 1 \\ 0 & 18 & -15 & -3 \end{bmatrix}$$

$$4.5R_2 + R_3 \to R_3 = \begin{bmatrix} 4 & 6 & 5 & 1 \\ 0 & -4 & 3 & 1 \\ 0 & 0 & -1.5 & 1.5 \end{bmatrix}, \quad \begin{matrix} 2R_3 + R_2 \to R_2 \\ R_3/(-1.5) \to R_3 \end{matrix} = \begin{bmatrix} 4 & 6 & 5 & 1 \\ 0 & -4 & 0 & 4 \\ 0 & 0 & 1 & -1 \end{bmatrix}$$

$$\begin{matrix} 1.5R_2 + 5R_3 + R_1 \to R_1 \\ R_2/(-4) \to R_2 \end{matrix} = \begin{bmatrix} 4 & 0 & 0 & 12 \\ 0 & 1 & 0 & -1 \\ 0 & 0 & 1 & -1 \end{bmatrix}, \quad R_1/(4) \to R_1 = \begin{bmatrix} 1 & 0 & 0 & 3 \\ 0 & 1 & 0 & -1 \\ 0 & 0 & 1 & -1 \end{bmatrix}$$

This reduced row echelon form indicates that the values that satisfy the original system of equations are $x = 3, y = -1$, and $z = -1$.

Trigonometry

Degrees, Radians, and the Unit Circle

It is important to understand the deep connection between trigonometry and circles. Specifically, the two main units, **degrees** (°) and **radians** (rad), that are used to measure angles are related this way: 360° in one full circle and 2π radians in one full circle: ($360° = 2\pi$ rad). The conversion factor relating the two is often stated as $\frac{180°}{\pi}$. For example, to convert $\frac{3\pi}{2}$ radians to degrees, multiply by the conversion factor: $\frac{3\pi}{2} \times \frac{180°}{\pi} = 270°$. As another example, to convert 60° to radians, divide by the conversion factor or multiply by the reciprocal: $60° \times \frac{\pi}{180°} = \frac{\pi}{3}$ radians.

Recall that the standard equation for a circle is $(x - h)^2 + (y - k)^2 = r^2$. A **unit circle** is a circle with a radius of 1 ($r = 1$) that has its center at the origin ($h = 0, k = 0$). Thus, the equation for the unit circle simplifies from the standard equation down to $x^2 + y^2 = 1$.

Standard position is the position of an angle of measure θ whose vertex is at the origin, the initial side crosses the unit circle at the point $(1, 0)$, and the terminal side crosses the unit circle at some other point (a, b). In the standard position, $\sin\theta = b$, $\cos\theta = a$, and $\tan\theta = \frac{b}{a}$.

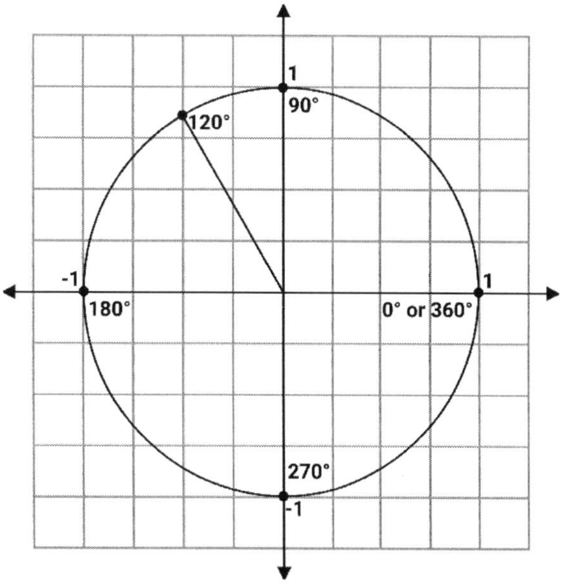

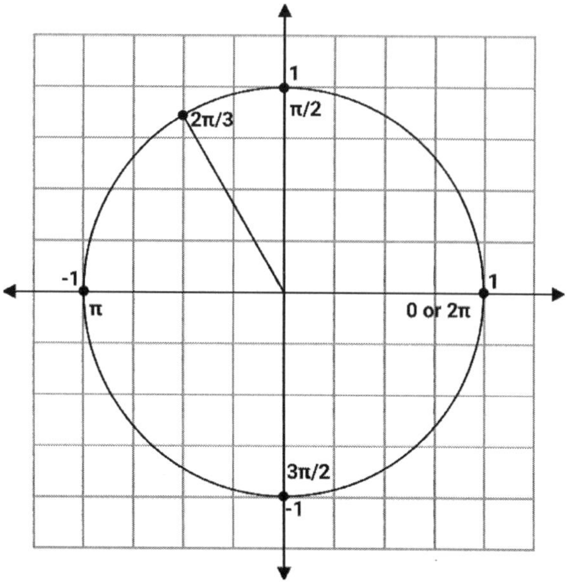

Review Video: Unit Circles and Standard Position
Visit mometrix.com/academy and enter code: 333922

Basic Trigonometric Functions

Sine

The **sine** (sin) function has a period of 360° or 2π radians. This means that its graph makes one complete cycle every 360° or 2π. Because $\sin 0 = 0$, the graph of $y = \sin x$ begins at the origin, with the x-axis representing the angle measure, and the y-axis representing the sine of the angle. The graph of the sine function is a smooth curve that begins at the origin, peaks at the point $\left(\frac{\pi}{2}, 1\right)$, crosses the x-axis at $(\pi, 0)$, has its lowest point at $\left(\frac{3\pi}{2}, -1\right)$, and returns to the x-axis to complete one cycle at $(2\pi, 0)$.

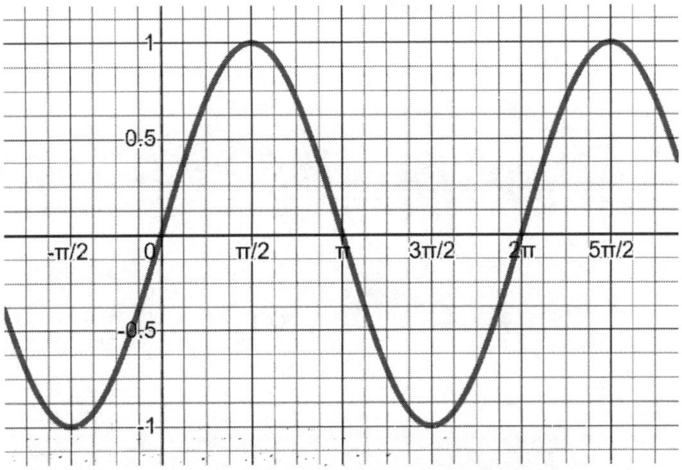

Review Video: Upper Level Trig: Sine
Visit mometrix.com/academy and enter code: 193339

Cosine

The **cosine** (cos) function also has a period of 360° or 2π radians, which means that its graph also makes one complete cycle every 360° or 2π. Because $\cos 0° = 1$, the graph of $y = \cos x$ begins at the point $(0, 1)$, with the x-axis representing the angle measure, and the y-axis representing the cosine of the angle. The graph of the cosine function is a smooth curve that begins at the point $(0,1)$, crosses the x-axis at the point $\left(\frac{\pi}{2}, 0\right)$, has its lowest point at $(\pi, -1)$, crosses the x-axis again at the point $\left(\frac{3\pi}{2}, 0\right)$, and returns to a peak at the point $(2\pi, 1)$ to complete one cycle.

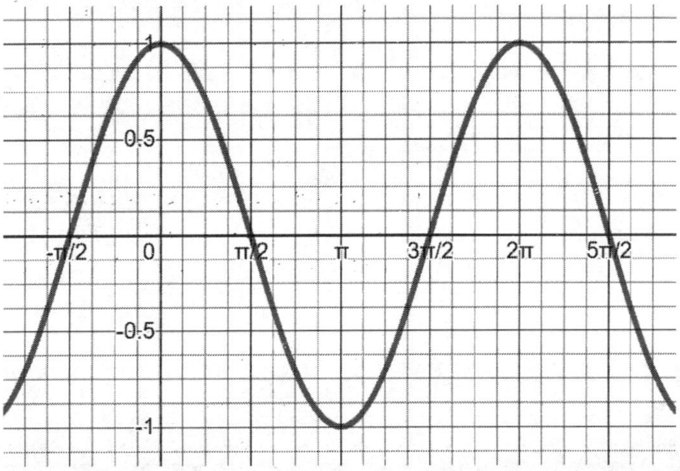

Review Video: Cosine
Visit mometrix.com/academy and enter code: 361120

Tangent

The **tangent** (tan) function has a period of 180° or π radians, which means that its graph makes one complete cycle every 180° or π radians. The x-axis represents the angle measure, and the y-axis represents the tangent of the angle. The graph of the tangent function is a series of smooth curves that cross the x-axis at every 180° or π radians and have an asymptote every $k \times 90°$ or $\frac{k\pi}{2}$ radians, where k is an odd integer. This can be explained by the fact that the tangent is calculated by dividing the sine by the cosine, since the cosine equals zero at those asymptote points.

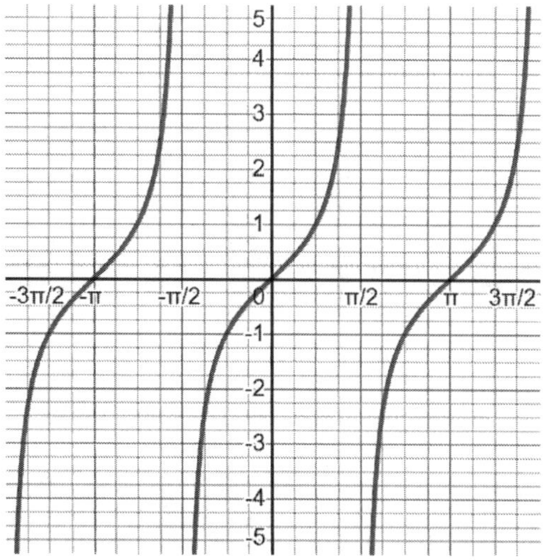

Review Video: Upper Level Trig: Tangent
Visit mometrix.com/academy and enter code: 947639

Defined and Reciprocal Functions

The tangent function is defined as the ratio of the sine to the cosine: $\tan x = \frac{\sin x}{\cos x}$

To take the reciprocal of a number means to place that number as the denominator of a fraction with a numerator of 1. The reciprocal functions are thus defined quite simply.

Cosecant	$\csc x$	$\frac{1}{\sin x}$
Secant	$\sec x$	$\frac{1}{\cos x}$
Cotangent	$\cot x$	$\frac{1}{\tan x}$

It is important to know these reciprocal functions, but they are not as commonly used as the three basic functions.

Review Video: Defined and Reciprocal Functions
Visit mometrix.com/academy and enter code: 996431

Inverse Functions

Each of the trigonometric functions accepts an angular measure, either degrees or radians, and gives a numerical value as the output. The inverse functions do the opposite; they accept a numerical value and give an angular measure as the output. The inverse of sine, or arcsine, commonly written as either $\sin^{-1} x$ or $\arcsin x$, gives the angle whose sine is x. Similarly:

The inverse of $\cos x$ is written as $\cos^{-1} x$ or $\arccos x$ and means the angle whose cosine is x.
The inverse of $\tan x$ is written as $\tan^{-1} x$ or $\arctan x$ and means the angle whose tangent is x.
The inverse of $\csc x$ is written as $\csc^{-1} x$ or $\text{arccsc}\, x$ and means the angle whose cosecant is x.
The inverse of $\sec x$ is written as $\sec^{-1} x$ or $\text{arcsec}\, x$ and means the angle whose secant is x.
The inverse of $\cot x$ is written as $\cot^{-1} x$ or $\text{arccot}\, x$ and means the angle whose cotangent is x.

Review Video: Inverse of a Cosine
Visit mometrix.com/academy and enter code: 156054

Review Video: Inverse of a Tangent
Visit mometrix.com/academy and enter code: 229055

Important Note About Solving Trigonometric Equations

Trigonometric and algebraic equations are solved following the same rules, but while algebraic expressions have one unique solution, trigonometric equations could have multiple solutions, and you must find them all. When solving for an angle with a known trigonometric value, you must consider the sign and include all angles with that value. Your calculator will probably only give one value as an answer, typically in the following ranges:

- For $\sin^{-1} x$, $\left[-\frac{\pi}{2}, \frac{\pi}{2}\right]$ or [–90°, 90°]
- For $\cos^{-1} x$, [0, π] or [0°, 180°]
- For $\tan^{-1} x$, $\left[-\frac{\pi}{2}, \frac{\pi}{2}\right]$ or [–90°, 90°]

It is important to determine if there is another angle in a different quadrant that also satisfies the problem. To do this, find the other quadrant(s) with the same sign for that trigonometric function and find the angle that has the same reference angle. Then check whether this angle is also a solution.

- In the first quadrant, all six trigonometric functions are positive.
- In the second quadrant, sin and csc are positive.
- In the third quadrant, tan and cot are positive.
- In the fourth quadrant, cos and sec are positive.

If you remember the phrase, "ALL Students Take Classes," you will be able to remember the sign of each trigonometric function in each quadrant. ALL represents all the signs in the first quadrant. The "S" in "Students" represents the sine function and its reciprocal in the second quadrant. The "T" in "Take" represents the tangent function and its reciprocal in the third quadrant. The "C" in "Classes" represents the cosine function and its reciprocal.

Domain, Range, and Asymptotes in Trigonometry

The domain is the set of all possible real number values of x on the graph of a trigonometric function. Some graphs will impose limits on the values of x.

The range is the set of all possible real number values of y on the graph of a trigonometric function. Some graphs will impose limits on the values of y.

Asymptotes are lines that the graph of a trigonometric function approaches but never reaches. Asymptotes exist for values of x in the graphs of the tangent, cotangent, secant, and cosecant. The sine and cosine graphs do not have any asymptotes.

Domain, Range, and Asymptotes of the Six Trigonometric Functions

The domain, range, and asymptotes for each of the trigonometric functions are as follows:

- In the **sine** function, the domain is all real numbers, the range is $-1 \leq y \leq 1$, and there are no asymptotes.
- In the **cosine** function, the domain is all real numbers, the range is $-1 \leq y \leq 1$, and there are no asymptotes.
- In the **tangent** function, the domain is $x \in$ all real numbers; $x \neq \frac{\pi}{2} + k\pi$, the range is all real numbers, and the asymptotes are the lines $x = \frac{\pi}{2} + k\pi$.
- In the **cosecant** function, the domain is $x \in$ all real numbers; $x \neq k\pi$, the range is $(-\infty, -1]$ and $[1, \infty)$, and the asymptotes are the lines $x = k\pi$.
- In the **secant** function, the domain is $x \in$ all real numbers; $x \neq \frac{\pi}{2} + k\pi$, the range is $(-\infty, 1]$ and $[1, \infty)$, and the asymptotes are the lines $x = \frac{\pi}{2} + k\pi$.
- In the **cotangent** function, the domain is $x \in$ all real numbers; $x \neq k\pi$, the range is all real numbers, and the asymptotes are the lines $x = k\pi$.

In each of the above cases, k represents any integer.

Trigonometric Identities

Sum and Difference

To find the sine, cosine, or tangent of the sum or difference of two angles, use one of the following formulas where α and β are two angles with known sine, cosine, or tangent values as needed:

$$\sin(\alpha \pm \beta) = \sin\alpha\cos\beta \pm \cos\alpha\sin\beta$$
$$\cos(\alpha \pm \beta) = \cos\alpha\cos\beta \mp \sin\alpha\sin\beta$$
$$\tan(\alpha \pm \beta) = \frac{\tan\alpha \pm \tan\beta}{1 \mp \tan\alpha\tan\beta}$$

Half Angle

To find the sine or cosine of half of a known angle, use the following formulas where θ is an angle with a known exact cosine value:

$$\sin(\theta/2) = \pm\sqrt{(1 - cos\theta)/2}$$
$$\cos(\theta/2) = \pm\sqrt{(1 + \cos\theta)/2}$$

To determine the sign of the answer, you must recognize which quadrant the given angle is in and apply the correct sign for the trigonometric function you are using. If you need to find an expression for the exact sine or cosine of an angle that you do not know, such as sine 22.5°, you can rewrite the given angle as a half angle, such as $\sin\left(\frac{45°}{2}\right)$, and use the formula above:

$$\sin\left(\frac{45°}{2}\right) = \pm\sqrt{(1 - \cos(45°))/2} = \pm\sqrt{\left(1 - \frac{\sqrt{2}}{2}\right)/2} = \pm\sqrt{(2 - \sqrt{2})/4} = \pm\frac{1}{2}\sqrt{(2 - \sqrt{2})}$$

To find the tangent or cotangent of half of a known angle, use the following formulas where θ is an angle with known exact sine and cosine values:

$$\tan\frac{\theta}{2} = \frac{sin\theta}{1+\cos\theta}$$
$$\cot\frac{\theta}{2} = \frac{\sin\theta}{1-\cos\theta}$$

These formulas will work for finding the tangent or cotangent of half of any angle unless the cosine of θ happens to make the denominator of the identity equal to 0.

The Pythagorean theorem states that $a^2 + b^2 = c^2$ for all right triangles. The trigonometric identity that derives from this principle is stated in this way: $\sin^2\theta + \cos^2\theta = 1$

Dividing each term by either $\sin^2\theta$ or $\cos^2\theta$ yields two other identities, respectively:

$$1 + \cot^2\theta = \csc^2\theta$$
$$\tan^2\theta + 1 = \sec^2\theta$$

Double Angles

In each case, use one of the double angle formulas. To find the sine or cosine of twice a known angle, use one of the following formulas:

$$\sin(2\theta) = 2\sin\theta\cos\theta$$

$$\begin{aligned}\cos(2\theta) &= \cos^2\theta - \sin^2\theta \\ &= 2\cos^2\theta - 1 \\ &= 1 - 2\sin^2\theta\end{aligned}$$

To find the tangent or cotangent of twice a known angle, use the formulas where θ is an angle with known exact sine, cosine, tangent, and cotangent values:

$$\tan(2\theta) = \frac{2\tan\theta}{1-\tan^2\theta}$$
$$\cot(2\theta) = \frac{\cot\theta - \tan\theta}{2}$$

Products

To find the product of the sines and cosines of two different angles, use one of the following formulas where α and β are two unique angles:

$$\sin\alpha\sin\beta = \frac{1}{2}[\cos(\alpha-\beta) - \cos(\alpha+\beta)]$$
$$\cos\alpha\cos\beta = \frac{1}{2}[\cos(\alpha+\beta) + \cos(\alpha-\beta)]$$
$$\sin\alpha\cos\beta = \frac{1}{2}[\sin(\alpha+\beta) + \sin(\alpha-\beta)]$$
$$\cos\alpha\sin\beta = \frac{1}{2}[\sin(\alpha+\beta) - \sin(\alpha-\beta)]$$

COMPLEMENTARY

The trigonometric cofunction identities use the trigonometric relationships of complementary angles (angles whose sum is 90°). These are:

$$\cos x = \sin(90° - x)$$
$$\csc x = \sec(90° - x)$$
$$\cot x = \tan(90° - x)$$

Review Video: Complementary Angles
Visit mometrix.com/academy and enter code: 919405

TABLE OF COMMONLY ENCOUNTERED ANGLES

$0° = 0$ radians, $30° = \frac{\pi}{6}$ radians, $45° = \frac{\pi}{4}$ radians, $60° = \frac{\pi}{3}$ radians, and $90° = \frac{\pi}{2}$ radians

$\sin 0° = 0$	$\cos 0° = 1$	$\tan 0° = 0$
$\sin 30° = \frac{1}{2}$	$\cos 30° = \frac{\sqrt{3}}{2}$	$\tan 30° = \frac{\sqrt{3}}{3}$
$\sin 45° = \frac{\sqrt{2}}{2}$	$\cos 45° = \frac{\sqrt{2}}{2}$	$\tan 45° = 1$
$\sin 60° = \frac{\sqrt{3}}{2}$	$\cos 60° = \frac{1}{2}$	$\tan 60° = \sqrt{3}$
$\sin 90° = 1$	$\cos 90° = 0$	$\tan 90° =$ undefined
$\csc 0° =$ undefined	$\sec 0° = 1$	$\cot 0° =$ undefined
$\csc 30° = 2$	$\sec 30° = \frac{2\sqrt{3}}{3}$	$\cot 30° = \sqrt{3}$
$\csc 45° = \sqrt{2}$	$\sec 45° = \sqrt{2}$	$\cot 45° = 1$
$\csc 60° = \frac{2\sqrt{3}}{3}$	$\sec 60° = 2$	$\cot 60° = \frac{\sqrt{3}}{3}$
$\csc 90° = 1$	$\sec 90° =$ undefined	$\cot 90° = 0$

The values in the upper half of this table are values you should have memorized or be able to find quickly and those in the lower half can easily be determined as the reciprocal of the corresponding function.

Review Video: Commonly Encountered Angles
Visit mometrix.com/academy and enter code: 204098

RECTANGULAR AND POLAR COORDINATES

Rectangular coordinates are those that lie on the square grids of the Cartesian plane. They should be quite familiar to you. The polar coordinate system is based on a circular graph, rather than the square grid of the Cartesian system. Points in the polar coordinate system are in the format (r, θ), where r is the distance from the origin (think radius of the circle) and θ is the smallest positive angle (moving counterclockwise around the circle) made with the positive horizontal axis.

To convert a point from rectangular (x, y) format to polar (r, θ) format, use the formula (x, y) to $(r, \theta) \Rightarrow r = \sqrt{x^2 + y^2}; \theta = \arctan\frac{y}{x}$ when $x \neq 0$

Review Video: Converting Between Polar and Rectangular Formats
Visit mometrix.com/academy and enter code: 281325

If x is positive, use the positive square root value for r. If x is negative, use the negative square root value for r. If $x = 0$, use the following rules:

- If $y = 0$, then $\theta = 0$
- If $y > 0$, then $\theta = \frac{\pi}{2}$
- If $y < 0$, then $\theta = \frac{3\pi}{2}$

To convert a point from polar (r, θ) format to rectangular (x, y) format, use the formula (r, θ) to $(x, y) \Rightarrow x = r\cos\theta\,; y = r\sin\theta$

De Moivre's Theorem

De Moivre's theorem is used to find the powers of complex numbers (numbers that contain the imaginary number i) written in polar form. Given a trigonometric expression that contains i, such as $z = r\cos x + ir\sin x$, where r is a real number and x is an angle measurement in polar form, use the formula $z^n = r^n(\cos nx + i\sin nx)$, where r and n are real numbers, x is the angle measure in polar form, and i is the imaginary number $i = \sqrt{-1}$. The expression $\cos x + i\sin x$ can be written cis x, making the formula appear in the format $z^n = r^n$ cis nx.

Note that De Moivre's theorem is only for angles in polar form. If you are given an angle in degrees, you must convert to polar form before using the formula.

Practice

P1. Convert the following angles from degrees to radians:

(a) 56°

(b) 12°

(c) 199°

P2. Convert the following angles from radians to degrees:

(a) 3

(b) 3π

(c) 33

P3. Simplify the following trigonometric expressions:

(a) $\frac{\sin x \tan x + \cos x}{\sec x}$

(b) $\frac{4\cos 2x}{\sin^2 2x} + \sec^2 x$

Practice Solutions

P1. Multiply each by the conversion factor $\frac{\pi}{180°}$:

(a) $56° \times \frac{\pi}{180°} \cong 0.977$

(b) $12° \times \frac{\pi}{180°} \cong 0.209$

(c) $199° \times \frac{\pi}{180°} \cong 3.473$

P2. Multiply each by the conversion factor $\frac{180°}{\pi}$:

(a) $3 \times \frac{180°}{\pi} \cong 171.9°$

(b) $3\pi \times \frac{180°}{\pi} = 540° = 180°$

(c) $33 \times \frac{180°}{\pi} \cong 1890.8° \cong 90.8°$

P3. (a) Utilize trigonometric identities and definitions to simplify. Specifically, $\tan x = \frac{\sin x}{\cos x}$, $\sec x = \frac{1}{\cos x}$, and $\sin^2 x + \cos^2 x = 1$:

$$\begin{aligned}\frac{\sin x \tan x + \cos x}{\sec x} &= \left(\sin x \frac{\sin x}{\cos x} + \cos x\right)\cos x \\ &= \frac{\sin^2 x}{\cos x}\cos x + \cos^2 x \\ &= \sin^2 x + \cos^2 x \\ &= 1\end{aligned}$$

(b) Utilize trigonometric identities and definitions to simplify. Specifically, double angle formulas, $\sin^2 x = (\sin x)^2$, and $\sin^2 x + \cos^2 x = 1$:

$$\begin{aligned}\frac{4\cos 2x}{\sin^2 2x} + \sec^2 x &= \frac{4(\cos^2 x - \sin^2 x)}{4\sin^2 x \cos^2 x} + \sec^2 x \\ &= \frac{\cos^2 x - \sin^2 x}{\sin^2 x \cos^2 x} + \sec^2 x \\ &= \frac{\cos^2 x}{\sin^2 x \cos^2 x} - \frac{\sin^2 x}{\sin^2 x \cos^2 x} + \sec^2 x \\ &= \frac{1}{\sin^2 x} - \frac{1}{\cos^2 x} + \sec^2 x \\ &= \csc^2 x - \sec^2 x + \sec^2 x \\ &= \csc^2 x\end{aligned}$$

Calculus

Calculus

Calculus, also called analysis, is the branch of mathematics that studies the length, area, and volume of objects, and the rate of change of quantities (which can be expressed as slopes of curves). The two principal branches of calculus are differential and integral. **Differential calculus** is based on derivatives and takes the form,

$$\frac{d}{dx}f(x)$$

Integral calculus is based on integrals and takes the form,

$$\int f(x)dx$$

Some of the basic ideas of calculus were utilized as far back in history as Archimedes. However, its modern forms were developed by Newton and Leibniz.

LIMITS

The **limit of a function** is represented by the notation $\lim_{x \to a} f(x)$. It is read as "the limit of *f* of *x* as *x* approaches *a*." In many cases, $\lim_{x \to a} f(x)$ will simply be equal to $f(a)$, but not always. Limits are important because some functions are not defined or are not easy to evaluate at certain values of *x*.

The limit at the point is said to exist only if the limit is the same when approached from the right side as from the left: $\lim_{x \to a^+} f(x) = \lim_{x \to a^-} f(x)$). Notice the symbol by the *a* in each case. When *x* approaches *a* from the right, it approaches from the positive end of the number line. When *x* approaches *a* from the left, it approaches from the negative end of the number line.

If the limit as *x* approaches *a* differs depending on the direction from which it approaches, then the limit does not exist at *a*. In other words, if $\lim_{x \to a^+} f(x)$ does not equal $\lim_{x \to a^-} f(x)$, then the limit does not exist at *a*. The limit also does not exist if either of the one-sided limits does not exist.

Situations in which the limit does not exist include a function that jumps from one value to another at *a*, one that oscillates between two different values as *x* approaches *a*, or one that increases or decreases without bounds as *x* approaches *a*. If the limit you calculate has a value of $\frac{c}{0}$, where *c* is any constant, this means the function goes to infinity and the limit does not exist.

It is possible for two functions that do not have limits to be multiplied to get a new function that does have a limit. Just because two functions do not have limits, do not assume that the product will not have a limit.

DIRECT SUBSTITUTION

The first thing to try when looking for a limit is direct substitution. To find the limit of a function $\lim_{x\to a} f(x)$ by direct substitution, substitute the value of a for x in the function and solve. The following patterns apply to finding the limit of a function by direct substitution:

$$\lim_{x\to a} b = b, \text{ where } b \text{ is any real number}$$
$$\lim_{x\to a} x = a$$
$$\lim_{x\to a} x^n = a^n, \text{ where } n \text{ is any positive integer}$$
$$\lim_{x\to a} \sqrt{x} = \sqrt{a}; a > 0$$
$$\lim_{x\to a} \sqrt[n]{x} = \sqrt[n]{a}, \text{ where } n \text{ is a positive integer and } a > 0 \text{ for all even values of } n$$
$$\lim_{x\to a} \frac{1}{x} = \frac{1}{a}; a \neq 0$$

You can also use substitution for finding the limit of a trigonometric function, a polynomial function, or a rational function. Be sure that in manipulating an expression to find a limit that you do not divide by terms equal to zero.

In finding the limit of a composite function, begin by finding the limit of the innermost function. For example, to find $\lim_{x\to a} f(g(x))$, first find the value of $\lim_{x\to a} g(x)$. Then substitute this value for x in $f(x)$ and solve. The result is the limit of the original problem.

LIMITS AND OPERATIONS

When finding the limit of the sum or difference of two functions, find the limit of each individual function and then add or subtract the results.
For example, $\lim_{x\to a}[f(x) \pm g(x)] = \lim_{x\to a} f(x) \pm \lim_{x\to a} g(x)$.

To find the limit of the product or quotient of two functions, find the limit of each individual function and then multiply or divide the results.
For example, $\lim_{x\to a}[f(x) \times g(x)] = \lim_{x\to a} f(x) \times \lim_{x\to a} g(x)$ and $\lim_{x\to a} \frac{f(x)}{g(x)} = \frac{\lim_{x\to a} f(x)}{\lim_{x\to a} g(x)}$, where $g(x) \neq 0$ and $\lim_{x\to a} g(x) \neq 0$. When finding the quotient of the limits of two functions, make sure the denominator is not equal to zero. If it is, use differentiation or L'Hôpital's rule to find the limit.

To find the limit of a power of a function or a root of a function, find the limit of the function and then raise the limit to the original power or take the root of the limit.
For example, $\lim_{x\to a}[f(x)]^n = \left[\lim_{x\to a} f(x)\right]^n$ and $\lim_{x\to a} \sqrt[n]{f(x)} = \sqrt[n]{\lim_{x\to a} f(x)}$, where n is a positive integer and $\lim_{x\to a} f(x) > 0$ for all even values of n.

To find the limit of a function multiplied by a scalar, find the limit of the function and multiply the result by the scalar. For example, $\lim_{x\to a} kf(x) = k \lim_{x\to a} f(x)$, where k is a real number.

L'HÔPITAL'S RULE

Sometimes solving $\lim_{x\to a} \frac{f(x)}{g(x)}$ by the direct substitution method will result in the numerator and denominator both being equal to zero, or both being equal to infinity. This outcome is called an indeterminate form. The limit cannot be directly found by substitution in these cases. L'Hôpital's rule is a useful method for finding the limit of a problem in the indeterminate form. L'Hôpital's rule allows you to find the limit using derivatives. Assuming both the numerator and denominator are differentiable, and that both are equal to zero when the direct substitution method is used, take the derivative of both the numerator and the denominator and then use the direct substitution method. For example, if $\lim_{x \to a} \frac{f(x)}{g(x)} = \frac{0}{0}$, take the derivatives of $f(x)$ and $g(x)$ and then find $\lim_{x \to a} \frac{f'(x)}{g'(x)}$. If $g'(x) \neq 0$, then you have found the limit of the original function. If $g'(x) = 0$ and $f'(x) = 0$, L'Hôpital's rule may be applied to the function $\frac{f'(x)}{g'(x)}$, and so on until either a limit is found, or it can be determined that the limit does not exist.

Squeeze Theorem

The squeeze theorem is known by many names, including the sandwich theorem, the sandwich rule, the squeeze lemma, the squeezing theorem, and the pinching theorem. No matter what you call it, the principle is the same. To prove the limit of a difficult function exists, find the limits of two functions, one on either side of the unknown, that are easy to compute. If the limits of these functions are equal, then that is also the limit of the unknown function. In mathematical terms, the theorem is:

If $g(x) \leq f(x) \leq h(x)$ for all values of x where $f(x)$ is the function with the unknown limit, and if $\lim_{x \to a} g(x) = \lim_{x \to a} h(x)$, then this limit is also equal to $\lim_{x \to a} f(x)$.

To find the limit of an expression containing an absolute value sign, take the absolute value of the limit. If $\lim_{n \to \infty} a_n = L$, where L is the numerical value for the limit, then $\lim_{n \to \infty} |a_n| = |L|$. Also, if $\lim_{n \to \infty} |a_n| = 0$, then $\lim_{n \to \infty} a_n = 0$. The trick comes when you are asked to find the limit as n approaches from the left. Whenever the limit is being approached from the left, it is being approached from the negative end of the domain. The absolute value sign makes everything in the equation positive, essentially eliminating the negative side of the domain. In this case, rewrite the equation without the absolute value signs and add a negative sign in front of the expression. For example, $\lim_{n \to 0^-} |x|$ becomes $\lim_{n \to 0^-} (-x)$.

Derivatives

The derivative of a function is a measure of how much that function is changing at a specific point, and is the slope of a line tangent to a curve at the specific point. The derivative of a function $f(x)$ is written $f'(x)$, and read, "f prime of x." Other notations for the derivative include $D_x f(x)$, y', $D_x y$, $\frac{dy}{dx}$, and $\frac{d}{dx} f(x)$. The definition of the derivative of a function is $f'(x) = \lim_{h \to 0} \frac{f(x+h) - f(x)}{h}$. However, this formula is rarely used.

There is a simpler method you can use to find the derivative of a polynomial. Given a function $f(x) = a_n x^n + a_{n-1} x^{n-1} + a_{n-2} x^{n-2} + \cdots + a_1 x + a_0$, multiply each exponent by its corresponding coefficient to get the new coefficient and reduce the value of the exponent by one. Coefficients with no variable are dropped. This gives $f'(x) = n a_n x^{n-1} + (n-1) a_{n-1} x^{n-2} + \cdots + a_1$, a pattern that can be repeated for each successive derivative.

Differentiable functions are functions that have a derivative. Some basic rules for finding derivatives of functions are:

$$f(x) = c \Rightarrow f'(x) = 0; \text{ where c is a constant}$$
$$f(x) = x \Rightarrow f'(x) = 1$$
$$f(x) = x^n \Rightarrow f'(x) = nx^{n-1}; \text{ where n is a real number}$$

$$\left(cf(x)\right)' = cf'(x); \text{ where c is a constant}$$
$$(f+g)'(x) = f'(x) + g'(x)$$
$$(fg)'(x) = f(x)g'(x) + f'(x)g(x)$$
$$\left(\frac{f}{g}\right)'(x) = \frac{f'(x)g(x) - f(x)g'(x)}{[g(x)]^2}$$
$$(f \circ g)'(x) = f'\left(g(x)\right) \times g'(x)$$

This last formula is also known as the **chain rule**. If you are finding the derivative of a polynomial that is raised to a power, let the polynomial be represented by $g(x)$ and use the chain rule. The chain rule is one of the most important concepts to grasp in the early stages of learning calculus. Many other rules and shortcuts are based upon the chain rule.

Review Video: Derivative Properties and Formulas
Visit mometrix.com/academy and enter code: 735227

Difference Quotient and Derivative

A secant is a line that connects two points on a curve. The **difference quotient** gives the slope of an arbitrary secant line that connects the point $\left(x, f(x)\right)$ with a nearby point $\left(x+h, f(x+h)\right)$ on the graph of the function f. The difference quotient is the same formula that is always used to determine a slope—the change in y divided by the change in x. It is written as $\frac{f(x+h)-f(x)}{h}$.

A tangent is a line that touches a curve at one point. The tangent and the curve have the same slope at the point where they touch. The derivative is the function that gives the slope of both the tangent and the curve of the function at that point. The derivative is written as the limit of the difference quotient, or:

$$\lim_{h \to 0} \frac{f(x+h) - f(x)}{h}$$

If the function is *f*, the derivative is denoted as $f'(x)$, and it is the slope of the function *f* at point $\left(x, f(x)\right)$. It is expressed as:

$$f'(x) = \lim_{h \to 0} \frac{f(x+h) - f(x)}{h}$$

Review Video: Definition of a Derivative
Visit mometrix.com/academy and enter code: 787269

Implicit Functions

An **implicit function** is one where it is impossible, or very difficult, to express one variable in terms of another by normal algebraic methods. This would include functions that have both variables raised to a power greater than 1, functions that have two variables multiplied by each other, or a combination of the two. To differentiate such a function with respect to *x*, take the derivative of each term that contains a variable, either x or y. When differentiating a term with y, use the chain rule, first taking the derivative with respect to y, and then multiplying by $\frac{dy}{dx}$. If a term contains both x and y, you will have to use the product rule as well as the chain rule. Once the derivative of each individual term has been found, use the rules of algebra to solve for $\frac{dy}{dx}$ to get the final answer.

Review Video: Upper Math: Implicit Differentiation
Visit mometrix.com/academy and enter code: 102151

Derivatives of Trigonometric Functions

Trigonometric functions are any functions that include one of the six trigonometric expressions. The following rules for derivatives apply for all trigonometric differentiation:

$$\frac{d}{dx}(\sin x) = \cos x, \quad \frac{d}{dx}(\cos x) = -\sin x, \quad \frac{d}{dx}(\tan x) = \sec^2 x$$

For functions that are a combination of trigonometric and algebraic expressions, use the chain rule:

$$\frac{d}{dx}(\sin u) = \cos u \frac{du}{dx} \qquad \frac{d}{dx}(\sec u) = \tan u \sec u \frac{du}{dx}$$
$$\frac{d}{dx}(\cos u) = -\sin u \frac{du}{dx} \qquad \frac{d}{dx}(\csc u) = -\csc u \cot u \frac{du}{dx}$$
$$\frac{d}{dx}(\tan u) = \sec^2 u \frac{du}{dx} \qquad \frac{d}{dx}(\cot u) = -\csc^2 u \frac{du}{dx}$$

Functions involving the inverses of the trigonometric functions can also be differentiated.

$$\frac{d}{dx}(\sin^{-1} u) = \frac{1}{\sqrt{1-u^2}}\frac{du}{dx} \qquad \frac{d}{dx}(\csc^{-1} u) = \frac{-1}{|u|\sqrt{u^2-1}}\frac{du}{dx}$$
$$\frac{d}{dx}(\cos^{-1} u) = \frac{-1}{\sqrt{1-u^2}}\frac{du}{dx} \qquad \frac{d}{dx}(\sec^{-1} u) = \frac{1}{|u|\sqrt{u^2-1}}\frac{du}{dx}$$
$$\frac{d}{dx}(\tan^{-1} u) = \frac{1}{1+u^2}\frac{du}{dx} \qquad \frac{d}{dx}(\cot^{-1} u) = \frac{-1}{1+u^2}\frac{du}{dx}$$

In each of the above expressions, u represents a differentiable function. Also, the value of u must be such that the radicand, if applicable, is a positive number. Remember the expression $\frac{du}{dx}$ means to take the derivative of the function u with respect to the variable x.

Review Video: Derivatives of Trigonometry Functions
Visit mometrix.com/academy and enter code: 132724

Derivatives of Exponential and Logarithmic Functions

Exponential functions are in the form e^x, which has itself as its derivative: $\frac{d}{dx}e^x = e^x$. For functions that have a function as the exponent rather than just an x, use the formula $\frac{d}{dx}e^u = e^u\frac{du}{dx}$. The inverse of the exponential function is the natural logarithm. To find the derivative of the natural logarithm, use the formula $\frac{d}{dx}\ln u = \frac{1}{u}\frac{du}{dx}$.

If you are trying to solve an expression with a variable in the exponent, use the formula $a^x = e^{x \ln a}$, where a is a positive real number and x is any real number. To find the derivative of a function in this format, use the formula $\frac{d}{dx}a^x = a^x \ln a$. If the exponent is a function rather than a single variable x, use the formula $\frac{d}{dx}a^u = a^u \ln a \frac{du}{dx}$. If you are trying to solve an expression involving a logarithm, use the formula $\frac{d}{dx}(\log_a x) = \frac{1}{x \ln a}$ or $\frac{d}{dx}(\log_a |u|) = \frac{1}{u \ln a}\frac{du}{dx}; u \neq 0$.

Continuity

A function can be either continuous or discontinuous. A conceptual way to describe continuity is this: A function is continuous if its graph can be traced with a pen without lifting the pen from the page. In other words, there are no breaks or gaps in the graph of the function. However, this is only a description, not a technical definition. A function is continuous at the point $x = a$ if the three following conditions are met:

1. $f(a)$ is defined
2. $\lim_{x \to a} f(x)$ exists
3. $\lim_{x \to a} f(x) = f(a)$

If any of these conditions are not met, the function is discontinuous at the point $x = a$.

A function can be continuous at a point, continuous over an interval, or continuous everywhere. The above rules define continuity at a point. A function that is continuous over an interval $[a, b]$ is continuous at the points a and b and at every point between them. A function that is continuous everywhere is continuous for every real number, that is, for all points in its domain.

Discontinuity

Discontinuous functions are categorized according to the type or cause of discontinuity. Three examples are point, infinite, and jump discontinuity. A function with a point discontinuity has one value of x for which it is not continuous. A function with infinite discontinuity has a vertical asymptote at $x = a$ and $f(a)$ is undefined. It is said to have an infinite discontinuity at $x = a$. A function with jump discontinuity has one-sided limits from the left and from the right, but they are not equal to one another, that is, $\lim_{x \to a^-} f(x) \neq \lim_{x \to a^+} f(x)$. It is said to have a jump discontinuity at $x = a$.

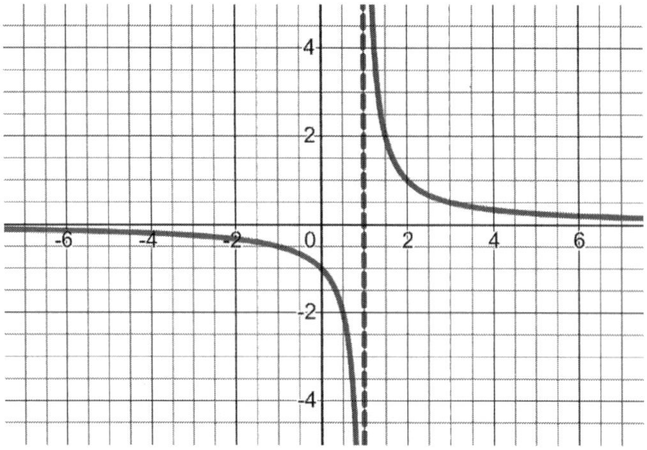

The function, $f(x) = \frac{1}{x-1}$, plotted in the graph has an infinite discontinuity. It has a vertical asymptote at $x = 1$, as such, the function is undefined at $x = 1$.

Differentiability

A function is said to be differentiable at point $x = a$ if it has a derivative at that point, that is, if $f'(a)$ exists. For a function to be differentiable, it must be continuous because the slope cannot be defined at a point of discontinuity. Furthermore, for a function to be differentiable, its graph must not have any sharp turn for which it is impossible to draw a tangent line. The sine function is an example of a differentiable function. It is continuous, and a tangent line can be drawn anywhere along its graph.

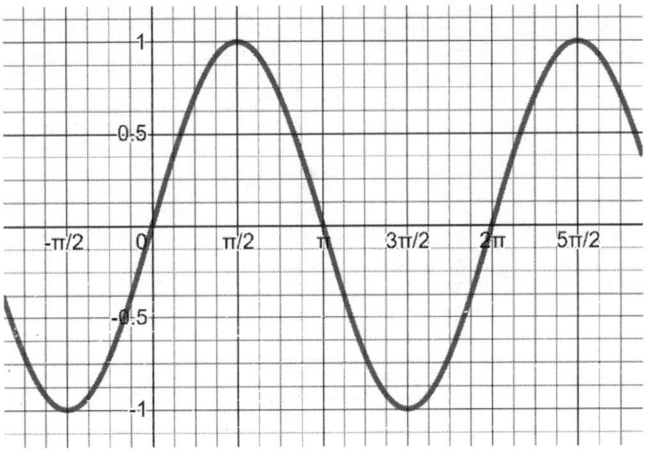

The absolute value function, $f(x) = |x|$, is an example of a function that is not differentiable:

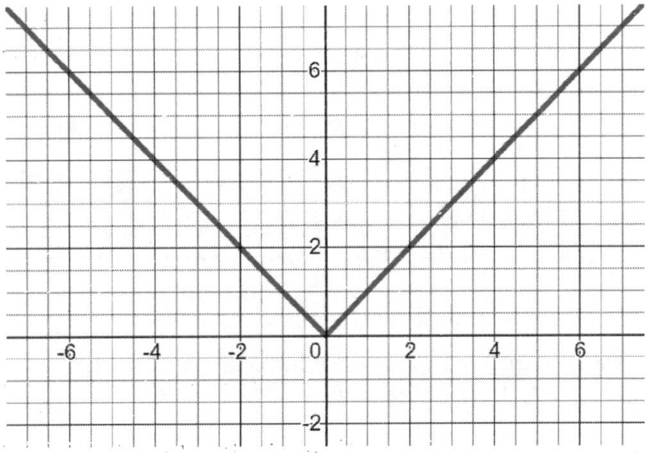

It is continuous, but it has a sharp turn at $x = 0$ which prohibits the drawing of a tangent at that point. All differentiable functions are continuous, but not all continuous functions are differentiable, as the absolute value function demonstrates.

The function $f(x) = \frac{1}{x-1}$ is not differentiable because it is not continuous. It has a discontinuity at $x = 1$. Therefore, a tangent could not be drawn at that point.

Approximating a Derivative from a Table of Values

The derivative of a function at a particular point is equal to the slope of the graph of the function at that point. For a nonlinear function, it can be thought of as the limit of the slope of a line drawn between two other points on the function as those points become closer to the point in question. Such a line drawn through two points on the function is called a **secant** of the function.

This definition of the derivative in terms of the secant allows us to approximate the derivative of a function at a point from a table of values: we take the slope of the line through the points on either side. That is, if the point lies between (x_1, y_1) and (x_2, y_2), the slope of the secant—the approximate derivative—is $\frac{y_2-y_1}{x_2-x_1}$. (This is also equal to the average slope over the interval $[x_1, x_2]$.)

For example, consider the function represented by the following table:

x	0	2	4	6	8	10
y	1	5	8	9	7	4

Suppose we want to know the derivative of the function when $x = 3$. This lies between the points $(2, 5)$ and $(4, 8)$; the approximate derivative is $\frac{8-5}{4-2} = \frac{3}{2}$.

Position, Velocity, and Acceleration

Velocity is a specific type of rate of change. It refers to the rate of change of the position of an object with relation to a reference frame. **Acceleration** is the rate of change of velocity.

Average velocity over a period of time is found using the formula $\bar{v} = \frac{s(t_2)-s(t_1)}{t_2-t_1}$, where t_1 and t_2 are specific points in time and $s(t_1)$ and $s(t_2)$ are the distances traveled at those points in time.

Instantaneous velocity at a specific time, *t*, is found using the limit $v = \lim_{h\to 0} \frac{s(t+h)-s(t)}{h}$, or $v = s'(t)$.

Remember that velocity at a given point is found using the first derivative, and acceleration at a given point is found using the second derivative. Therefore, the formula for acceleration at a given point in time is found using the formula $a(t) = v'(t) = s''(t)$, where *a* is acceleration, *v* is velocity, and *s* is distance or location.

Using First and Second Derivatives

The **first derivative** of a function is equal to the **rate of change** of the function. The sign of the rate of change shows whether the value of the function is **increasing** or **decreasing**. A positive rate of change—and therefore a positive first derivative—represents that the function is increasing at that point. A negative rate of change represents that the function is decreasing. If the rate of change is zero, the function is not changing, i.e. it is constant.

For example, consider the function $f(x) = x^3 - 6x^2 - 15x + 12$. The derivative of this function is $f'(x) = 3x^2 - 12x - 15 = 3(x^2 - 4x - 5) = 3(x - 5)(x + 1)$. This derivative is a quadratic function with zeroes at $x = 5$ and $x = -1$; by plugging in points in each interval we can find that $f'(x)$ is positive when $x < -1$ and when $x > 5$ and negative when $-1 < x < 5$. Thus $f(x)$ is increasing in the interval $(-\infty, -1) \cup (5, \infty)$ and decreasing in the interval $(-1, 5)$.

Extrema

The **maximum** and **minimum** values of a function are collectively called the **extrema** of the function. Both maxima and minima can be local, also known as relative, or absolute. A local maximum or minimum refers to the value of a function near a certain value of *x*. An absolute maximum or minimum refers to the value of a function on a given interval.

The local maximum of a function is the largest value that the function attains near a certain value of *x*. For example, function *f* has a local maximum at $x = b$ if $f(b)$ is the largest value that *f* attains as it approaches *b*.

Conversely, the local minimum is the smallest value that the function attains near a certain value of x. In other words, function f has a local minimum at $x = b$ if $f(b)$ is the smallest value that f attains as it approaches b.

The absolute maximum of a function is the largest value of the function over a certain interval. The function f has an absolute maximum at $x = b$ if $f(b) \geq f(x)$ for all x in the domain of f.

The absolute minimum of a function is the smallest value of the function over a certain interval. The function f has an absolute minimum at $x = b$ if $f(b) \leq f(x)$ for all x in the domain of f.

Critical Points

Remember Rolle's theorem, which states that if two points have the same value in the range that there must be a point between them where the slope of the graph is zero. This point is located at a peak or valley on the graph. A **peak** is a maximum point, and a **valley** is a minimum point. The relative minimum is the lowest point on a graph for a given section of the graph. It may or may not be the same as the absolute minimum, which is the lowest point on the entire graph. The relative maximum is the highest point on one section of the graph. Again, it may or may not be the same as the absolute maximum. A relative extremum (plural extrema) is a relative minimum or relative maximum point on a graph.

A **critical point** is a point $\big(x, f(x)\big)$ that is part of the domain of a function, such that either $f'(x) = 0$ or $f'(x)$ does not exist. If either of these conditions is true, then x is either an inflection point or a point at which the slope of the curve changes sign. If the slope changes sign, then a relative minimum or maximum occurs.

In graphing an equation with relative extrema, use a sign diagram to approximate the shape of the graph. Once you have determined the relative extrema, calculate the sign of a point on either side of each critical point. This will give a general shape of the graph, and you will know whether each critical point is a relative minimum, a relative maximum, or a point of inflection.

First Derivative Test

Remember that critical points occur where the slope of the curve is 0. Also remember that the **first derivative** of a function gives the slope of the curve at a particular point on the curve. Because of this property of the first derivative, the first derivative test can be used to determine if a critical point is a minimum or maximum. If $f'(x)$ is negative at a point to the left of a critical number and $f'(x)$ is positive at a point to the right of a critical number, then the critical number is a relative minimum. If $f'(x)$ is positive to the left of a critical number and $f'(x)$ is negative to the right of a critical number, then the critical number is a relative maximum. If $f'(x)$ has the same sign on both sides, then the critical number is a point of inflection.

Second Derivative Test

The **second derivative**, designated by $f''(x)$, is helpful in determining whether the relative extrema of a function are relative maximums or relative minimums. If the second derivative at the critical point is greater than zero, the critical point is a relative minimum. If the second derivative at the critical point is less than zero, the critical point is a relative maximum. If the second derivative at the critical point is equal to zero, you must use the first derivative test to determine whether the point is a relative minimum or a relative maximum.

There are a couple of ways to determine the concavity of the graph of a function. To test a portion of the graph that contains a point with domain p, find the second derivative of the function and evaluate it for p. If $f''(p) > 0$, then the graph is concave upward at that point. If $f''(p) < 0$, then the graph is concave downward at that point.

The **point of inflection** on the graph of a function is the point at which the concavity changes from concave downward to concave upward or from concave upward to concave downward. The easiest way to find the points of inflection is to find the second derivative of the function and then solve the equation $f''(x) = 0$. Remember that if $f''(p) > 0$, the graph is concave upward, and if $f''(p) < 0$, the graph is concave downward. Logically, the concavity changes at the point when $f''(p) = 0$:

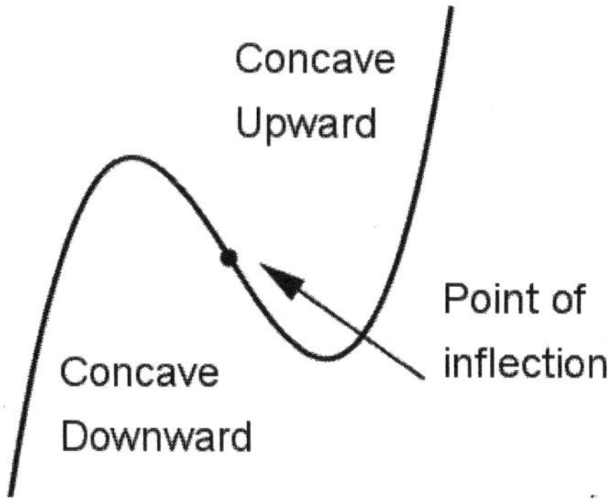

The derivative tests that have been discussed thus far can help you get a rough picture of what the graph of an unfamiliar function looks like. Begin by solving the equation $f(x) = 0$ to find all the zeros of the function, if they exist. Plot these points on the graph. Then, find the first derivative of the function and solve the equation $f'(x) = 0$ to find the critical points. Remember the numbers obtained here are the x portions of the coordinates. Substitute these values for x in the original function and solve for y to get the full coordinates of the points. Plot these points on the graph. Take the second derivative of the function and solve the equation $f''(x) = 0$ to find the points of inflection. Substitute in the original function to get the coordinates and graph these points. Test points on both sides of the critical points to test for concavity and draw the curve.

Derivative Problems

A derivative represents the rate of change of a function; thus, derivatives are a useful tool for solving any problem that involves finding the rate at which a function is changing. In its simplest form, such a problem might provide a formula for a quantity as a function of time and ask for its rate of change at a particular time.

If the temperature in a chamber in degrees Celsius is equal to $T(t) = 20 + e^{-t/2}$, where t is the time in seconds, then the derivative of the function represents the rate of change of the temperature over time. The rate of change is equal to $\frac{dT}{dt} = \frac{d}{dt}\left(20 + e^{-t/2}\right) = -\frac{1}{2}e^{-t/2}$, and the initial rate of change is $T'(0) = -\frac{1}{2}e^{-0/2} = -\frac{1}{2}\frac{°C}{s}$.

Suppose we are told that the net profit that a small company makes when it produces and sells x units of a product is equal to $P(x) = 200x - 20000$. The derivative of this function would be the *additional profit for each additional unit sold*, a quantity known as the marginal profit. The marginal profit in this case is $P'(x) = 200$.

Solving Related Rates Problems

A **related rate problem** is one in which one variable has a relation with another variable, and the rate of change of one of the variables is known. With that information, the rate of change of the other variable can be determined. The first step in solving related rates problems is defining the known rate of change. Then, determine the relationship between the two variables, then the derivatives (the rates of change), and finally substitute the problem's specific values. Consider the following example:

The side of a cube is increasing at a rate of 2 feet per second. Determine the rate at which the volume of the cube is increasing when the side of the cube is 4 feet long.

For the problem in question, the known rate of change can be expressed as $s'(t) = \frac{ds}{dt} = 2\frac{\text{ft}}{\text{s}}$, where s is the length of the side and t is the elapsed time in seconds. The relationship between the two variables of the cube is $v = s^3$, where v is the volume of the cube and s is the length of the side. The unknown rate of change to determine is the volume. As both v and s change with time, $v = s^3$ becomes $v(t) = [s(t)]^3$

Now, the chain rule is applied to differentiate both sides of the equation with respect to t.

$$d\frac{v(t)}{dt} = \frac{d[s(t)]^3}{dt}; \ \frac{dv}{dt} = \frac{(3[s(t)]^2)ds}{dt}$$

Finally, the specific value of $s = 4$ feet is substituted, and the equation is evaluated.

$$\begin{aligned} \frac{dv}{dt} &= \frac{(3[s(t)]^2)ds}{dt} \\ &= 3(4)^2 \times 2 = 96\frac{\text{ft}^3}{\text{s}} \\ &= 96 \text{ cubic}\frac{\text{ft}}{\text{s}} \end{aligned}$$

Therefore, when a side of the cube is 4 feet long, the volume of the cube is increasing at a rate of 96 cubic feet/second .

Solving Optimization Problems

An **optimization problem** is a problem in which we are asked to find the value of a variable that maximizes or minimizes a particular value. Because the maximum or maximum occurs at a critical point, and because the critical point occurs when the derivative of the function is zero, we can solve an optimization problem by setting the derivative of the function to zero and solving for the desired variable.

For example, suppose a farmer has 720 m of fencing, and wants to use it to fence in a 2 by 3 block of identical rectangular pens. What dimensions of the pens will maximize their area?

We can draw a diagram:

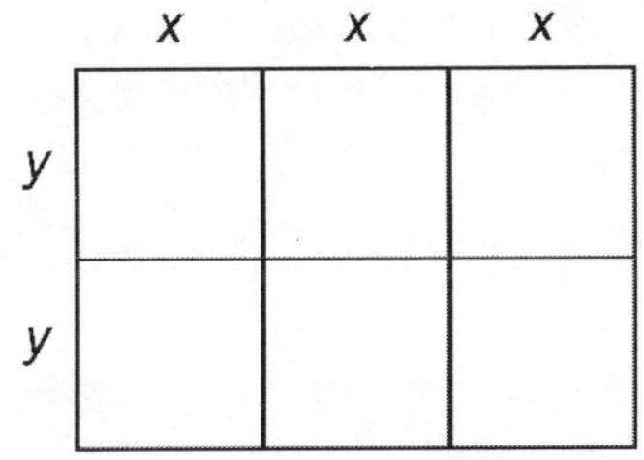

We want to maximize the area of each pen, $A(x, y) = xy$. However, we have the additional constraint that the farmer has only 720 m of fencing. In terms of x and y, we can count the number of segments of each length, 9 for x and 8 for y, so the total amount of fencing required will be $9x + 8y$. Our constraint becomes $9x + 8y = 720$; solving for y yields $y = -\frac{9}{8}x + 90$. We can substitute that into the area equation to get $A(x) = x\left(-\frac{9}{8}x + 90\right) = -\frac{9}{8}x^2 + 90x$. Taking the derivative yields $A'(x) = -\frac{9}{4}x + 90$; setting that equal to zero and solving for x yields $x = 40$. $y = -\frac{9}{8}(40) + 90 = 45$, thus, the maximum dimensions of the pen are 40 by 45 meters.

Characteristics of Functions (Using Calculus)

Rolle's theorem states that if a differentiable function has two different values in the domain that correspond to a single value in the range, then the function must have a point between them where the slope of the tangent to the graph is zero. This point will be a maximum or a minimum value of the function between those two points. The maximum or minimum point is the point at which $f'(c) = 0$, where c is within the appropriate interval of the function's domain. The following graph shows a function with one maximum in the second quadrant and one minimum in the fourth quadrant.

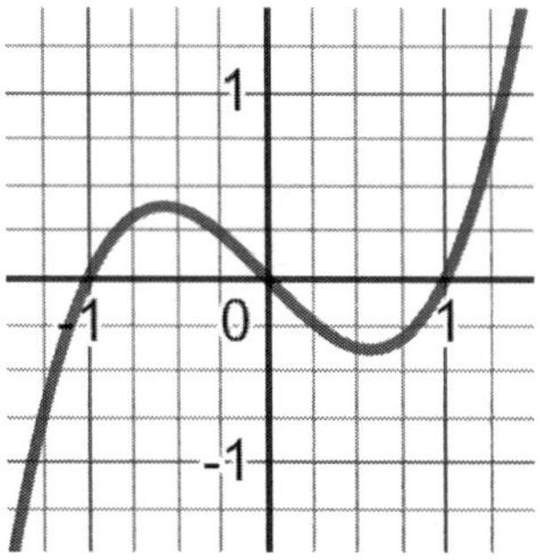

Mean Value Theorem

According to the **mean value theorem**, between any two points on a curve, there exists a tangent to the curve whose slope is parallel to the chord formed by joining those two points. Remember the formula for slope: $m = \frac{\Delta x}{\Delta y}$. In a function, $f(x)$ represents the value for y. Therefore, if you have two points on a curve, m and n, the corresponding points are $(m, f(m))$ and $(n, f(n))$. Assuming $m < n$, the formula for the slope of the chord joining those two points is $\frac{f(n)-f(m)}{n-m}$. This must also be the slope of a line parallel to the chord, since parallel lines have equal slopes. Therefore, there must be a value p between m and n such that $f'(p) = \frac{f(n)-f(m)}{n-m}$.

For a function to have continuity, its graph must be an unbroken curve. That is, it is a function that can be graphed without having to lift the pencil to move it to a different point. To say a function is continuous at point p, you must show the function satisfies three requirements. First, $f(p)$ must exist. If you evaluate the function at p, it must yield a real number. Second, there must exist a relationship such that $\lim_{x\to p} f(x) = f(p)$. Finally, the following relationship must be true:

$$\lim_{x\to p^+} F(x) = \lim_{x\to p^-} F(x) = F(p)$$

If all three of these requirements are met, a function is considered continuous at p. If any one of them is not true, the function is not continuous at p.

Tangents

Tangents are lines that touch a curve in exactly one point and have the same slope as the curve at that point. To find the slope of a curve at a given point and the slope of its tangent line at that point, find the derivative of the function of the curve. If the slope is undefined, the tangent is a vertical line. If the slope is zero, the tangent is a horizontal line.

A line that is normal to a curve at a given point is perpendicular to the tangent at that point. Assuming $f'(x) \neq 0$, the equation for the normal line at point (a, b) is: $y - b = -\frac{1}{f'(a)}(x - a)$. The easiest way to find the slope of the normal is to take the negative reciprocal of the slope of the tangent. If the slope of the tangent is zero, the slope of the normal is undefined. If the slope of the tangent is undefined, the slope of the normal is zero.

Antiderivatives (Integrals)

The antiderivative of a function is the function whose first derivative is the original function. Antiderivatives are typically represented by capital letters, while their first derivatives are represented by lower case letters. For example, if $F' = f$, then F is the antiderivative of f. Antiderivatives are also known as indefinite integrals. When taking the derivative of a function, any constant terms in the function are eliminated because their derivative is 0. To account for this possibility, when you take the indefinite integral of a function, you must add an unknown constant C to the end of the function. Because there is no way to know what the value of the original constant was when looking just at the first derivative, the integral is indefinite.

To find the indefinite integral, reverse the process of differentiation. Below are the formulas for constants and powers of x.

$$\int 0\,dx = C$$

$$\int k\,dx = kx + C$$

$$\int x^n\,dx = \frac{x^{n+1}}{n+1} + C, \text{where } n \neq -1$$

Recall that in the differentiation of powers of x, you multiplied the coefficient of the term by the exponent of the variable and then reduced the exponent by one. In integration, the process is reversed: add one to the value of the exponent, and then divide the coefficient of the term by this number to get the integral. Because you do not know the value of any constant term that might have been in the original function, add C to the end of the function once you have completed this process for each term.

Review Video: Indefinite Integrals
Visit mometrix.com/academy and enter code: 541913

Finding the integral of a function is the opposite of finding the derivative of the function. Where possible, you can use the trigonometric or logarithmic differentiation formulas in reverse, and add C to the end to compensate for the unknown term. In instances where a negative sign appears in the differentiation formula, move the negative sign to the opposite side (multiply both sides by -1) to reverse for the integration formula. You should end up with the following formulas:

$$\int \cos x \; dx = \sin x + C$$

$$\int \sec x \tan x \; dx = \sec x + C$$

$$\int \sin x \; dx = -\cos x + C$$

$$\int \csc x \cot x \; dx = -\csc x + C$$

$$\int \sec^2 x \; dx = \tan x + C$$

$$\int \csc^2 x \; dx = -\cot x + C$$

$$\int \frac{1}{x} \, dx = \ln |x| + C$$

$$\int e^x \, dx = e^x + C$$

Integration by substitution is the integration version of the chain rule for differentiation. The formula for integration by substitution is given by the equation

$$f(g(x))g'(x)dx = \int f(u)du\,; \quad u = g(x) \text{ and } du = g'(x)dx$$

When a function is in a format that is difficult or impossible to integrate using traditional integration methods and formulas due to multiple functions being combined, use the formula shown above to convert the function to a simpler format that can be integrated directly.

Integration by parts is the integration version of the product rule for differentiation. Whenever you are asked to find the integral of the product of two different functions or parts, integration by parts can make the process simpler. Recall for differentiation $(fg)'(x) = f(x)g'(x) + g(x)f'(x)$. This can also be written $\frac{d}{dx}(u \times v) = u\frac{dv}{dx} + v\frac{du}{dx}$, where $u = f(x)$ and $v = g(x)$. Rearranging to integral form gives the formula:

$$\int u \, dv = uv - \int v \, du$$

$$\int f(x)g'(x) \, dx = f(x)g(x) - \int f'(x)g(x) \, dx$$

When using integration by parts, the key is selecting the best functions to substitute for u and v so that you make the integral easier to solve and not harder.

While the indefinite integral has an undefined constant added at the end, the definite integral can be calculated as an exact real number. To find the definite integral of a function over a closed interval, use the formula $\int_n^m f(x) \, dx = F(m) - F(n)$ where F is the integral of f. Because you have been given the boundaries of n and m, no undefined constant C is needed.

First Fundamental Theorem of Calculus

The **first fundamental theorem of calculus** shows that the process of indefinite integration can be reversed by finding the first derivative of the resulting function. It also gives the relationship between differentiation and integration over a closed interval of the function. For example, assuming a function is continuous over the interval $[m, n]$, you can find the definite integral by using the formula

$$\int_m^n f(x) \, dx = F(n) - F(m)$$

To find the **average value** of the function over the given interval, use the formula:

$$\frac{1}{n-m}\int_{m}^{n} f(x)\,dx$$

Second Fundamental Theorem of Calculus

The **second fundamental theorem of calculus** is related to the first. This theorem states that, assuming the function is continuous over the interval you are considering, taking the derivative of the integral of a function will yield the original function. The general format for this theorem for any point having a domain value equal to *c* in the given interval is:

$$\frac{d}{dx}\int_{c}^{x} f(x)\,dx = f(x)$$

For each of the following **properties of integrals** of function *f*, the variables *m*, *n*, and *p* represent values in the domain of the given interval of $f(x)$. The function is assumed to be integrable across all relevant intervals.

Swapping the limits of integration:	$\int_{m}^{n} f(x)\,dx = -\int_{n}^{m} f(x)\,dx$
Function multiplied by a constant:	$\int_{m}^{n} kf(x)dx = k\int_{m}^{n} f(x)\,dx$
Separating the integral into parts:	$\int_{m}^{n} f(x)\,dx = \int_{m}^{p} f(x)\,dx + \int_{p}^{n} f(x)\,dx$
If the limits of integration are equivalent:	$\int_{n}^{n} f(x)\,dx = 0$
If $f(x)$ is an even function and the limits of integration are symmetric:	$\int_{-m}^{m} f(x)\,dx = 2\int_{0}^{m} f(x)\,dx$
If $f(x)$ is an odd function and the limits of integration are symmetric:	$\int_{-m}^{m} f(x)\,dx = 0$

Matching Functions to Derivatives or Accumulations

Derivatives

We can use what we know about the meaning of a derivative to match the graph of a function with a graph of its derivative. For one thing, we know that where the function has a critical point, the derivative is zero. Therefore, at every *x* value at which the graph of a function has a maximum or minimum, the derivative must cross the *x* axis—and conversely, everywhere the graph of the derivative crosses the *x* axis, the function must have a critical point: either a maximum, a minimum, or an inflection point. If this is still not enough to identify the correct match, we can also use the fact that the sign of the derivative corresponds to whether the function is increasing or decreasing: everywhere the graph of the derivative is above the *x* axis, the function must be increasing (its slope is positive), and everywhere the graph of the derivative is below the *x* axis, the function must be decreasing (its slope is negative).

For example, below are graphs of the function and its derivative. The maxima and minima of the function (left) are circled, and the zeroes of the derivative (right) are circled.

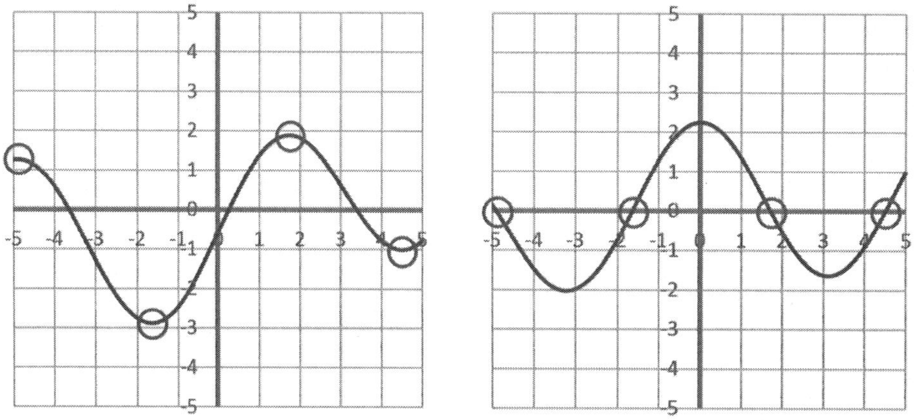

ACCUMULATIONS

The **accumulation** of a function is another name for its antiderivative, or integral. We can use the relationship between a function and its antiderivative to match the corresponding graphs. For example, we know that where the graph of the function is above the *x* axis, the function is positive, thus the accumulation must be increasing (its slope is positive); where the graph of the function is below the *x* axis, the accumulation must be decreasing (its slope is negative). It follows that where the function changes from positive to negative—where the graph crosses the *x* axis with a negative slope—, its accumulation changes from increasing to decreasing—so the accumulation has a local maximum. Where the function changes from negative to positive—where its graph crosses the *x* axis with a positive slope—, the accumulation has a local minimum.

For example, below are graphs of a function and its accumulation. The points on the function (left) where the graph crosses the *x* axis are circled; the local minima and maxima of the accumulation (right) are circled.

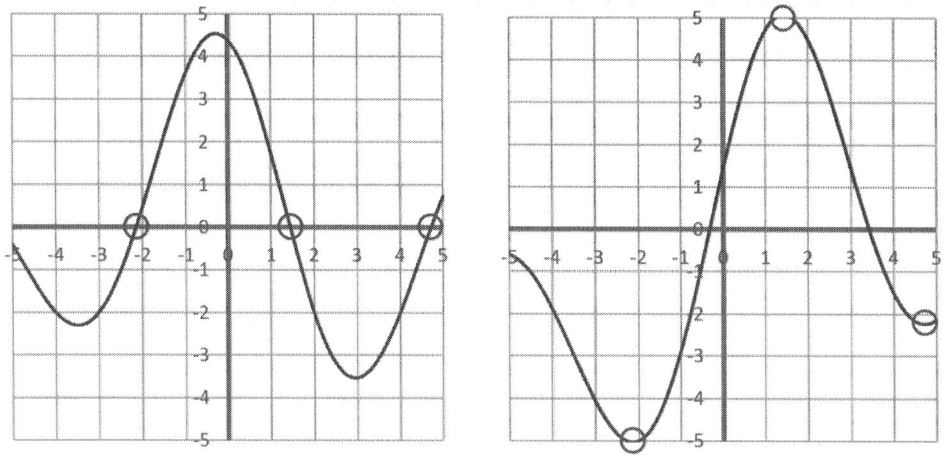

RIEMANN SUMS

A **Riemann sum** is a sum used to approximate the definite integral of a function over a particular interval by dividing the area under the function into vertical rectangular strips and adding the areas of the strips. The height of each strip is equal to the value of the function at some point within the interval covered by the strip. Formally, if we divide the interval over which we are finding the area into n intervals bounded by the n +1 points $\{x_i\}$ (where x_0 and x_n are the left and right bounds of the interval), then the Riemann sum is $\sum_{i=1}^{n} f(x_i^*)\Delta x_i$, where $\Delta x_i = x_i - x_{i-1}$ and x_i^* is some point in the interval $[x_{i-1}, x_i]$. In principle, any point in the interval can be chosen, but common choices include the left endpoint of the interval (yielding the **left Riemann sum**), the right endpoint (yielding the **right Riemann sum**), and the midpoint of the interval (the basis of the **midpoint rule**). Usually it is convenient to set all the intervals to the same width, although the definition of the Riemann sum does not require this.

The following graphic shows the rectangular strips used for one possible Riemann sum of a particular function:

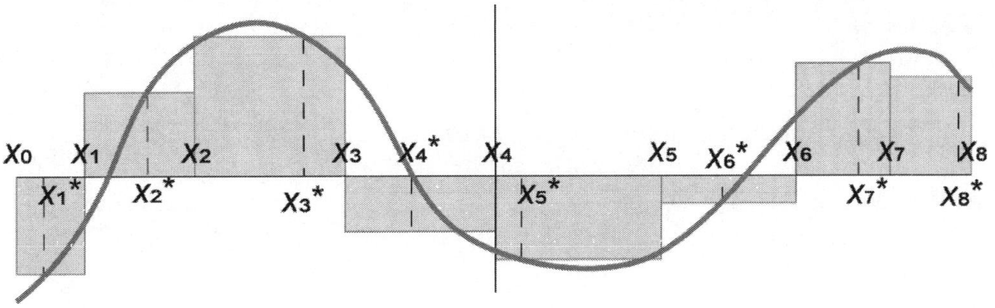

Left and Right Riemann Sums

A **Riemann sum** is an approximation to the definite integral of a function over a particular interval performed by dividing it into smaller intervals and summing the products of the width of each interval and the value of the function evaluated at some point within the interval. The **left Riemann sum** is a Riemann sum in which the function is evaluated at the left endpoint of each interval. In the **right Riemann sum**, the function is evaluated at the right endpoint of each interval.

When the function is increasing, the left Riemann sum will always underestimate the function. This is because we are evaluating the function at the minimum point within each interval; the integral of the function in the interval will be larger than the estimate. Conversely, the right Riemann sum is evaluating the function at the maximum point within each interval, thus it will always overestimate the function. Consider the following diagrams, in which the area under the same increasing function is shown approximated by a left Riemann sum and a right Riemann sum:

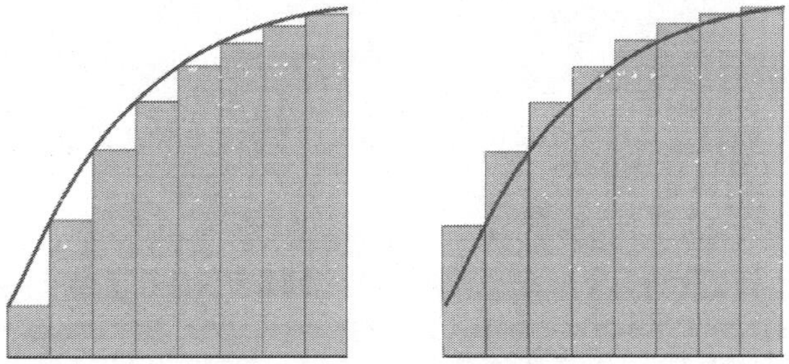

For a decreasing function these considerations are reversed: a left Riemann sum will overestimate the integral, and a right Riemann sum will underestimate it.

Midpoint Rule

The **midpoint rule** is a way of approximating the definite integral of a function over an interval by dividing the interval into smaller sub-intervals, multiplying the width of each sub-interval by the value of the function at the midpoint of the sub-interval, and then summing these products. This is a special case of the Riemann sum, specifying the midpoint of the interval as the point at which the function is to be evaluated. The approximation found using the midpoint rule is usually more accurate than that found using the left or right Riemann sum, though as the number of intervals becomes very large the difference becomes negligible.

For example, suppose we are asked to estimate by the midpoint rule the integral of $f(x) = \frac{1}{x}$ in the interval [2, 4]. We can divide this interval into four intervals of width $\frac{1}{2}$: [2, 2.5], [2.5, 3], [3, 3.5], and [3.5, 4]. (The more intervals, the more accurate the estimate, but we'll use a small number of intervals in this example to keep it simple.) The midpoint rule then gives an estimate of $\frac{1}{2}(f(2.25)) + \frac{1}{2}(f(2.75)) + \frac{1}{2}(f(3.25)) + \frac{1}{2}(f(3.75)) = \frac{1}{2}\left(\frac{4}{9}\right) + \frac{1}{2}\left(\frac{4}{11}\right) + \frac{1}{2}\left(\frac{4}{13}\right) + \frac{1}{2}\left(\frac{4}{15}\right) \approx 0.691$, not far from the actual value of $\int_2^4 \frac{1}{x} dx = [\ln x]_2^4 \approx 0.693$.

TRAPEZOID RULE

The **trapezoid rule** is a method of approximating the definite integral of a function by dividing the area under the function into a series of trapezoidal strips, the upper corners of the trapezoid touching the function, and adding the areas of the strips. The following diagram shows the use of the trapezoid rule to estimate the integral of the function $y = 2^x$ in the interval $[0, 3]$:

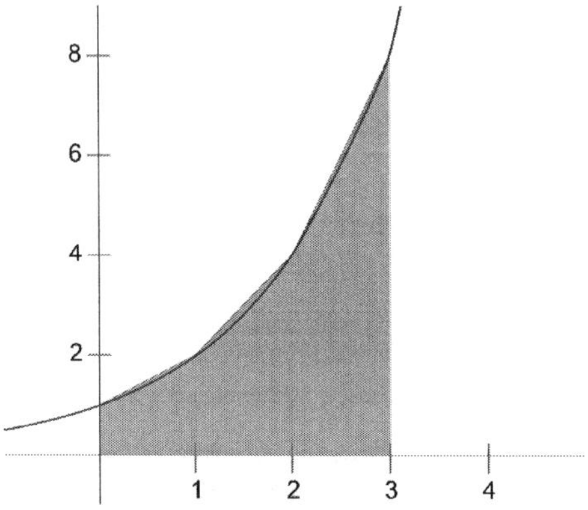

Mathematically, if we define the endpoints of the n subdivisions to be $\{x_i\}$, where x_0 and x_n are the endpoints of the entire interval over which we are estimating the integral, then the result of the application of the trapezoid rule is equal to $\sum_{i=1}^{n} \left(\frac{x_{i-1}+x_i}{2}\right)(x_i - x_{i-1})$. For the example shown above, that yields $\left(\frac{2^1+2^0}{2}\right)(1-0) + \left(\frac{2^2+2^1}{2}\right)(2-1) + \left(\frac{2^3+2^2}{2}\right)(3-2) = \frac{21}{2}$, or 10.5—not far from the actual value of $\int_0^3 2^x dx = \int_0^3 e^{x \ln 2} dx = \left[\frac{2^x}{\ln 2}\right]_0^3 \approx 10.1$. (Of course, we could have achieved more accuracy by using smaller subdivisions.)

The trapezoid rule is related to the Riemann sum, but usually gives more accurate results than the left or right Riemann sum for the same number of intervals. In fact, it isn't hard to prove that the answer given by the trapezoid rule is equal to the average of the left and right Riemann sums using the same partition.

LIMIT OF RIEMANN SUMS

As the number of sub-intervals becomes larger, and the width of each sub-interval becomes smaller, the approximation becomes increasingly accurate, and at the limit as the number of sub-intervals approaches infinity and their width approaches zero, the value becomes exact. In fact, the definite integral is often defined as a limit of Riemann sums.

It's possible to find the definite integral by this method. Suppose we want to find the integral of $f(x) = x^2$ over the interval [0, 2]. We'll divide this interval into n sub-intervals of equal width and evaluate the function at the right endpoint of each sub-interval. (This choice is arbitrary; at the limit the answer would be the same if we chose the left endpoint, or any other point within the interval.) Our Riemann sum becomes $\sum_{i=1}^{n} \frac{2}{n}\left(\frac{2}{n}i\right)^2 = \frac{8}{n^3}\sum_{i=1}^{n} i^2$, where $\sum_{i=1}^{n} i^2 = \frac{1}{6}n(n+1)(2n+1)$, thus this becomes $\frac{8}{n^3} \cdot \frac{1}{6}n(n+1)(2n+1) = \frac{4}{3}\left(1+\frac{1}{n}\right)\left(2+\frac{1}{n}\right)$. At the limit as $n \to \infty$, this becomes $\frac{4}{3}(1)(2) = \frac{8}{3}$. This is the same result as we get by integrating directly: $\int_0^2 x^2 dx = \left[\frac{1}{3}x^3\right]_0^2 = \frac{1}{3}2^3 - \frac{1}{3}0^3 = \frac{8}{3}$.

Uses for Integration

Calculating Distances

When given the velocity of an object over time, it's possible to find a distance by integration. The velocity is the rate of change of the position; therefore, the displacement is the accumulation of the velocity: that is, the integral of the velocity is the displacement. However, if asked to find the total distance traveled (as opposed to the displacement), it's important to take the sign into account: we must integrate not just the velocity, but the absolute value of the velocity, which essentially means integrating separately over each interval in which the velocity has a different sign.

For example, suppose we're asked to find the total distance traveled from $t = 0$ to $t = 8$ by an object moving with a velocity in meters per second given by the equation $v(t) = 2\sqrt{t} - t$. This function is zero when $2\sqrt{t} - t = 0 \Rightarrow \sqrt{t}(2-\sqrt{t}) = 0 \Rightarrow t = 0$ or 4. $v(t)$ is positive when $0 < t < 4$ and negative when $t > 4$. Thus, the distance travelled is

$$\begin{aligned}
\int_0^8 |v(t)|dt &= \int_0^8 \left|2\sqrt{t} - t\right| dt \\
&= \int_0^4 (2\sqrt{t} - t)dt - \int_4^8 (2\sqrt{t} - t)dt \\
&= \left[\frac{4}{3}t^{3/2} - \frac{1}{2}t^2\right]_0^4 - \left[\frac{4}{3}t^{3/2} - \frac{1}{2}t^2\right]_4^8 \\
&= \left(\left[\frac{4}{3}4^{3/2} - \frac{1}{2}4^2\right] - \left[\frac{4}{3}0^{3/2} - \frac{1}{2}0^2\right]\right) - \left(\left[\frac{4}{3}8^{3/2} - \frac{1}{2}8^2\right] - \left[\frac{4}{3}4^{3/2} - \frac{1}{2}4^2\right]\right) \\
&= \left(\left[\frac{32}{3} - 8\right] - 0\right) - \left(\left[\frac{64}{3}\sqrt{2} - 32\right] - \left[\frac{32}{3} - 8\right]\right) \\
&= \frac{8}{3} - \frac{64}{3}\sqrt{2} + \frac{96}{3} + \frac{8}{3} \\
&= \frac{8}{3}(1 - 8\sqrt{2} + 12 + 1) \\
&= \frac{8}{3}(14 - 8\sqrt{2}) \approx 7.16 \text{ meters}
\end{aligned}$$

Calculating Areas

One way to calculate the area of an irregular shape is to find a formula for the width of the shape along the *x* direction as a function of the *y* coordinate, and then integrate over *y*, or vice versa. What this amounts to is dividing the area into thin strips and adding the areas of the strips—and then taking the limit as the width of the strips approaches zero.

For example, suppose we want to find the area enclosed by the functions $y_1 = x^2$ and $y_2 = (2 - x^2)$. The height of this enclosure is equal to $y_2 - y_1 = 2 - 2x^2$; we can find the area by integrating this height over x. The two shapes intersect at the points $(1, 1)$ and $(-1, 1)$, thus our limits of integration are -1 and 1. Thus the area can be found as:

$$\int_{-1}^{1} (2 - 2x^2)dx = \left[2x - \frac{2}{3}x^3\right]_{-1}^{1} = \left(2 - \frac{2}{3}\right) - \left(-2 + \frac{2}{3}\right) = \frac{8}{3}$$

CALCULATING VOLUMES

One way to calculate the volume of a three-dimensional shape is to find a formula for its cross-sectional area perpendicular to some axis and then integrate over that axis. Effectively, this divides the shape into thin, flat slices and adds the volumes of the slices—and then takes the limit as the thickness of the slices approaches zero.

For example, suppose we want to find the area of the ellipsoid $4x^2 + 4y^2 + z^2 = 36$. If we take a cross-section parallel to the z-axis, this has the formula $4x^2 + 4y^2 = 36 - z^2$, or $x^2 + y^2 = 9 - \frac{z^2}{4}$; this is the formula of a circle with a radius of $\sqrt{9 - \frac{z^2}{4}}$, and thus has an area of $\pi\left(9 - \frac{z^2}{4}\right)$. To find the volume, we integrate this formula over z. The maximum and minimum values of z occur when $x = y = 0$, and then $z^2 = 36$, thus $z = \pm 6$; these are our limits of integration. Thus, the volume is:

$$\int_{-6}^{6} \pi\left(9 - \frac{z^2}{4}\right)dz = \pi\left[9z - \frac{z^3}{12}\right]_{-6}^{6}$$
$$= 72\pi \approx 226.2$$

PRACTICE

P1. Evaluate $\lim_{x\to4} f(x)$ for the following functions:

(a) $f(x) = 7$

(b) $f(x) = \frac{x-4}{x^2-16}$

(c) $f(x) = \begin{cases} x + 1, \text{when } x < 4 \\ x - 1, \text{when } x \geq 4 \end{cases}$

P2. Given that $\lim_{x\to3} f(x) = 2$, $\lim_{x\to3} g(x) = 6$, and $k = 5$, solve the following:

(a) $\lim_{x\to3} kg(x)$

(b) $\lim_{x\to3}(f(x) + g(x))$

(c) $\lim_{x\to3} f(x) \times g(x)$

(d) $\lim_{x\to3} g(x) \div f(x)$

(e) $\lim_{x\to3}[f(x)]^n = C^n$, where $n = 3$

P3. Find $f'(x)$ for the following functions:

(a) $f(x) = 3x$

(b) $f(x) = x^2$

P4. Use the power rule of differentiation to differentiate the following:

(a) $f(x) = 4x^2$

(b) $f(x) = x^4$

(c) $f(x) = 3x^2 - 5x + 6$

P5. Calculate the area under the curve of the function $f(x) = x^2 + 3$ on the interval [2,5] using:

(a) right-hand approximation with 6 subdivisions.

(b) left-hand approximation with 3 subdivisions.

P6. Find the position, velocity, and acceleration for the following at $t = 3$ s:

(a) A train begins moving and its displacement (in meters) is: $s(t) = t^2 + 4t + 5$

(b) A car begins moving and its displacement (in feet) is: $s(t) = t^3$

P7. Find $\frac{dy}{dx}$ given the equation $xy^2 = 3y + 2x$.

P8. Use the first fundamental theorem of calculus to evaluate:

(a) $\int_0^1 (x^3 + 2x)dx$

(b) $\int_{-1}^0 (3x^2 + 2)dx$

P9. Find the total distance traveled from $t = 0$ to $t = 10$ by an object moving with a velocity in meters per second given by the equation $v(t) = 6t - t^2$.

Practice Solutions

P1. (a) 7 is a constant function, so therefore, $\lim_{x\to 4} 7 = 7$

(b) $\lim_{x\to 4} \frac{x-4}{x^2-16}$ can be simplified by factoring:

$$\lim_{x\to 4} \frac{x-4}{x^2-16} = \lim_{x\to 4} \frac{x-4}{(x+4)(x-4)} = \lim_{x\to 4} \frac{1}{x+4} = \frac{1}{8}$$

(c) $\lim_{x\to 4} f(x)$, when $f(x) = x + 1$ for $x < 4$ and $f(x) = x - 1$ for $x \geq 4$

$$\lim_{x\to 4^+} f(x) = x - 1 = 4 - 1 = 3$$
$$\lim_{x\to 4^-} f(x) = x + 1 = 4 + 1 = 5$$

Therefore, $\lim_{x\to 4} f(x)$, does not exist.

P2. (a) $\lim_{x\to a} kf(x) = kC$, where k is a constant, so $\lim_{x\to 3} kg(x) = 5 \times 6 = 30$

(b) $\lim_{x\to a}(f(x) \pm g(x)) = C \pm D$, so $\lim_{x\to 3}\big(f(x) + g(x)\big) = 2 + 6 = 8$

(c) $\lim_{x\to a} f(x) \times g(x) = C \times D$, so $\lim_{x\to 3} f(x) \times g(x) = 2 \times 6 = 12$

(d) $\lim_{x\to a} f(x) \div g(x) = C \div D$, if $D \neq 0$, so $\lim_{x\to 3} \frac{g(x)}{f(x)} = \frac{6}{2} = 3$

(e) $\lim_{x\to a}[f(x)]^n = C^n$, so $\lim_{x\to 3}[f(x)]^n = C^n = 2^3 = 8$

P3. Using the formula $f'(x) = \lim_{h\to 0} \frac{f(x+h)-f(x)}{h}$:

(a)
$$\begin{aligned} f'(x) &= \lim_{h\to 0} \frac{3x + 3h - 3x}{h} \\ &= \lim_{h\to 0} \frac{3h}{h} \\ &= \lim_{h\to 0} 3 \\ &= 3 \end{aligned}$$

(b)
$$\begin{aligned} f'(x) &= \lim_{h\to 0} \frac{x^2 + 2xh + h^2 - x^2}{h} \\ &= \lim_{h\to 0} \frac{2xh + h^2}{h} \\ &= \lim_{h\to 0} 2x + h \\ &= 2x \end{aligned}$$

P4. The power rule is useful for finding the derivative of polynomial functions. It states that the derivative of $x^n = nx^{n-1}$.

(a) $f(x) = 4x^2 \to f'(x) = 2 \times 4x^2 - 1 = 8x$

(b) $f(x) = x^4 \to f'(x) = 4 \times x^{4-1} = 4x^3$

(c) $f(x) = 3x^2 - 5x + 6 \to f'(x) = 2 \times 3x^{2-1} - 1 \times 5x^{1-1} = 6x - 5$

P5. (a) First, divide the interval [2,5] by the number of subdivisions, $\Delta x = \frac{b-a}{n} = \frac{5-2}{6} = 0.5$, thus each rectangle has a width of 0.5.

The height of the right-hand side of each rectangle is given by the value of the function at the points $x = 2.5, 3, 3.5, 4, 4.5, 5$. Summing these heights and multiplying by the width of each rectangle gives the approximate total area under the curve.

$$\begin{aligned} &= 0.5\big(f(2.5) + f(3) + f(3.5) + f(4) + f(4.5) + f(5)\big) \\ &= 0.5(9.25 + 12 + 15.25 + 19 + 23.25 + 28) = 53.375 \end{aligned}$$

The total area under the curve of the function $f(x) = x^2 + 3$ on the interval [2,5], calculated using right-hand approximation, is found to be approximately 53.375.

(b) First, divide the interval [2,5] by the number of subdivisions, $\Delta x = \frac{b-a}{n} = \frac{5-2}{3} = 1$, thus each rectangle has a width of 1.

The height of the left-hand side of each rectangle is given by the value of the function at $x = 2, 3, 4$. Summing these heights and multiplying by the width of each rectangle gives the approximate area under the curve.

$$1\big(f(2) + f(3) + f(4)\big) = (7 + 12 + 19) = 38$$

The total area under the curve of the function $f(x) = x^2 + 3$ on the interval [2,5], calculated using left-hand approximation, is found to be approximately 38.

P6. Find each derivative and evaluate at $t = 3$:

(a) $s(t) = t^2 + 4t + 5$ $\quad v(t) = s'(t) = 2t + 4$ $\quad a(t) = v'(t) = 2$

$$s(3) = 3^2 + 4(3) + 5 = 26 \text{ m} \qquad v(3) = 2(3) + 4 = 10\frac{\text{m}}{\text{s}} \qquad a(3) = 2\frac{\text{m}}{\text{s}^2}$$

(b) $s(t) = t^3$ $\quad v(t) = s'(t) = 3t^2$ $\quad a(t) = v'(t) = 6t$

$$s(3) = 3^3 = 27 \text{ ft} \qquad v(3) = 3(3)^2 = 27\frac{\text{ft}}{\text{s}} \qquad a(3) = 6(3) = 18\frac{\text{ft}}{\text{s}^2}$$

P7. Take the derivative of each term with respect to x: $\frac{d}{dx}(xy^2) = \frac{d}{dx}(3y + 2x)$. In order to take the derivative of the left side, we will need to use the product rule $\left(\frac{d}{dx}(u \times v) = v\frac{du}{dx} + u\frac{dv}{dx}\right)$ where $u = x$ and $v = y^2$:

$$\frac{d}{dx}(x)y^2 + \frac{d}{dx}(y^2)x = \frac{d}{dx}(3y + 2x)$$
$$y^2 + \frac{d}{dx}(y^2)x = \frac{d}{dx}(3y) + \frac{d}{dx}(2x)$$

Now we will use the chain rule $\left(\frac{d}{dx}f(u) = \frac{df}{du} \times \frac{du}{dx}\right)$ where $f(u) = y^2$ and $u = y$:

$$y^2 + \left(\frac{d(y^2)}{dy} \times \frac{dy}{dx}\right)x = \frac{d}{dx}(3y) + \frac{d}{dx}(2x)$$
$$y^2 + \left(2y\frac{dy}{dx}\right)x = \frac{d}{dx}(3y) + \frac{d}{dx}(2x)$$
$$y^2 + 2xy\frac{dy}{dx} = 3\frac{dy}{dx} + 2$$
$$2xy\frac{dy}{dx} - 3\frac{dy}{dx} = 2 - y^2$$
$$\frac{dy}{dx} = \frac{2 - y^2}{2xy - 3}$$

P8. (a) By the first fundamental theorem of calculus: $\int_a^b f(x)dx = F(b) - F(a)$

$$\begin{aligned}\int_0^1 (x^3 + 2x)dx &= \left[\frac{x^4}{4} + x^2\right]_{x=0}^1 \\ &= \frac{(1)^4}{4} + (1)^2 - \left(\frac{(0)^4}{4} + (0)^2\right) \\ &= \frac{5}{4} - 0 = \frac{5}{4}\end{aligned}$$

(b) By the first fundamental theorem of calculus: $\int_a^b f(x)dx = F(b) - F(a)$

$$\begin{aligned}\int_{-1}^0 (3x^2 + 2)dx &= [x^3 + 2x]_{x=-1}^0 \\ &= (0)^3 + 2(0) - \left((-1)^3 + 2(-1)\right) \\ &= 0 - (-3) = 3\end{aligned}$$

P9. This velocity function is zero when $6t - t^2 = 0 \Rightarrow t(6 - t) = 0 \Rightarrow t = 0$ or 6. $v(t)$ is positive when $0 < t < 6$ and negative when $t > 6$. Thus, the distance travelled is

$$\begin{aligned}\int_0^{10} |v(t)|dt &= \int_0^{10} |6t - t^2|dt \\ &= \int_0^6 (6t - t^2)dt - \int_6^{10} (6t - t^2)dt \\ &= \left[3t^2 - \frac{t^3}{3}\right]_0^6 - \left[3t^2 - \frac{t^3}{3}\right]_6^{10} \\ &= \left(\left[3(6)^2 - \frac{6^3}{3}\right] - \left[3(0)^2 - \frac{0^3}{3}\right]\right) - \left(\left[3(10)^2 - \frac{10^3}{3}\right] - \left[3(6)^2 - \frac{6^3}{3}\right]\right) \\ &= ([108 - 72] - 0) - \left(\left[300 - \frac{1000}{3}\right] - [108 - 72]\right) \\ &= 36 - \left[\frac{900}{3} - \frac{1000}{3}\right] + 36 \\ &= 72 - \left[-\frac{100}{3}\right] \approx 105.3 \text{ meters}\end{aligned}$$